custom SOCKS

 knit to fit your feet

KATE ATHERLEY

INTERWEAVE.
interweave.com

Editor Ann Budd

Technical Editor Therese Chynoweth

Assistant Art Director Charlene Tiedemann

Photographer Joe Hancock

Photo Stylist Allie Liebgott

Cover & Interior Design Kerry Jackson

Illustration Kathie Kelleher

Interweave
A division of F+W Media, Inc.
4868 Innovation Drive
Fort Collins, CO 80525
Interweave.com

Manufactured in China by RR Donnelley Shenzhen

Library of Congress Cataloging-in-Publication Data
not available at time of printing.

ISBN 978-1-62033-775-2 (pbk.)
ISBN 978-1-62033-776-9 (PDF)

10 9 8 7 6 5 4 3 2 1

In Thanks

The following people offered enormous help in making this book a reality.

Readers and Test Knitters: Cari Angold, Fiona Ballard, Jennifer Batt, Anne Blayney, Karen Crouch, Rayna Curtis Fegan, Sue Frost, Catherine Goykhmann, Kim McBrien-Evans, Lisa McGlade, Lara Neel, Stephannie Roy, Lori Sanders, Lynne Sosnowski, Keri Williams, and Liz Wilson.

Interweave/F+W Media: Anne Merrow for saying hello in the hotel lobby and for making many important introductions. Kerry Bogert for thinking this was a good idea, and Ann Budd for helping me turn a good idea into a good book.

Yarn Suppliers: Anzula Luxury Fibers, Brown Sheep Company, Garnstudio, Handmaiden Fine Yarn, Indigodragonfly, Madelinetosh, Miss Babs Hand-Dye Yarns and Fibers, Patons, The Plucky Knitter, Skacel Collection (Austermann), Skeinny Dipping, Space Cadet Creations, Sweet Georgia Yarns, Westminster Fibers (Regia and Rowan), and Zen Yarn Garden.

Other Support: Sue Frost for making the leftovers socks and weaving in a million ends; Fiona Ellis for cheerleading and a clever trick; Café Unwind for strong coffee and goodies when I needed them the most; Dexter the dog for mostly staying away from the yarn. And Norman, for everything.

Contents

Introduction

Everyone's feet are different. Even two people who wear exactly the same size shoes can—and usually do—have very differently shaped feet.

Yet not all sock patterns address that reality. A good sock pattern comes in multiple sizes, but, even so, a particular design might not accommodate your particular needs.

I've got smaller-than-average feet, and my first few pairs of handknitted socks were disappointing. In some cases, it was because I used patterns that didn't provide an appropriate size for me; in other cases, it was because I didn't understand the sizing information given.

Custom Socks is designed to help you knit socks that really fit by helping you understand sock sizing information, by teaching you how to properly measure your feet, and by explaining how to customize a sock for your specific needs.

There are two basic templates in this book: one for a basic top-down sock (see page 40) and one for a basic toe-up sock (see page 54). I've provided handy tables of all the key numbers for finished sock circumferences from 5 inches (12.5 cm) to 10½ inches (26.5 cm)—to fit feet ranging from 5½ inches (14 cm) to 12 inches (30.5 cm) in circumference—in gauges that range from 4 to 9 stitches per inch (2.5 cm). If you're knitting for a foot with an "average" size and shape, these tables will give you all the numbers you need to make socks that fit perfectly, whether you work from the toe up or from the cuff down.

But, because not everyone is "average," I've also provided all the formulas you need to easily calculate the numbers that will work for you. I've also included information on foot shapes and sizes to help you determine what shape sock will fit you best and detailed instructions for modifying the basic patterns for special needs.

Proper-fitting socks not only look great, but they feel great—and they last longer. The information in this book will ensure that you have the best-fitting and the best-wearing socks ever!

Chapter 1
On Sock Sizing

The first step in knitting a pair of well-fitting socks is to understand how a sock fits a foot and how your particular foot is shaped.

How a Sock Is Supposed to Fit

Socks should be worn with a little bit of **negative ease**—that is, they should be smaller than the foot (and leg) they're to cover. You want the sock to have to stretch a bit so that it will stay up on your leg and stay in place on your foot. A common problem cited with handknitted socks is that the legs don't stay up (see page 156)—in many cases, this is simply because the sock is too big.

A handknitted sock (especially one made out of wool or other animal fibers; see Chapter 2) will stretch out over the day. Unless the sock stretches somewhat to fit your foot, this added stretch can cause the sock to become floppy as the day wears on. In addition to feeling uncomfortable, loose floppy socks will move around inside shoes and wear out much quicker due to the added friction. A sock that has to stretch to fit your foot will stay put on your foot, feel comfortable, and resist abrasion.

For the best fit, a sock for an adult should measure about 10 percent—practically speaking, that corresponds to about 1 inch (2.5 cm)—smaller than the actual leg or foot circumference, and about ½ inch (1.3 cm) shorter than the actual foot length. A sock for a child should also measure about 10 percent smaller in circumference—about ½ inch (1.3 cm) for a foot with a 5 inch (12.5 cm) circumference—and about ¼ inch to ½ inch (6 mm to 1.3 cm) shorter in length.

If you haven't been choosing your sock size based on these rules, chances are that you haven't enjoyed well-fitting socks. Follow these guidelines for your next pair of socks and you'll find an instant improvement in fit, even if you're following a standard pattern.

HOW SOCK PATTERNS ARE SIZED

Before we continue, let's take a look at how typical sock patterns are sized. The finished size of the majority of sock patterns—whether they're knitted toe up or top down—is based on the foot or ankle circumference. This makes sense—the socks have to fit around the foot and ankle, whereas the foot length and the leg length can be easily adjusted by working more or fewer rounds.

When we talk about **foot circumference,** we mean the measurement taken around the ball of the foot, discounting any bunions. You don't want to include a bunion in this measurement because that bony protuberance typically occupies less than 1 inch (2.5 cm), or 10 percent, of the foot circumference or foot length. The inherent stretch in knitted fabric will accommodate this amount of variation. If you based the sock size on that larger circumference, the sock would be too big for 90 percent of your foot. This is why it's good to be a knitter—we make a fabric that stretches. A sock with 10 percent negative ease will still stretch to fit comfortably around an area that's a bit larger.

When we talk about **ankle circumference,** we mean the measurement around the narrowest part of your ankle—usually just above those characteristic rounded bones.

Most sock patterns assume that the wearer's foot circumference and ankle circumference are the same. Most sock patterns call this measurement the "leg circumference" because, for the majority of calf-length sock patterns, the circumference of the sock leg is constant from the top of cuff to the top of the heel (we'll talk later about making adjustments to the sock leg circumference). So, assuming your foot confirms to this standard, you can base your size on either measurement. But remember that you want to allow for negative ease, so the finished size that you want to follow should be 10 percent—that's about 1 inch (2.5 cm) for an adult sock—smaller than your actual foot or ankle circumference.

Not all sock patterns provide the same sizing information. Ideally, you want to know the "finished" measurements or "actual size" of the sock. This will tell you exactly what to expect in the knitted sock. Sizes that are described as "to fit" or "foot size" describe the foot intended to wear the sock, not the actual sock measurements. Unless you know exactly how much (if any) negative ease is allowed, these measurements won't tell you the actual size of the finished sock.

If the sock sizes are given as a finished ankle or foot circumference: Choose a size that has about 10 percent negative ease—about 1 inch (2.5 cm) for an "average" adult sock; about ¼ inch to ½ inch (6 mm to 1.3 cm) for an "average" child's sock.

If the sock sizes are given as shoe size: First check where the pattern was published—shoe sizes differ regionally and a U.S. size 7 shoe is different than a U.K. size 7 shoe.

In general, shoes are designed with the expectation that a longer foot (larger shoe size) corresponds to a larger foot circumference, and shoe sizes assume that the foot has an "average" or medium width. If your foot is narrow, you'll probably find the socks too big; if your foot is wide, you'll probably find the socks too small.

The only way to know for sure what the finished sock will measure around the foot or leg is to divide the number of stitches in the foot or leg by the number of stitches per inch in the stitch pattern used (assuming the stitch gauge for the pattern used on the foot or leg is provided).

For example, if the pattern calls for 64 stitches in the foot or leg and the gauge is 8 stitches per inch (2.5 cm), the finished sock will measure 8 inches (20.5 cm) in circumference.

64 stitches ÷ 8 stitches/inch = 8 inches

If the sock sizes are given as foot length: Be careful. The typical assumption is that foot circumference increases proportionally with foot length. But the relationship

isn't this simple. If the pattern doesn't include the finished foot or leg circumference, you'll want to calculate it yourself based on the number of stitches and the gauge. If you can't find (or calculate) the finished measurement, these patterns are best avoided.

If the sock sizes are given as standard names, "small," "medium," "large": Again, be careful—if there's no indication of the actual size, you can't be sure of what you'll get unless you can calculate the finished measurement from the stitch count and gauge.

If the sock only has one size: Beware—one size does not fit all! Unless the finished measurement is also given, there's no way to know how it will fit unless there's enough information for you to calculate the finished measurement yourself.

All of this is to say that you need to know the finished measurements—foot and leg circumference and foot and leg lengths—to know if a knitted sock is going to fit. That's why I've given finished measurements for all the patterns in this book. If only one circumference measurement is given, the sock has the same circumference for both the leg and the foot. Unless indicated otherwise, choose the size that has about 10 percent negative ease. In other words, the finished sock should be 10 percent smaller than your actual foot measurements. For patterns that have slightly different foot and ankle circumferences, choose the size that corresponds to your foot circumference (again, allowing for negative ease).

The Foot Size Survey

There are disadvantages to the way that socks are typically sized. In general, we need to know more details about the size and shape of a foot to properly fit a sock. At a minimum, we need to know the foot and ankle circumferences, as well as the foot length. Ideally, we'd also like to know about the circumference at the arch of the foot, the circumference of the leg, and the length of the toes.

To compile a meaningful database, I ran a foot size survey in 2011 in which I asked knitters for five key measurements of their own feet and the feet of as many of their friends and family members as they could manage. Although I received replies from all over the world, most of the data I received was from North American knitters. I received more data for women's feet than men's. There is inherent risk in getting respondents to take their own measurements—I have to trust that they measured in the right places. Although this

THE FOOT SIZE SURVEY RESULTS

FOOT CIRCUM	FOOT LENGTH (in inches)				ANKLE CIRCUMFERENCE (in inches)				GUSSET CIRCUMFERENCE (in inches)			
	min	max	avg	avg as % of foot circum	min	max	avg	avg as % of foot circum	min	max	avg	as % of foot circum
8	8.00	10	8.9	1.11	7.50	9.75	8.5	1.06	8.66	9.66	9.1	1.14
8¼	8.75	9.75	9.1	1.1	7.60	8.5	8.1	0.98	8.50	9.5	9.1	1.1
8½	8.75	10.5	9.4	1.11	7.50	9	8.6	1.01	9.00	10	9.5	1.12
8¾	9.00	11	9.4	1.07	8.00	9.5	8.5	0.97	8.86	10.5	9.5	1.09
9	8.75	11	9.5	1.06	8.25	10.5	9	1	9.00	10.5	9.78	1.09
9¼	9.25	10.5	9.7	1.05	8.25	10	9.15	0.99	9.25	11	9.9	1.07
9½	9.50	10.5	9.9	1.04	8.75	10	9.35	0.98	9.25	11	10.4	1.09
9¾	9.00	10.5	10	1.03	8.50	10.75	9.6	0.98	9.75	11.75	10.7	1.1
10	9.75	11	10.3	1.03	8.75	11	9.77	0.98	9.75	11.75	10.8	1.08
10¼	9.50	11	10.4	1.01	8.75	10.75	9.9	0.97	9.75	11	10.5	1.02
10½	10.40	11.3	10.6	1.01	10.50	11.9	10.5	1	11.00	12.5	11.7	1.11
10¾	10.00	11	10.3	0.96	9.00	10	9.86	0.92	10.50	12	11.3	1.05
11	9.50	11	10.7	0.97	9.00	13	10.6	0.96	11.00	12.6	11.7	1.06

Notes: All measurements are in inches; multiply by 2.54 to get metric equivalents. The minimum (min) number is the smallest number reported for that measurement; the maximum (max) number is the largest number reported. The average was calculated by taking all of the numbers reported for that measurement and dividing by the total number of responses; it therefore may not be a simple average of the reported max and min numbers.

data only represents about 500 feet, it provides a significant sampling of foot circumferences that range from about 8 inches to 11 inches (20.5 to 28 cm), foot lengths that range from 8 inches to 11¼ inches (20.5 to 28.5 cm), and ankle circumferences that range from 7½ inches (19 cm) to almost 12 inches (30.5 cm). The data is compiled in the table above.

The measurements used in the table are shown in the illustration on page 9 and, taken as a whole, account for most of the nuances that can affect "standard" sock fit.

Foot Circumference (A): The circumference around the ball of the foot (avoid any bunions).

Ankle Circumference (B): The circumference around the narrowest part of the ankle.

Gusset Circumference (C): The circumference around the arch of the foot, just in front of the heel.

Foot Length (D): The length of the foot, from the tip of the longest toe from the back of the heel (this measurement is best taken when standing on a tape measure).

In addition, the following three measurements are handy for fine tuning.

Low Calf Circumference (E): The circumference of the leg, measured 6 inches (15 cm) up from the ground.

Heel Diagonal (F): The circumference of the diagonal from the top of the foot at the front of the ankle to the back of the heel, at the floor.

Toe Length (G): The length of the longest toe. It wasn't until after taking the survey that I discovered that toe length is also an important measurement.

In the vast majority of cases, **the ankle circumference is just about the same as the foot circumference.** The

HEEL DIAGONAL CIRCUMFERENCE (in inches)				LOW CALF CIRCUM 6" (15 cm) from floor	
min	max	avg	avg as % of foot circum	avg	avg as % of ankle circum
11	12	11.5	1.44	9.2	1.08
11	12	11.5	1.39	9.3	1.15
11	13	11.8	1.39	11.3	1.31
11	12.8	11.5	1.31	8.9	1.05
11.75	13.5	12.2	1.36	10.1	1.12
11.5	13.5	12.4	1.34	9.85	1.08
12.	14	12.9	1.36	10.2	1.09
12.4	14	13	1.33	9.76	1.02
12.8	14	13.1	1.31	10.7	1.1
10.5	15	13	1.27	9.6	0.97
13.	14.5	13	1.24	11.4	1.09
13.5	14.2	13.8	1.28	11	1.12
13.5	14.8	14.3	1.3	13	1.23

(E) low calf circumference

(B) ankle circumference

(A) foot circumference

(F) heel diagonal

6" (15 cm)

(C) gusset circumference

(G) toe length

(D) foot length

foot circumference is either the same or larger (only very rarely is it smaller). If the foot circumference is larger, it's only by about 5 percent. This means that you can expect the ankle circumference to be the same or possibly slightly smaller than the foot circumference.

I found a remarkable correlation between foot circumference and foot length. On average, **the foot length is about 5 percent to 10 percent larger than the foot circumference.** For example, if the foot circumference is 9 inches (23 cm), the foot length is about 9½ to 10 inches (24 to 25.5 cm).

$$9" \times 1.05 = 9.45"$$
$$or$$
$$9" \times 1.1 = 9.9"$$

On average, **the gusset circumference is about 10 percent to 15 percent larger than the foot circumference.** For example, if the foot circumference is 8 inches (20.5 cm), the gusset circumference will be about 9 inches (23 cm).

$$8" \times 1.1 = 8.8"$$
$$or$$
$$8" \times 1.15 = 9.2"$$

On average, the **heel diagonal** is about 35 percent larger than the foot circumference. For example, if the foot circumference is 8½ inches (21.5 cm), the heel diagonal will be about 11½ inches (29 cm).

$$8.5" \times 1.35 = 11.475"$$

The final measurement I asked for was the **low calf circumference**—the circumference of the leg 6 inches (15 cm) up from the floor (for an adult). This is the point where a "standard" leg (if there is such a thing) becomes wider as the calf muscle begins to curve out. A typical sock leg covers this curve, yet there's no shaping included to account for it. Remarkably, nearly half of the survey respondents reported a significant increase in leg circumference between the ankle and the low calf.

On average, the low calf circumference is 12 percent larger than the ankle circumference, but a huge variance was reported—some respondents had calf circumferences that were twice that of the foot.

For about 15 percent of the respondents, the low calf circumference is the same or smaller than the ankle circumference. These people have very thin legs below the calf muscles—they tend to be the ones described as having "athletic" builds or are naturally tall and skinny. "Standard" sock legs may very well fall down their thin legs, making customization a good idea.

For the majority of respondents—nearly 40 percent—this low calf circumference is between 1 percent and 10 percent larger than the ankle circumference. This means that a 9 inches (23 cm) ankle circumference corresponds to a low calf circumference between 9 inches and 10 inches (23 and 25.5 cm).

$$9" \times 1 = 9"$$
$$or$$
$$9" \times 1.1 = 9.9"$$

This is the typical shape we expect in legs, and it's the standard that most sock patterns follow. For the lucky people in this group, the difference between the two circumferences is not enough to affect how a sock fits—no leg shaping is required for a calf-length sock.

But for 30 percent of respondents (that's nearly one third!), the low calf circumference is 10 percent to 20 percent larger than the ankle circumference. In these cases, a 9 inches (23 cm) ankle circumference corresponds to a low calf circumference between 10 inches and 11 inches (25.5 and 28 cm).

$$9" \times 1.1 = 9.9"$$
$$or$$
$$9" \times 1.2 = 10.8"$$

The difference between the two circumferences can be significant—up to nearly 2 inches (5 cm)—which can have a sizable impact on how a standard sock will fit, particularly if the fabric isn't very stretchy.

For about 18 percent of the total respondents, the low calf circumference was more than 20 percent larger—2 inches (5 cm) or larger—than the ankle circumference. For these feet, calf shaping in the sock is a must!

How Do Your Feet Measure Up?

It's time to get a tape measure and ruler and measure both your bare feet according to the measurements in the Personal Foot Measurements table at right. Use the tape measure to measure circumferences, pulling the tape snug to eliminate any slack, but not so tight that it pinches. When measuring foot and toe lengths, step on a ruler that's placed on the floor.

Next, grab a calculator for a bit of analysis that will help you determine your sock-fit needs. The following ratios are indicative of whether or not standard patterns will fit your feet. Don't despair if your measurements don't match the expected ratios—we'll get to how to accommodate variations in Chapter 5.

Foot Circumference/Ankle Circumference Ratio: Divide your foot circumference by your ankle circumference.

If your answer is close to 1 (.95 to about 1.05), you can consider the two circumferences to be effectively the same—standard sock constructions should work just fine for you.

But if your answer is greater than 1.1, your foot is larger than your ankle and you'll benefit from some adjustments to the fit. Similarly, if your answer is less than 0.9, your foot is smaller than your ankle and you'll also be better off making some adjustments.

Gusset Circumference/Foot Circumference Ratio: Divide your gusset circumference by your foot circumference.

For an average foot, this ratio is 1.1. If your number is more than 1.15, you have a high arch and will want to adjust the fit. If your number is significantly smaller (1.0 or less), then you have a lower arch (or "flat" foot) that will also benefit from an adjusted fit.

Heel Diagonal/Foot Circumference Ratio: Divide your heel diagonal by your foot circumference.

For an average foot, this number is about 1.35, which is the ratio assumed in standard patterns. But if there's a sizeable difference in your ankle and foot circumferences, this number can vary significantly. Whether it's much bigger or much smaller, you'll want to make adjustments to your sock.

Foot Length/Foot Circumference Ratio: Divide your foot length by your foot circumference.

For an average foot, this ratio is between 1.05 and 1.1. If your number is much different—either higher or lower—then you need to be very wary about choosing sock patterns that are sized by foot length. In addition, if you're working a sock pattern in which the foot length is fixed for a given circumference, then you'll likely need adjustments. No adjustment is needed when working the standard patterns provided in this book because they permit on-the-fly foot length adjustment.

Toe Length: After taking the main survey, I asked knitters in my sock classes and on Twitter, as well as friends and family, to take this measurement. From a data set of about 100 responses, the average length of an adult's longest toe is between 1¾ inches and 2¼ inches (4.5 and 5.5 cm). Anything outside this range may require a pattern adjustment.

Estimating Missing Measurements

Rather remarkably, for an "average" shaped foot, as long as you have one of the three key measurements—foot (or ankle) circumference, foot length, or gusset circumference—you can use the following simple equations to determine the rest.

Foot circumference = foot length × 1.05

Ankle circumference = foot length × 1.05

Gusset circumference = foot length × 1.15

Foot length = foot circumference × 0.95

Foot length = ankle circumference × 0.95

Gusset circumference = foot circumference × 1.10

Gusset circumference = ankle circumference × 1.10

Most adult feet will be comfortable in standard socks patterns that are worked to these dimensions.

PERSONAL FOOT MEASUREMENTS

ACTUAL MEASUREMENTS	LEFT	RIGHT
Foot circumference (A) =		
Ankle circumference (B) =		
Gusset circumference (C) =		
Foot length (D) =		
Low calf cirfumference (E) =		
Heel diagonal (F) =		
Toe length (G) =		

RELATIONSHIPS	LEFT	RIGHT
Foot circumference ÷ ankle circumference = (standard fit = 0.95 to 1.05)		
Gusset circumference ÷ foot circumference = (standard fit = 1.1 to 1.15)		
Heel diagonal ÷ foot circumference = (standard fit = 1.3 to 1.4)		
Foot length ÷ foot circumference = (average fit = 1.05 to 1.1)		

Sock Sizing Tables

As a result of my foot size survey, I've compiled tables for what I believe to be "standard" sock sizes. If you know only the shoe size or foot circumference, you can find the other necessary measurements in the following tables.

SHOE SIZE, FOOT CIRCUMFERENCE, AND FOOT LENGTH

The following three tables provide sock circumference and finished sock length based on age, gender, shoe size, foot circumference, and actual foot length. If you know only one of these dimensions, the table will provide the other necessary measurements, assuming a "standard" foot.

WOMEN'S SHOE SIZES

US/ Canadian	EUR	UK	ESTIMATED FOOT CIRCUMFERENCE in	cm	SOCK CIRCUMFERENCE in	cm	ACTUAL FOOT LENGTH in	cm	FINISHED SOCK FOOT LENGTH in	cm
2½	33	1	7½	19	6¾	17	8	20.5	7¼	18.5
3		1.5	7¾	19.5	7	18	8	20.5	7½	19
3½	34	2	7¾	19.5	7	18	8	20.5	7¾	19.5
4	35	2.5	8	20.5	7¼	18.5	8¼	21	8	20.5
4½		3	8	20.5	7¼	18.5	8½	21.5	8	20.5
5	36	3.5	8¼	21	7½	19	8½	21.5	8	20.5
5½		4	8½	21.5	7½	19	8¾	22	8¼	21
6	37	4.5	8½	21.5	7½	19	9	23	8¼	21
6½	38	5	8¾	22	7¾	19.5	9	23	8½	21.5
7		5.5	9	23	8	20.5	9¼	23.5	8¾	22
7½	39	6	9	23	8	20.5	9½	24	9	23
8	40	6.5	9¼	23.5	8¼	21	9½	24	9	23
8½	41	7	9½	24	8½	21.5	9¾	25	9½	24
9		7.5	9½	24	8½	21.5	10	25.5	9½	24
9½	42	8	9¾	25	8¾	22	10	25.5	9¾	25
10	43	8.5	9¾	25	8¾	22	10½	26.5	9¾	25
10½		9	10	25.5	9	23	10½	26.5	10	25.5
11	44	9.5	10¼	26	9¼	23.5	10¾	27.5	10	25.5
11½		10	10¼	26	9¼	23.5	10¾	27.5	10½	26.5
12	45	10.5	10½	26.5	9½	24	11	28	10½	26.5
12½		11	10½	26.5	9½	24	11	28	10½	26.5
13	46	11.5	10¾	27.5	9¾	25	11½	29	10¾	27.5
13½	47	12	11	28	10	25.5	11½	29	11	28

Notes: There are minor disagreements among various sources about conversions between U.S./Canadian, European, and U.K. shoe sizes. Because of this, it's obviously most accurate to work with the actual foot length rather than shoe size, if possible. You might find slightly different numbers in your own research, but they shouldn't affect your results significantly. For ease of measurement, all of the numbers have been rounded to the nearest ¼ inch (6 mm) and 2 inches (5 cm).

The foot lengths are derived from industry standards for shoe sizes. The other numbers are calculated—based on "average" foot shapes—and rounded to the nearest ⅛ inch (3 mm). For simplicity, metric measurements are rounded to the nearest .5 centimeter. If your measuring tape/ruler isn't that accurate, just round down. Knitted fabric stretches and you're better erring on the small side!

For a child's sock, the general rule is to allow ¼ inch (6 mm) of negative ease in foot length. For an adult's sock, allow for ½ inch (1.3 cm) of negative ease in the foot length.

Sock foot length can be a guessing game, too. Patterns typically approach it one of two ways. The pattern may

MEN'S SHOE SIZES

US/ Canadian	EUR	UK	ESTIMATED FOOT CIRCUMFERENCE		SOCK CIRCUMFERENCE		ACTUAL FOOT LENGTH		FINISHED SOCK FOOT LENGTH	
			in	cm	in	cm	in	cm	in	cm
5	37	4.5	8½	21.5	7½	19	9	23	8½	21.5
5½	38	5	8¾	22	7¾	19.5	9	23	8¾	22
6		5.5	9	23	8	20.5	9½	24	8¾	22
6½	39	6	9	23	8	20.5	9½	24	9	23
7	40	6.5	9¼	23.5	8¼	21	9¾	25	9	23
7½	41	7	9½	24	8½	21.5	9¾	25	9½	24
8		7.5	9½	24	8½	21.5	10	25.5	9½	24
8½	42	8	9¾	25	8¾	22	10	25.5	9¾	25
9	43	8.5	9¾	25	8¾	22	10½	26.5	9¾	25
9½		9	10	25.5	9	23	10½	26.5	10	25.5
10	44	9.5	10¼	26	9¼	23.5	10¾	27.5	10	25.5
10½		10	10¼	26	9¼	23.5	10¾	27.5	10½	26.5
11	45	10.5	10½	26.5	9½	24	11	28	10½	26.5
11½		11	10½	26.5	9½	24	11	28	10¾	27.5
12	46	11.5	10¾	27.5	9¾	25	11½	29	10¾	27.5
12½	47	12	11	28	10	25.5	11½	29	11	28
13		12.5	11	28	10	25.5	11¾	30	11	28
13½	48	13	11¼	28.5	10¼	26	11¾	30	11½	29
14	49	13.5	11½	29	10¼	26	12	30.5	11½	29
14½		14	11½	29	10¼	26	12¼	31	11¾	30
15	50	14.5	11¾	30	10½	26.5	12½	31.5	11¾	30
15½	51	15	12	30.5	10¾	27.5	12½	31.5	12	30.5

CHILDREN'S SHOE SIZES

US/ Canadian	EUR	UK	ESTIMATED FOOT CIRCUMFERENCE		SOCK CIRCUMFERENCE		ACTUAL FOOT LENGTH		FINISHED SOCK FOOT LENGTH	
			inches	cm	inches	cm	inches	cm	inches	cm
1	16	0.5	3¼	8.5	3	7.5	3½	9	3¼	8.5
1½		1	3½	9	3¼	8.5	3¾	9.5	3½	9
2	17	1.5	3¾	9.5	3½	9	4	10	3¾	9.5
2½	18	2	3¾	9.5	3½	9	4	10	4	10
3		2.5	4	10	3½	9	4¼	11	4	10
3½	19	3	4¼	11	3¾	9.5	4½	11.5	4¼	11
4	20	3.5	4½	11.5	4	10	4½	11.5	4¼	11
4½		4	4½	11.5	4	10	4¾	12	4½	11.5
5	21	4.5	4¾	12	4¼	11	5	12.5	4¾	12
5½		5	4¾	12	4¼	11	5	12.5	5	12.5
6	22	5.5	5	12.5	4½	11.5	5¼	13.5	5	12.5
6½	23	6	5¼	13.5	4¾	12	5½	14	5¼	13.5
7		6.5	5½	14	5	12.5	5¾	14.5	5¼	13.5
7½	24	7	5½	14	5	12.5	5¾	14.5	5½	14
8	25	7.5	5¾	14.5	5¼	13.5	6	15	5¾	14.5
8½		8	5¾	14.5	5¼	13.5	6¼	16	6	15
9	26	8.5	6	15	5½	14	6¼	16	6	15
9½		9	6¼	16	5¾	14.5	6½	16.5	6¼	16
10	27	9.5	6¼	16	5¾	14.5	6¾	17	6¼	16
10½	28	10	6½	16.5	6	15	6¾	17	6¾	17
11	29	10.5	6¾	17	6	15	7	18	6¾	17
11½		11	6¾	17	6	15	7	18	7	18
12	30	11.5	7	18	6¼	16	7¼	18.5	7	18
12½		12	7	18	6¼	16	7½	19	7¼	18.5
13	31	12.5	7¼	18.5	6½	16.5	7¾	19.5	7¼	18.5
13½		13	7½	19	6¾	17	7¾	19.5	7¾	19.5
1	32	13.5	7¾	19.5	7	18	8	20.5	7¾	19.5
1½	33	1	7¾	19.5	7	18	8	20.5	8	20.5
2	34	1.5	8	20.5	7¼	18.5	8¾	22	8	20.5
2½		2	8	20.5	7¼	18.5	8½	21.5	8¼	21
3	35	2.5	8¼	21	7½	19	8¾	22	8½	21.5
3½	36	3	8½	21.5	7½	19	8¾	22	8¾	22
4		3.5	8½	21.5	7½	19	9	23	8¾	22
4½	37	4	8¾	22	7¾	19.5	9	23	9	23
5		4.5	9	23	8	20.5	9½	24	9	23
6	38	5	9	23	8	20.5	9½	24	9¼	23.5

give a set foot length for a given size—which isn't at all helpful if you're knitting for a foot that doesn't conform to the expected averages. Or the pattern may specify the distance to work, such as "work foot until it's 2 inches (5 cm) short of desired length," before starting the toe, which isn't very helpful if you're knitting the socks as a gift and don't know the wearer's actual foot length.

To help with these situations, I've provided a table of suggested sock foot lengths based on shoe size and sock circumference. If all you know is a shoe size, you can use this table to ensure your socks will fit well.

SOCK LEG LENGTHS

Many sock patterns relate sock leg length to sock size (foot circumference), but this isn't always an accurate approach. After all, sock size is no predictor of height, and

it certainly doesn't reflect individual preferences. Rather than relating leg length to sock size, I find it's better to base it on the age of the wearer for children or on gender and height for adults.

Use this table to choose leg lengths based on age and gender. I've provided three lengths for adults—short for those of less-than-average height, or those who prefer a shorter-than-average sock; regular for a standard fit; tall for those of taller-than-average height. Keep in mind that if you want to extend the leg length beyond what's given here, you may have to add leg circumference adjustments as described in Chapter 5.

The numbers here have been rounded to the nearest ¼ inch and .5 cm.

SOCK LEG LENGTHS

AGE/GENDER	ANKLE LENGTH	CALF LENGTH
4 to 6 years		4½"–5½" (11.5–14 cm)
6 to 8 years	1" (2.5 cm)	5"–6" (12.5–15 cm)
8 to 10 years		5½"–6½" (14–16.5 cm)
10 to 13 years		6"–7" (15–18 cm)

		Short	Regular	Tall
Women	1" (2.5 cm)	5"–6" (12.5–15 cm)	7" (18 cm)	8" (20.5 cm)
Men	1½" (3.8 cm)	7" (18 cm)	8" (20.5 cm)	9" (23 cm)

The Marpleridge Sock, page 82

Chapter 2
On Yarn, Needles, and Gauge

Because socks are subject to repeated stretching and abrasion, the fabric needs to withstand wear and abuse. A successful sock depends on the careful pairing of yarn and needles to get a sturdy fabric.

Yarn

The best yarns for sock knitters are those designed for knitting socks. Look for yarns that are specifically labeled "sock" yarn. In general, most sock yarns are fingering weight, but it doesn't follow that all fingering-weight yarns make good sock yarns. A good sock yarn is tightly spun with very little loft or "squish." The best sock yarns have multiple strands that are plied together. More strands form a denser yarn that's more resistant to abrasion.

When it comes to socks, beware of soft yarns! Softness is often an indicator of fragility. Although the temptation is to choose a yarn based on how it feels against your bare skin—your hands or your neck, for example—it's not a good way to choose a sock yarn. In most cases (unless you suffer from swollen and sore feet), feet are much less sensitive than hands when it comes to scratchy fibers. You don't want a fiber that makes you itchy, but you do want to avoid something that feels *too* good on your hands. A sock yarn should feel solid, substantial, and

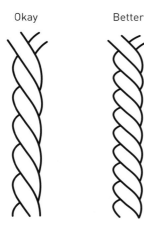

Okay   Better

A tightly spun yarn.

Good   Better   Best

Multiple plies.

strong—maybe even a little bit harsher than you'd like in a mitten or hat. In most cases, these are yarns that are made up of multiple plies. To test for itchiness, rub a potential sock yarn around the less sensitive skin of your elbow, not on the inside of your wrist or neck.

Many yarns are soft because they're loosely spun—something you don't want in a sock yarn. The softer and drapier the yarn, the quicker it's going to wear out, no matter how tightly you knit it. And softer yarns tend to pill more, so that the finished socks take on an old and tired look very quickly. The exception is the group of luxury sock yarns that include a percentage (typically 10 percent to 20 percent) of extra-soft fiber, such as angora, alpaca, cashmere, silk, or even qiviut. These yarns are more expensive, but they can be wonderful to wear.

FIBER CONTENT

Wool is the best fiber of all for sock knitting—it wicks away moisture to keep sweaty or rain-soaked feet amazingly dry and comfortable. It's insulating, but it also breathes, which makes it warm on a cold day and surprisingly cool on a warm day. It's got elasticity, so, although it will stretch out over the day with wear, it always bounces back to shape when washed. Wool doesn't hold odors, so it's ideal for those with "fragrant" feet. In fact, smelly feet are often smelly because sweat isn't given a chance to evaporate. The moisture is wicked away in wool socks, so there's no opportunity for odor to develop.

My favorite sock yarns are blends of superwash wool and nylon, especially those with 75–80 percent wool and 25–20 percent nylon. The nylon, which is spun along with the wool fibers, adds toughness and longevity. Some of my earliest socks knitted with this type of blend are still going strong, more than fifteen years later.

Silk is also a great addition to sock yarn, adding strength, warmth, and a nice sheen. If you can't find a suitable wool-nylon blend, a wool-silk blend is an excellent second choice. For a more summery alternative, try a blend of wool, cotton, and nylon.

Yarns made of pure wool generally don't wear as well as those blended with nylon. Although it's not uncommon to see a pure wool yarn labeled as sock yarn, I recommend caution. Socks knitted from 100 percent wool yarn just won't last as long. If you do choose pure wool for your socks, make sure that they fit your feet well, wash them gently, and be careful in how you wear them. It may seem counterintuitive, but a sock will last longer if it's worn in a shoe. If worn as a slipper against the floor, the sock experiences more friction and movement. In a shoe, on the other hand, the sock is relatively still so it doesn't rub and wear out.

You can help extend the life of socks made from non-sock yarns by working the fabric more densely than you normally would.

Wool Sensitivity

Many people believe that they're sensitive to wool and shy away from sock yarns that contain wool. To test if you're allergic to the fiber in a yarn, tie a short length around your wrist or ankle and wear it for a day. If a rash or sensitivity develops in that area, remove the yarn and, by all means, avoid knitting with that yarn or fiber.

Some people insist that they're allergic when, in fact, they just had a bad experience with an itchy sweater as a child or can't shake the perception that wool is scratchy. If tying the yarn around the wrist or ankle doesn't cause a reaction, wool socks shouldn't either. If the reaction is minor, try a yarn with less wool—one that blends wool, cotton, and nylon, for example—or choose a yarn composed of a softer wool, such as merino. Many of the sock yarns on the market now are spun from fine merino, which many people who thought they had wool sensitivities can wear comfortably.

Sometimes the allergy isn't about the fiber at all. It's quite possible that the problem lies in the chemicals that were added during the spinning and dyeing processes. In these cases, the problem can disappear down the drain with a thorough washing.

I'm not unsympathetic to a genuine allergy, but I do want to dispel misconceptions and bad memories. Wool really is best for socks if you can wear it comfortably. If you or someone you're knitting for experience uncomfortable reactions (itchiness or a rash) when wool comes in contact with the skin, you'll need to be diligent about reading yarn labels—even sock yarns sold as "cotton" can contain some percentage of wool. For a wool-sensitive foot, I recommend cotton-elastic-blend sock yarns. The elastic helps the socks bounce back into shape after a day of wear, and the cotton feels great on the feet. I've also seen blends of bamboo and elastic that should work equally well.

YARN AMOUNT

To determine if you have enough yarn for the socks you want to knit, check out the table below, which provides estimates for how much yarn you'll need for socks of various sizes and gauges. Note that two lengths are provided for each size—the standard calf length and the shorter ankle length. Keep in mind that your requirements will vary based on your own gauge, the foot and leg length of the sock, and any pattern adjustments. The numbers here are generous and include about a 15 percent "fudge factor" to help ensure you don't run out of yarn.

WASHING AND BLOCKING

Although I do sometimes handwash my socks—particularly those knitted from hand-dyed yarn, as I want to keep the colors at their best, or those knitted in colors that might bleed when wet—I don't want to *have* to do it. That's why I prefer sock yarns that are knitted from superwash wool. However, "superwash" doesn't include machine drying. Socks will last much longer if they air-dry—the friction a sock undergoes in a dryer creates unnecessary wear and tear (all those clothes rubbing against each other!). And the heat of the dryer can cause colors to fade.

YARN REQUIREMENTS FOR SOCKS

SOCK CIRCUMFERENCE		GAUGE (sts/inch)									
		4	5	5.5	6	6.5	7	7.5	8	9	
5" (12.5 cm)	calf length	80	85	90	100	110	120	130	140	160	yd
		73	78	82	91	101	110	119	128	146	m
	ankle length	53	56	59	66	73	79	86	92	106	yd
		48	51	54	60	67	72	79	84	97	m
5½" (14 cm)	calf length	100	110	120	130	140	150	160	170	180	yd
		91	101	110	119	128	137	146	155	165	m
	ankle length	65	72	78	85	91	98	104	111	117	yd
		59	66	71	78	83	90	95	101	107	m
6" (15 cm)	calf length	110	120	140	160	170	180	190	200	220	yd
		101	110	128	146	155	165	174	183	201	m
	ankle length	69	76	88	101	110	113	120	126	139	yd
		63	69	80	92	101	103	110	115	127	m
6½" (16.5 cm)	calf length	120	140	160	180	190	200	220	240	260	yd
		110	128	146	165	174	183	201	219	238	m
	ankle length	74	87	99	112	118	124	136	149	161	yd
		68	80	91	102	108	113	124	136	147	m
7" (18 cm)	calf length	150	160	200	210	225	250	265	285	305	yd
		137	146	183	192	206	229	242	261	279	m
	ankle length	92	98	123	129	138	154	163	175	188	yd
		84	90	112	118	126	141	149	160	172	m
7½" (19 cm)	calf length	175	190	240	260	275	295	310	325	350	yd
		160	174	219	238	251	270	283	297	320	m
	ankle length	106	115	145	157	166	178	188	197	212	yd
		97	105	133	144	152	163	172	180	194	m

For socks knitted with superwash wool, I recommend a cool or cold wash using normal laundry detergent. Wash them as you'd wash your best jeans. After the spin cycle is complete, hang the damp socks over a laundry or towel rack, or on "clippy hangers," to air-dry.

Contrary to popular belief, handwashing socks is not a major ordeal. Simply fill a sink, basin, or bucket with lukewarm water, add a squirt of wool wash, and swish it around to mix thoroughly. I'm very fond of the no-rinse wool washes, such as Soak and Eucalan, that are gentle on wool fibers and specifically formulated to eliminate the need to rinse. Add the socks to the water and let them soak for at least twenty minutes to fully absorb the water. Drain the water, then roll the socks in a towel (or put them in your washing machine's spin cycle) to squeeze out excess moisture. Then simply hang them to dry.

Because not all yarns are colorfast (and hand-dyed yarns often run), I always test a new yarn to see if the color will bleed before I wash socks with items of other colors. Either dunk the socks on their own in water, or just wet a length

YARN REQUIREMENTS FOR SOCKS, CONT.

SOCK CIRCUMFERENCE		GAUGE (sts/inch)									
		4	5	5.5	6	6.5	7	7.5	8	9	
8" (20.5 cm)	calf length	210	225	275	310	330	350	375	385	425	yd
		192	206	251	283	302	320	343	352	389	m
	ankle length	133	148	177	207	221	236	251	266	280	yd
		122	135	162	189	202	216	229	243	256	m
8½" (21.5 cm)	calf length	225	250	300	350	375	400	425	450	475	yd
		206	229	274	320	343	366	389	411	434	m
	ankle length	133	148	177	207	221	236	251	266	280	yd
		122	135	162	189	202	216	230	243	256	m
9" (23 cm)	calf length	250	280	350	390	420	440	460	475	525	yd
		229	256	320	357	384	402	421	434	480	m
	ankle length	146	164	205	228	246	257	269	278	307	yd
		134	150	187	208	225	235	246	254	281	m
9½" (24 cm)	calf length	300	325	375	440	460	475	500	525	575	yd
		274	297	343	402	421	434	457	480	526	m
	ankle length	174	189	218	255	267	276	290	305	334	yd
		159	173	199	233	244	252	265	279	305	m
10" (25.5 cm)	calf length	325	350	400	480	520	550	575	600	650	yd
		297	320	366	439	475	503	526	549	594	m
	ankle length	187	201	230	276	299	316	331	345	374	yd
		171	184	210	252	273	289	303	315	342	m
10½" (26.5 cm)	calf length	330	380	460	525	580	625	650	675	700	yd
		302	347	421	480	530	572	594	617	640	m
	ankle length	188	217	262	299	331	356	371	385	399	yd
		172	198	240	273	303	326	339	352	365	m

of the yarn and wrap it around a bunch of paper towels. Either way, you'll quickly see if the dye bleeds. The yarn may only bleed with the first wash, or the color may run for some time. If the color runs, wash the socks separately by hand until the wash water is completely clear.

Many knitters ask me if socks need to be blocked. Blocking—traditionally referred to as "dressing"—is the process by which we bring the fabric to its finished state. In general, knitted pieces are blocked to smooth and even out the fabric, stretch the piece to its finished size, wash off any substance that might have been applied during the spinning or dyeing process, and to remove any dirt or foreign substances picked up during the knitting process.

Although it sounds complicated and onerous, blocking socks is actually very simple. Certain fibers and fabrics require special treatments—notably fragile fibers and delicate lace fabrics—but we're not going to run into those when knitting socks.

To block your socks, wash them. Yes, that's it! Wash them as you intend to wash them going forward. If they're worked in a lace, cable, or colorwork fabric (something that benefits from a stretching and smoothing), then when they're still damp, put them on your feet to stretch them to fit; immediately remove them and let them dry.

And what about sock blockers, you ask? Those wooden or metal sock-shaped drying racks aren't really required these days. Their usage dates back to when knitters worked with yarns that were likely to felt—I believe that blockers were used to help stave off the shrinking that was likely to happen. After washing, the socks would be stretched over the blocker to help maintain the original size and shape as they dried. Unless you're working with a non-superwash yarn that might felt—which I don't recommend for a number of reasons—you don't need sock blockers.

To be honest, when I knit socks for myself, I often skip the blocking process entirely—they'll be washed soon enough anyway! If the socks are for a gift, or are going to be photographed for publication, I will take the time to tidy them up with a quick wash. The only time I will use sock blockers is if the socks are too big for me and too small for my husband, in which case, the blocker ensures that they're stretched to the correct size. Otherwise, I use the feet that are available to me.

Needles

Although there are patterns for knitting socks flat and seaming them, I don't recommend this type of construction because the seam creates bulk and can rub against the foot for an uncomfortable fit. The exception, of course, is socks that are never walked in—those knitted for babies, those in wheelchairs, or to wear in bed.

Traditionally, knitters have used double-pointed needles to knit socks in tubes. But in the past decade or so, sock knitters have taken to using the magic-loop method of knitting on a single long circular needle or working with two shorter circular needles. Needle manufacturers have recently begun to offer very short—8-inch (20.5 cm) to 9-inch (23 cm)—circular needles specifically for sock knitting.

There are pros and cons to each type of needle, and the type to use is largely personal choice. Double-pointed needles can make for quick progress, but some knitters find ladders of loose stitches form at the needle boundaries. If you're prone to dropping needles, you might prefer using two circular needles or the magic-loop method, although some knitters are annoyed by the extra needle tips and cable loops. Some knitters swear by the small circular needle, while others find them uncomfortable.

Ultimately, it doesn't matter what needle configuration you use—the results are the same. I strongly believe in letting the knitter choose the method that's most comfortable, and that patterns should be written to encourage any needle configuration. To that end, the patterns in this book are needle agnostic. That's to say, no specifications are given for needle arrangement. This takes a little more awareness on the part of the knitter—you need to know that the stitches should be divided up and how to navigate the different sections (such as the instep or sole stitches), rather than relying on specific needle designation. The discussion that follows will help with that.

DOUBLE-POINTED NEEDLES

Double-pointed needles (abbreviated dpn) are relatively short needles that have points at both ends. They are the classic, and still much-favored, method for working small circumferences in the round. Stitches are divided across three (or four) needles, and a fourth (or fifth) needle is used to knit around and around. The use of four versus five needles stems from regional differences—five needles were more common in Europe and Japan; four needles more common in the United Kingdom, Canada, Australia, and the United States.

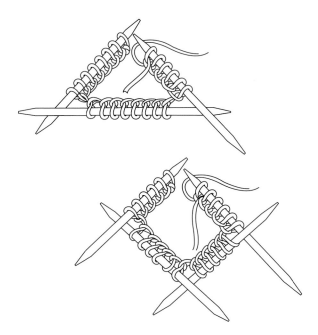

Sock stitches arranged on three (top) or four (bottom) double-pointed needles. A fourth or fifth needle will be used to knit with.

For a Top-Down Sock

When knitting a sock from the top down on double-pointed needles, it doesn't matter how the stitches are divided for the leg. It's a good idea to divide them relatively evenly, but it doesn't have to be precise. It's most important to have even multiples of your stitch pattern on each needle. For example, if you're working a sock leg in k2, p2 ribbing, arrange the stitches so that there is a multiple of four stitches on each needle. That way, each needle will begin with k2 and end with p2, which makes it easy to keep your place in the pattern.

For example, if your sock has 56 stitches and is worked in k1, p1 ribbing on a set of four double-pointed needles, divide the stitches so that there are 20 stitches on the first needle, 18 stitches on the second, and 18 stitches on the third. With this arrangement, there's an even number of stitches on each needle, and each needle will begin with a "k1, p1" repeat.

If, on the other hand, a k2, p2 ribbing is used, divide the stitches so that there are 20 stitches on the first needle, 20 stitches on the second, and 16 on the third. This ensures that each needle has a multiple of four stitches so that each will begin with a "k2, p2" repeat.

If you were working the same sock on a set of five double-pointed needles, you'd want to arrange 14 stitches (a multiple of 2 stitches) each on four needles for k1, p1 ribbing. For k2, p2 ribbing, you'd want 16 stitches each on two needles and 12 stitches each on the remaining needles so that there's a multiple of 4 stitches on each needle.

Whether you're working on four or five double-pointed needles, when you get to the heel adjust the stitches so that all of the heel stitches are on the same needle. After the heel is turned and it's time to pick up the gusset stitches, arrange the stitches so that the instep stitches are all on one needle (if you're using four needles) or divided between two needles (if you're using five needles). Pick up the stitches for one gusset with the needle that holds the heel stitches, work the instep stitches as established, then use an empty needle to pick up stitches for the other gusset and end by working the first half of the heel stitches (again) onto this needle. The stitches for one gusset and half of the heel are on one needle and the stitches for the other half of the heel and the other gusset are on another needle. At this point, the rounds begin at the bottom of the foot.

Gusset decreases are worked at the end of the first needle of the round and at the start of the last needle of the round. Maintain this arrangement after the gusset decreases have been completed so that the toe decreases are worked at the boundaries between the needles that hold the sole stitches and the needle(s) that hold(s) the instep stitches.

For a Toe-Up Sock

When knitting a sock from the toe up on four double-pointed needles, the instep (top of foot) stitches should be on one needle and the sole (bottom of foot) stitches divided equally between the two other needles. If five needles are used, divide the instep stitches between two needles.

When it comes time to shape the gussets, group the gusset increases and heel/sole stitches together—on one needle if you're working with four; divided equally between two needles if you're working with five—and divide the instep stitches between two needles. After the heel is completed, divide the stitches as you wish, remembering to keep track of the start of the round and making sure there are even multiples of the pattern repeat on each needle as for the top-down version.

TWO CIRCULAR NEEDLES OR THE MAGIC-LOOP METHOD

The method for using two circular needles was popularized by Cat Bordhi and Joyce Williams near the turn of the twenty-first century. This method relies on two circular needles—each 16 inches to 24 inches (40 to 60 cm) long—with half of the sock on each needle. The front of the leg or instep stitches are on one needle, while the back of the leg, heel, or sole stitches are on the other needle. As the stitches are worked in rounds, each needle only works the stitches that it holds.

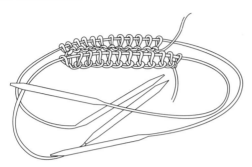

Sock stitches arranged on two circular needles.

The magic-loop method, invented by Sarah Hauschka and popularized by Bev Galeskas and *Fiber Trends* in 2002, uses a single circular needle that's 32 inches to 40 inches (80 to 100 cm) long. It's worked much the same as the two circular method, but only a single needle is used. The sock stitches are divided in half on the needle—the front of the leg/instep stitches in one half and the back of leg/heel/sole stitches in the other—with loops of the cord pulled out at the breaks between the halves. Only the half of the round actively being worked sits on the needle tips; the other half of the round rests on the cord.

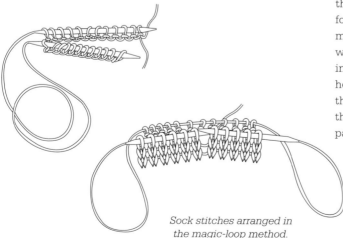

Sock stitches arranged in the magic-loop method.

For a Top-Down Sock

When knitting a sock from the top down on two circular needles or the magic-loop method, divide the stitches in half, making adjustments as necessary to maintain an even multiple of the stitch pattern on each half.

For example, if your sock has 58 stitches and is worked in k1, p1 ribbing, divide the stitches so that there are 30 stitches in one half and 28 stitches in the other half. With this arrangement, there's an even number of stitches in each half and each will begin with a "k1, p1" repeat. Once the ribbing is complete, you can rearrange the stitches so that there's the same number on each needle, taking care to not accidentally shift the start of the round when you shift the stitches.

Work the heel flap and heel turn on half of the stitches that are one needle. Once the heel is turned, use that same needle to pick up the first set of gusset stitches. Work across the instep stitches with the other needle and then use the heel needle to pick up the second set of gusset stitches. This will position all the instep stitches on one needle (or one half if using the magic-loop method) and all the heel stitches as well as both sets of gusset stitches on the other needle (or other half if using the magic-loop method). If you're using the magic-loop method, the loops will be pulled out at the boundaries between the instep and gusset stitches.

Keep in mind that this arrangement puts the beginning of the round at the center of the heel/bottom of foot stitches, which is in the center of the needle holding the heel and gusset stitches. Be sure to place a marker so you'll know when you come to it.

For a Toe-Up Sock

When knitting a sock from the top up on two circular needles or the magic-loop method, divide the stitches so that half are for the instep/top of foot and the other half are for the sole/bottom of foot. Unless adjustments have to be made to accommodate a stitch pattern on the instep (in which case there may be a different number of stitches in each half), this arrangement can continue through the heel shaping (the heel is shaped on the stitches that form the sole) and on to the ribbing at the top of the leg. For the ribbing, make sure that each needle begins with full pattern repeat.

For example, if your sock has 62 stitches and has a k1, p1 ribbing, you'll want 30 stitches in one half and 32 stitches in the other half. With this arrangement, there's an even number of stitches on each needle and each begins with a "k1, p1" repeat.

Keep in mind that if you have to adjust the stitch distribution to accommodate a stitch pattern for the leg, you'll need to rearrange them again before starting the heel to ensure that all the sole stitches are on one needle and the instep stitches on the other.

A SHORT CIRCULAR NEEDLE

A very short 8-inch or 9-inch (20.5 or 23 cm) circular needle may be a perfect solution for sock knitting—the stitches for most adult socks fit perfectly around the small circumference.

Sock stitches arranged on a very short circular needle.

Once you place a marker and join for working in rounds, you don't have to worry about needle breaks interrupting pattern repeats. But you will need to add markers to keep track of the boundaries between the instep and sole stitches.

Unfortunately, this method hasn't taken the sock world by storm because many knitters find the exceptionally short needle tips awkward to work with.

If you're knitting a sock with a large circumference, it's possible that the stitches will be too crowded on such a short needle. If this becomes a problem, use one of the other needle arrangements when the gussets are at their fullest.

Marking the Start of the Round

Most patterns specify placing a marker at the start of the round. This is easily done if you're working on a small circular needle, but if you're using double-pointed needles or two circulars or the magic-loop method, the marker will fall off the needle.

In these cases, it's a good idea to come up with other ways to identify the start of the round.

Top-Down Sock

The start of the round is easy to keep track of when you're working the leg of a top-down sock—it's aligned with the cast-on tail. You're at the start of the round when you're aligned with the cast-on tail at the end of a needle.

After you've turned the heel and picked up the gusset stitches, the start of the round is at the center of the heel/sole stitches. If you're using double-pointed needles, this coincides with the break between the first and last needles of the round. You can place a removable stitch marker in the fabric at this point to help you keep track of where you are. If you're working on two circulars or the magic-loop method, the start of the round is located in the center of the sole stitches. Because the sole stitches are all on the same needle, it's safe to place a marker in the appropriate place in the center of them.

Toe-Up Sock

For socks that are worked from the toe up, the start of the round is located at the side of the foot. Because it's difficult to keep track of the cast-on tail—it gets hidden in the cup that forms the toe—attach a removable stitch marker or safety pin to the outside of the sock near the break between the sole and instep stitches. You don't have to be precise about the marker placement; as long as it's closer to one side than the other, you'll be able to keep track of it. Move the marker up every few rounds so that it's always easy to see.

Whether you're working top down or toe up, you'll have to substitute a different type of needle—double-pointed, two circulars, or the magic loop—when it's time to decrease for the toe. A short circular needle can't accommodate the diminishing circumferences of toe shaping.

MANAGING PATTERN REPEATS

Your choice of needle configuration can help you manage your stitches if you're working a stitch or color pattern. When working a sock with cables that travel all around the leg, it's better to have fewer breaks—turning a cable over a break between two needles requires rearranging the stitches. If your sock has a very large pattern repeat— a lace motif over half the leg, for example—then either the magic-loop or two circulars method will allow you to group all of the stitches in the motif together, making the design easier both to work and to track. (Double-pointed needles can work just as well for a sock with a patterned foot and plain sole; just group the patterned stitches together on one needle and divide the plain sole across two needles.) Of course, a small circular is great for managing any size or number of pattern repeats—just add markers to keep track of the boundaries.

MINIMIZING LADDERS OF LOOSE STITCHES

When knitting in rounds, it's pretty common to experience "ladders"—columns of loose strands between stitches at the breaks between the needles. These ladders are formed when more yarn is used to bridge the gap between needles than needed to bridge the gap between two adjacent stitches. This typically results in the first stitch on the new needle "taking on" that extra yarn and becoming larger in doing so.

Round in progress, with a visible ladder.

To prevent distinct vertical lines of loose stitches, some knitters move the stitches around every now and then, changing the breaks between the needles. This doesn't really solve the problem, but rather disguises it by distributing the looseness around the round.

Many knitters find that they can minimize ladders by their choice of needle type. Some reduce the number of ladders by choosing to work with two circulars or the magic-loop method instead of working with double-pointed needles. Their reasoning is that there are only two needle breaks instead of

three or four. Others find that their ladders are worse when they use two circulars or the magic-loop method, and these knitters have better luck when there are more needle breaks and not such a sharp angle between each needle. These knitters prefer to use five double-pointed needles.

There are two factors that contribute to ladders—the type of stitch that's being worked and how the needles are held. Ladders tend to be worse when a needle begins with a purl stitch. This is because the yarn has a bit farther to go to get into position for a purl stitch. This can be exacerbated by the extra distance that's inherently between two needles. To mitigate this possibility, distribute the stitches as necessary so that each needle begins with a knit stitch, not a purl.

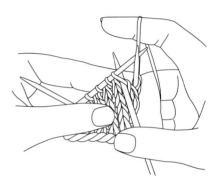

Needle setup, tips close to each other, old needle tip under new needle tip.

Another trick is to hold your needles so that there's as little distance as possible between the last stitch on the previous needle and the first stitch on the next needle. I have good luck when I position the previous needle tip below the tip of the next needle.

You can consciously snug up the first stitch of each needle to help remove some of the extra yarn. But pulling the first stitch tight only helps so much—you can't pull the stitch any tighter than the needle it sits on will allow. Although it seems counter intuitive, I've found that pulling the *second* stitch tight takes care of the problem. Simply pull extra tight when working the second stitch on a needle, thereby pulling the first stitch up close to it and removing excess slack.

Over the years, I've noticed that my laddering problem has gotten a little worse. As I've gained experience as a sock knitter, I've developed the habit of tugging on every stitch to ensure a tight fabric. Therefore, pulling the second stitch doesn't change things that much for me. But I've also learned not to worry about my ladders too much—most of them come out with washing and wearing. The little bit of extra yarn in that start-of-needle stitch gets distributed throughout the fabric after a few washes and eventually disappears entirely.

Examine some of your newest socks and some of your older socks to get a sense of how big a problem laddering is for you. You, too, may be pleasantly surprised to see that it solves itself over time.

If you find that your ladders are visible even after washing and wearing, or if you're presenting the socks as a gift and want them to look perfect right out of the gate, there's a nice little trick that I call the "hungry stitch." Slip the first stitch of each needle knitwise while holding the yarn in the back of the work, which will leave a short strand of yarn behind the stitch **(Figure 1)**. On the following round, work that slipped stitch by pulling the previous round's strand through the stitch **(Figure 2)**—it's effectively slipped on each subsequent round because it's worked with the strand from the previous round; not the current round's **(Figure 3)**. This makes the first stitch on the needle extra tight because the float created by slipping the stitch is shorter than the length of yarn needed for a normal stitch. Once you get the hang of it, you'll find that you can settle into a comfortable rhythm.

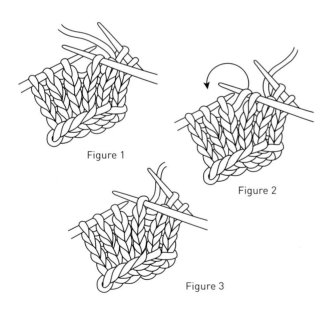

Figure 1

Figure 2

Figure 3

If you're unhappy with ladders that aren't eliminated with washing, there's still hope. Find yourself a tiny crochet hook one or two sizes smaller in diameter than the needles you knitted with. Then turn the lowest rung of the ladder into a new stitch—pick up the strand at the base of the leg, twist it to take up the slack **(Figure 1)**, then ladder up

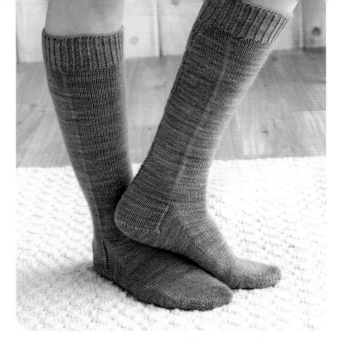

The Fitzcarraldo Knee Sock, page 178.

the rungs to the ribbing at the top of the leg **(Figure 2)**. Pull the final loop to the wrong side, then use a bit of extra yarn to secure it in place.

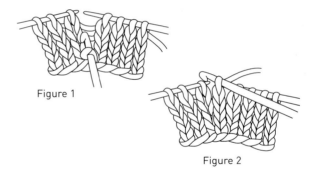

Figure 1

Figure 2

Be aware that this isn't an invisible fix—it leaves a bit of a ridge that could be uncomfortable along the bottom of the foot and potentially along the instep if worn with somewhat tight shoes. Therefore, it's best to limit this trick to ladders along the sides of the leg.

But, there's no reason you can't use this as a design element. When knitting the Fitzcarraldo Knee Socks on page 178, I didn't worry about the ladders as I went. After the socks were off the needles, I worked this "faux seam" on the sides of the legs for an attractive look.

If you're working toe up and you know in advance that you want this look, create the seam stitch after the leg is complete but before you start the ribbing. Once you've worked the new stitch to the top, slip it onto your needles and work it together with its neighbor as you start the ribbing.

Gauge

If you want the socks you knit to fit, yes, you do need to knit a gauge swatch. And in the round at that.

In addition to indicating the finished size of a knitted piece, a gauge swatch is a great way to get a sense of the yarn. It's far better to find that you're allergic to one of the fibers—or that you don't like working with it, or that the colorway doesn't work the way you want, or that it doesn't machine wash well—after committing to just a swatch than after knitting an entire pair of socks!

It's important to knit your swatch in the round because that's the way you'll knit the socks. Many knitters knit and purl at different gauges—most often the purl stitches are looser than their knit stitches. When worked back and forth in rows, stockinette stitch is produced by alternating rows of knit stitches with rows of purl stitches. But when worked in rounds, as socks are knitted, stockinette stitch is produced by only knit stitches. If your purl stitches are a little looser than your knit stitches (or vice versa), it's quite possible that the gauge you get when working in rounds will be different than the gauge you get when working back and forth in rows.

THE GAUGE SWATCH

To determine your gauge, you'll need to knit a swatch that's about 6 inches (15 cm) in circumference. To determine how many stitches to cast on for this circumference, multiply the number of stitches suggested for 4 inches (10 cm) on the ball band by 1.5 if you're using a sock yarn; multiply the number by 2 if you're using a yarn that isn't manufactured specifically for knitting socks. If necessary, round up to the nearest even number.

For example, if the ball band on a sock yarn is reported as 28 stitches = 4" (10 cm), you'll want to cast on 42 stitches.

28 stitches × 1.5 = 42 stitches

If the ball band on a non-sock yarn is reported as 20 stitches = 4" (10 cm), you'll want to cast on 40 stitches.

20 stitches × 2 = 40 stitches

Note: Some yarns list the gauge on the ball band as stitches per 1 inch or 2 inches (2.5 or 5 cm). Read carefully! You'll have to adjust these numbers to match the "per 4 inches (10 cm)" gauge.

If you're using yarn designed for sock knitting (read the label), use the needles recommended on the ball band. If you're using yarn that's not labeled as sock yarn, use needles two to three sizes smaller than recommended on the ball band. This will ensure a dense, sturdy fabric suitable for socks.

Using your choice of double-pointed or circular needles, cast on the determined number of stitches and join for working in rounds. Working in rounds, work in k1, p1 ribbing for at least ½ inch (1.3 cm), work in the stockinette stitch (or the pattern stitch you plan to use; see page 62) for about 3 inches (7.5 cm), then loosely bind off all the stitches. I don't work ribbing at both the top and bottom of the swatch because it can prevent the swatch from lying flat and make it difficult to get a good measurement of the stockinette stitch.

Wash the swatch the way you intend to wash the finished socks, then let it air-dry completely.

Don't be tempted to skip the step on washing the swatch. Some yarns (and therefore knitted fabrics) can change shape with washing. Superwash wools often relax a little when washed—you don't want to knit a pair of socks that only fit the first time they're worn! In addition, washing the swatch will let you know if the color is going to run—it's better to know this before you wash a new pair of red socks in the same load as your favorite white ones. And many yarns soften up and bloom beautifully with washing; washing the swatch will give you a good sense of how the finished sock fabric will look and feel.

MEASURING THE GAUGE SWATCH

To measure the swatch, lay a ruler on the fabric (do not press down on the ruler) and count the number of stitches, including partial stitches, in a 2-inch (5 cm) width. You need to measure and count precisely—partial stitches do matter!

Measure in two or three places—a yarn that's a little slubby or inconsistently spun might have different gauges at different places. If this is the case, take the average of the gauges you measure.

The number of stitches you count will be your stitch gauge over 2 inches (5 cm) of knitting. Note that you'll have to divide that number by 2 in order to determine the stitch gauge over 1 inch (2.5 cm). For example, if you count 11 stitches across 2 inches (5 cm) in the horizontal direction, your stitch gauge is 5.5 stitches per inch (2.5 cm).

11 stitches per 2" ÷ 2 = 5.5 stitches per inch

If you plan to knit your socks from the toe up, you'll also need to know the vertical, or "round" gauge, or the number of rounds per inch (2.5 cm). Simply reorient the ruler and count the number of stitches in 2 inches (5 cm) of vertical length. Then divide this number by 2 to determine the round gauge. For example, if you count 16 stitches across 2 inches (5 cm) in the vertical direction, your round gauge is 8 rounds per inch (2.5 cm).

16 rounds per 2" ÷ 2 = 8 rounds per inch

It's important to measure over 2 inches (5 cm) to get an accurate result. Fractions of stitches, which can be difficult to properly estimate over a short distance, can become significant when multiplied over the entire circumference of a sock. For example, when measuring over just 1 inch (2.5 cm), it can be difficult to discern the difference between a half and a quarter of a stitch. But the difference is more clearly apparent when averaged over 2 inches (5 cm).

FABRIC DENSITY

Socks that wear the longest are knitted in dense fabrics. A loosely knitted fabric will wear out faster and will stretch more and feel less comfortable against the foot. Yarns designed for sock knitting (spun and blended with longevity in mind) typically recommend tighter gauges than normal for yarns of similar sizes.

If you plan to use a yarn that's not designed specifically for sock knitting, you'll want to knit it tighter than the gauge specified on the ball band. In most cases, this means you'll use smaller needles than the size recommended. For example, a worsted-weight yarn that normally would be worked at a gauge of 20 stitches/4" (10 cm) should be worked at a gauge of 22 stitches/4" (10 cm) for socks. It's not unusual to use needles several sizes smaller than recommended on the ball band to achieve this tighter gauge.

Swatching in the Round: A Shortcut

There is a handy shortcut for swatching in the round. Working on two double-pointed needles or a single circular needle, cast on the necessary number of stitches. Knit the first row, but don't turn the work at the end of the row. Instead, slide the stitches to the other end of the needle, bringing the working yarn *loosely* across the wrong side of the piece, and knit again, starting with the first stitch of the previous row, as if knitting a very wide (and very loose) bit of I-cord. To keep the edge stitches tidy, twist the first and last stitch of every row by knitting them through their back loops.

Be careful not to pull the loose strands too tightly across the back of the work—the idea is to have them long enough to span the width without causing puckers.

Once you've got about 3 inches (7.5 cm) of stockinette stitch, work about ½ inch (1.3 cm) of k1, p1 ribbing, then bind off loosely in pattern.

Wash the swatch as usual, then cut the loose strands to ensure the swatch will lie flat when you measure the gauge.

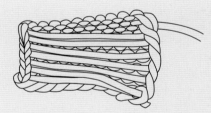

Loose strands carried across the back of the work for the I-cord method of swatching in rounds.

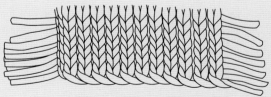

When the loose strands are cut, the gauge is easily measured.

The table below gives guidelines for appropriate sock gauges for yarns of different weights. Because sock-appropriate yarns can be difficult to find in some weights, I've included information for combining finer yarns to achieve standard yarn weights.

A good rule of thumb is that combining two strands of the same yarn together will produce a gauge of about two-thirds of the gauge of the yarn worked single-stranded. That is, if you expect a gauge of 30 stitches in 4 inches (10 cm) with a single strand of fingering-weight yarn, you can expect a gauge of about 20 stitches in 4 inches (10 cm) with the yarn doubled, which amounts to the equivalent of a worsted-weight yarn.

$$30 \; stitches \times {}^2/_3 = 20 \; stitches$$

In addition, you'll want to use smaller needles to ensure a suitable dense fabric. Keep in mind that these are only guidelines—always knit a swatch to know for sure if the fabric will be appropriate.

A Note About Stitch Proportions

The tables in this book make the (big) assumption that your stitches adhere to the typical 3:4 ratio—that is, there are three stitches in width for every four rows in length. Put another way, the width of three stitches is the same as the height of four rows. In general, your stitch gauge should be the same as your round gauge multiplied by about 0.75.

For example, the gauge for many of the yarns I've chosen is 8 stitches and 11 rounds per inch (2.5 cm). These numbers adhere to the 3:4 ratio necessary for the formulas in this book:

$$8 \; stitches \div 11 \; rounds = 0.73$$

Anything between about .7 and .8 is fine. If your stitch and round gauge don't conform to this ratio, don't panic. You'll just need to calculate your own measurements for the numbers in the tables according to the formulas that are provided in Chapter 5.

YARN EQUIVALENTS TABLE

YARN WEIGHT	USUAL GAUGE & NEEDLES	RECOMMENDED SOCK GAUGE & NEEDLES	EQUIVALENTS
"Light fingering"	30–32 sts/4" (10 cm) on 2.25–2.5mm/US 1–1.5	If designed for sock knitting, use as stated. If not, recommend 32–36 sts/4" (10 cm) on 2.0–2.25/US 0–1	Combining two laceweight yarns might get you the gauge you need, but you'll need to experiment as laceweight yarns vary in thickness.
"Heavy fingering"	28 sts/4" (10 cm) on 2.75mm/US 2	If a sock yarn, use as stated. If not, aim for 30–32 sts/4" on 2.25–2.5mm/US 1–1.5	
Baby/Sport	25–26 sts/4" (10 cm) on 3–3.5mm/US 2.5–4	28 sts/4" (10 cm) on 2.75mm/US 2	
Double Knitting (DK)/ Light Worsted	22–24 sts/4" (10 cm) on 3.5–4mm/US 4–6	25–26 sts/4" (10 cm) on 3–3.5mmUS 2.5–4	two strands light fingering weight
Worsted	20 sts/4" (10 cm) on 4.5mm/US 7	22 sts/4" (10 cm) on 3.5–4mm/US 4–6	two strands heavy fingering weight
Aran/Heavy Worsted	18 sts/4" (10 cm) on 5mm/US 8	20 sts/4" (10 cm) on 4–4.5mm/US 6–7	two strands baby/ sportweight
Chunky/Bulky	14 sts/4" (10 cm) on 6mm/US 10	16 sts/4" (10 cm) on 5mm/US 8	two strands worsted weight

Reinforcement

To help socks wear longer, it can be a good idea to reinforce areas that are subject to abrasion and friction. Because everyone has a different foot, and everyone has a different gait, and everyone wears shoes differently, the stress areas on socks are different for everyone. Examine a pair of your well-loved, frequently worn socks for signs of wear. Outright holes are easy to find, but also look for areas where the fabric might be pilling or thinning.

HEEL FLAPS

Most top-down sock patterns specify that a special dense pattern be worked on the heel flap to add thickness and strength to an area that can be subject to a lot of stress and abrasion. I've even seen Christmas stockings with reinforced heels, although I believe the only place that needs reinforcement on a Christmas stocking is the toe—oranges are heavy!

I typically don't add this type of reinforced stitch pattern to my sock patterns because I don't feel it's always necessary. The slipped-stitch patterns used for heel flap reinforcement do three things that aren't always desirable—they make the heel flaps thicker (which makes for a tighter fit in shoes), they remove the lateral stretch in this area, and they change the look of the fabric. None of these is a major issue, but if it's not necessary, then why bother?

But if you find that your socks wear thin along the back of the heel, a little reinforcement is a good idea. The two slip-stitch patterns in the box on page 30 are excellent and can be added to any heel flap.

Another option is to work the heel flap in a color-stranded pattern, such as The Carpita Sock on page 116. If you don't want a color pattern, simply alternate 1 stitch each from two different balls of the same-color yarn.

I sometimes choose to extend the pattern that's on the back of the leg along the heel flap of a sock. This choice is a design flourish, and I fully admit that it may not always be practical. A cabled heel, such as the one in Man of Aran Sock on page 146, does all the things the heel stitch patterns do—it makes a thicker fabric, removes the stretch, and changes the look—but it also looks great. If you don't like the look of a patterned heel flap, it's perfectly fine to work stockinette stitch or one of the more conventional reinforced heel patterns instead. But keep in mind that doing so may require an adjustment to the stitch count so that the heel flap is worked on the same number of stitches as the sole. In most cases, you

The Man of Aran Sock, page 146.

can simply increase or decrease to the necessary number of stitches—on a top-down sock, work the increases to decreases before you begin the flap; on a toe-up sock, work the increases or decreases after completing the flap.

OTHER AREAS

The dense heel stitch patterns don't have to be limited to the heel flaps—you can use them wherever you need a little reinforcement. For example, my big toe tends to poke through the tops of the toes in the socks. To help the fabric last longer, I often work the standard heel stitch pattern on the top of the toes of my socks. You could add the same pattern to the bottom of the heel or ball of the foot as well if you find that those areas wear out more quickly on your socks.

The square heel turn that's used for the templates and projects in this book lends itself well to reinforcement at the bottom of the heel. Because the same number of stitches remain in the center section of the heel in a top-down sock, it's easy to add a reinforcing pattern.

It's a little more challenging to reinforce the bottom of the heel in a toe-up sock, but it can be done. Establish the reinforced stitch pattern on the first row of the heel turn, then continue working the pattern throughout the short-row section.

Because the heel stitch patterns will reduce the horizontal (stitch-wise) stretch of the fabric, I don't recommend

Heel Stitch Patterns

Standard Pattern

The most common reinforcement pattern for heel flaps is worked over 2 rows or rounds. The first row or round alternates a slipped stitch with a knit stitch, while the second is worked "plain." There are slight differences in the way the 2 rows are worked, depending on whether the heel flap is worked in rows or rounds and depending on whether there is an even or odd number of stitches. The instructions that follow are for working socks from the top down; when working the heel stitch patterns on toe-up socks, the last stitch of every row is worked together with the nearest instep stitch to join them together.

Worked in Rows; Even Number of Stitches
ROW 1: (right side) *Slip 1 purlwise while holding yarn in back, knit 1; repeat from *.

ROW 2: (wrong side) Slip 1 purlwise while holding yarn in front, purl to end.

Repeat Rows 1 and 2 for pattern.

Worked in Rows; Odd Number of Stitches
ROW 1: (right side) *Slip 1 purlwise while holding yarn in back, knit 1; repeat from * to last stitch, knit 1.

ROW 2: (wrong side) Slip 1 purlwise while holding yarn in front, purl to end.

Repeat Rows 1 and 2 for pattern.

Eye-Of-Partridge Pattern

The eye-of-partridge pattern is worked over 4 rows or rounds. The first 2 rows or rounds are worked the same as the standard pattern. The slipped and knitted stitches are reversed on the third row or round, then the fourth is worked "plain." The result is a decorative honeycomb pattern.

Worked in Rows; Even Number of Stitches
ROW 1: (right side) *Slip 1 purlwise while holding yarn in back, knit 1; repeat from *.

ROW 2: (wrong side) Purl.

ROW 3: (right side) Slip 1 purlwise while holding yarn in back, *slip 1 purlwise while holding yarn in back, knit 1; repeat from * to last stitch, knit 1.

ROW 4: (wrong side) Purl.

Repeat Rows 1–4 for pattern.

Worked in Rows; Odd Number of Stitches
ROW 1: (right side) *Slip 1 purlwise while holding yarn in back, knit 1; repeat from * to last stitch, knit 1.

ROW 2: (wrong side) Purl.

ROW 3: (right side) Slip 1 purlwise while holding yarn in back, *slip 1 purlwise while holding yarn in back, knit 1; repeat from *.

ROW 4: (wrong side) Purl.

Repeat Rows 1–4 for pattern.

Worked in Rounds; Even Number of Stitches

ROUND 1: *Slip 1 purlwise while holding yarn in back, knit 1; repeat from *.

ROUND 2: Knit.

Repeat Rounds 1 and 2 for pattern.

Worked in Rounds; Odd Number of Stitches

ROUND 1: *Slip 1 purlwise while holding yarn in back, knit 1; repeat from * to last stitch, knit 1.

ROUND 2: Knit.

Repeat Rounds 1 and 2 for pattern.

Worked In Round; Even Number of Stitches

ROUND 1: *Slip 1 purlwise while holding yarn in back, knit 1; repeat from *.

ROUND 2: Knit.

ROUND 3: Slip 1 purlwise while holding yarn in back, *slip 1 purlwise while holding yarn in back, knit 1; repeat from * to last stitch, knit 1.

ROUND 4: Knit.

Repeat Rounds 1–4 for pattern.

Worked In Rounds; Odd Number of Stitches

ROUND 1: *Slip 1 purlwise while holding yarn in back, knit 1; repeat from * to last stitch, knit 1.

ROUND 2: Knit.

ROUND 3: Slip 1 purlwise while holding yarn in back, *slip 1 purlwise while holding yarn in back, knit 1; repeat from * to last stitch, knit 1.

ROUND 4: Knit.

Repeat Rounds 1–4 for pattern.

using them for more than about 30 percent of the sock circumference at any point (unless, of course you're using it on the heel flap; the lack of stretch in the flap is compensated for with a little extra length in the foot).

REINFORCEMENT YARNS

Reinforcement yarn, made specifically to strengthen the heels and toes of socks, is available in an assortment of colors. Some sock yarns even include a spool of finer yarn that's been dyed to match for this purpose. Reinforcement yarn is particularly helpful if the working yarn isn't designed specifically for knitting socks or if it doesn't contain any nylon. They typically contain some percentage of nylon for strength, but even a strand of pure wool will help make the fabric denser and tighter.

Simply carry the reinforcement yarn along with the working yarn in any area that you wish to reinforce. In general, these yarns are very fine, and they don't significantly change the gauge of the fabric.

When choosing a reinforcement yarn, choose one that has the same tensile strength as the working yarn. If you add something that's stronger (such as polyester or nylon sewing thread, for example), there's a risk that the stronger reinforcement fibers will cut through the working yarn and actually accelerate wear. Reinforcement yarns designed for sock knitting take this into account.

If you can't find reinforcement yarn, you can always hold two strands of the working yarn together without changing the needle size. Although this will alter the gauge somewhat, the thick fabric will wear like iron. If worked over a relatively small area, such as the heel flap, the gauge change will have minimal structural impact.

Chapter 3
On the Basic Patterns

If you're knitting for a foot that conforms to the rules for average foot shape, and you're working a relatively "plain" sock, then you can use these patterns as written without adjustment. By "plain," I mean a sock with a stockinette-stitch foot and the leg worked entirely in ribbing or partly in ribbing and partly in stockinette stitch.

These rules also apply if you're working in a pattern stitch that doesn't affect your gauge (see Chapter 4).

I've provided two such patterns in this chapter—one worked from the cuff to the toe, the other worked from the toe to the cuff. Each version includes instructions for twelve foot circumferences and each at nine possible gauges.

Finished Sock Measurements

To begin, you need to know what size sock to knit. Measure your foot as described in Chapter 1 to determine the proper finished size (keeping in mind that you want to allow for about 10 percent negative ease). Note that all the measurements given in the tables below are for the finished sock, not the foot measurements.

FOOT OR ANKLE CIRCUMFERENCE

If you know the circumference of the foot or ankle you're knitting for, multiply it by 0.9 (which allows for 10 percent negative ease) to get the finished sock circumference. For example, if your foot measures 10 inches (25.5 cm), you'd want to follow the instructions for a sock with a finished circumference of 9 inches (23 cm).

$$10'' \times 0.9 = 9''$$

If you're knitting for someone else and only know the shoe size, turn to the Shoe Size/Sock Length Tables on pages 12–14 to determine the appropriate foot (and ankle) circumference. For example, if the shoe size is a U.S. Men's 12, then you can assume a foot circumference of 11½ inches (29 cm).

Again, multiply this foot circumference by 0.9 to determine the appropriate finished sock circumference.

FOOT LENGTH

If you know the length of the foot you're knitting for, calculate the sock foot length by subtracting ¼ inch (6 mm) for a child's sock or subtracting ½ inch (1.3 cm) for an adult's sock. For example, if an adult foot measures 9¼ inches (23.5 cm) long, you'll want the finished foot of the sock to measure 8¾ inches (22 cm).

$$9\tfrac{1}{4}'' - \tfrac{1}{2}'' = 8\tfrac{3}{4}''$$

If you're knitting for someone else and only know the shoe size, turn to the Shoe Size/Sock Length Tables on pages 12–14 to determine the appropriate length of the sock foot. For example, if the adult shoe size is a U.S. Women's 10, then you can assume a foot length of 10½ inches (26.5 cm). Again, subtract ½ inch (1.3 cm) from this length to determine the appropriate finished length of the foot portion of the sock.

$$10\tfrac{1}{2}'' - \tfrac{1}{2}'' = 10''$$

LEG LENGTH

Finally, decide how long you want the leg of the sock. You can use a ruler to measure the distance up from the floor, or you can find an appropriate length for the age or gender you're knitting for on the Sock Leg Lengths table on page 15.

The Top-Down Sock

The standard top-down sock instructions that follow include a square heel, which includes a heel flap and gussets and a wedge toe. The sock begins with a flexible cast-on followed by 2 inches (5 cm) of ribbing for the cuff. The leg is worked in stockinette stitch to the top of the heel, at which point half of the stitches are worked back and forth in rows to shape the heel flap and heel turn. Stitches are then picked up for the gussets, and the stitches are rejoined for working in rounds as the gusset stitches are decreased to the original cast-on number for the foot. The foot is worked for the specified length, then the toe is shaped with decreases at each side of the foot. Decreases are worked every other round until about half of the original stitches remain, then decreases are worked every round until 8 or 10 stitches remain. The remaining stitches are gathered to close the hole at the tip of the toe.

Let's look at each part in detail.

CUFF

The cuff of a sock knitted from the top down begins with a flexible cast-on (see pages 34 and 35) that can withstand stretching on and off over the heel. The cuff typically is worked in ribbing to ensure a snug fit. The basic instructions on page 40 specify an even number of stitches, which allows for k1, p1 (single) ribbing on the cuff (or all along the leg). If you'd prefer to use k2, p2 (double) ribbing, you'll need a number of stitches that's evenly divisible by 4. If the size/gauge you've chosen is not a multiple of 4, simply increase or decrease up to 2 stitches as necessary to obtain the necessary number of stitches for the ribbing. Then decrease or increase the same number of stitches at the end of the ribbing to return to the specified number of stitches.

Typically, ribbing is worked for 1 inch (2.5 cm) to 2 inches (5 cm), but it can extend all the way to the heel if you'd like.

LEG

The leg begins when the stitch pattern is changed from ribbing to stockinette stitch. The leg is typically worked on the same number of stitches as the cuff. The reported length of the sock leg usually includes the length of the cuff as well (see the table on page 15 for standard lengths).

If you want very short legs on your socks, as for anklets or "sport" socks, omit the leg portion and go straight from the cuff to the heel. If you do so, use needles a couple of sizes smaller for the cuff ribbing or work a twisted ribbing (work the knit stitches through their back loops) to ensure a very snug fit around the ankle. Consider adding a pom-pom to the back of the ankle to prevent the sock from slipping down into the shoe.

HEEL FLAP

The top-down socks in this book have a square heel that begins with a heel flap that's worked back and forth in rows. Slipped stitches at the beginning of each row provide a foundation for picking up the gusset stitches later.

HEEL TURN

The heel cap is shaped with short-rows (without wraps at the turning point), while stitches are decreased along each edge until all of the heel flap stitches have been worked.

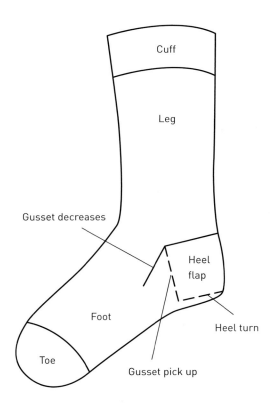

Anatomy of a top-down sock.

Flexible Cast-Ons

A sock that's knitted from the top down requires a stretchy and flexible cast-on. My two favorites are the long-tail and the twisted German (also called "old Norwegian") methods. The long-tail cast-on is excellent for most purposes; the twisted German is a bit trickier to work, but results in a stretchier edge.

There's a common misperception that casting on over a larger needle (or two needles held together) will result in a stretchier edge. This isn't the case! The key is to leave a bit of space—one to two needle widths—between the stitches on the needle as you cast on.

The Long-Tail Method

The long-tail method creates an attractive and flexible edge. It's worked by effectively knitting the first row of stitches as they're created. When set up for working in rounds, the "knit" side of the cast-on stitches will be facing outward.

Leaving a long tail—about ½ inch (1.3 cm) per stitch to be cast on with fingering-weight yarn or 1 inch (2.5 cm) per stitch for thicker yarns will be more than enough and provides room for error and cavalier measurement—make a slipknot. (Some recommend skipping the slipknot, just twisting the yarn around the needle instead; but I like the stability of a slipknot, particularly for those learning this method, and the way it makes a nicer join.)

Place the slipknot on a needle held in your right hand (**Figure 1**). As you work, use your right index finger to hold the knot in place.

SET-UP: Use your left hand to make a fist around the two ends of yarn extending from the slipknot; use your left thumb and forefinger to separate the two strands—as if you were opening the curtains a crack, then swing your left hand so that your thumb and forefinger point upward (**Figure 1**).

CREATING STITCHES, STEP 1: Use your right hand to bring the needle toward you, over the tops of the two thumb strands, then up through the loop around your thumb (**Figure 2**).

CREATING STITCHES, STEP 2: Swing the needle away from you and around the outside and over top of the nearest finger strand to catch a loop, then bring this strand toward you through the thumb loop (**Figure 3**).

CREATING STITCHES, STEP 3: Pull your thumb out of the thumb loop, then catch the strand again and pull to tension the stitch on the needle (**Figure 4**).

Although you want the stitches to be snug to the needle, don't pull the yarn so tight that the stitches are right next to each other. The elasticity of this cast-on method depends on there being at least a needle's width between each of the cast-on stitches.

Reposition your hand and repeat from Step 1 for each additional stitch.

Once you get fluid with the motions, you can leave the strand draped around your finger, and "kick" the stitches snug with your thumb at the same time as you reposition the yarn.

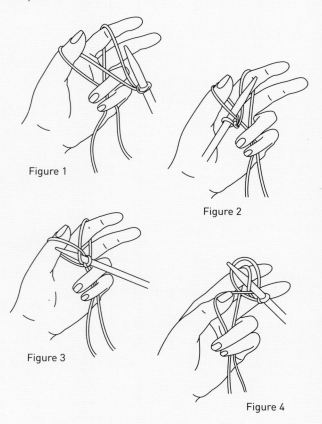

Figure 1

Figure 2

Figure 3

Figure 4

The Twisted German/ Old Norwegian Method

The Twisted German (also known as the Old Norwegian) method is worked very much like the long-tail method, but with an extra twist of yarn at the base of each stitch, which creates more flexibility.

This method is set up the same as the long-tail method (Figure 1).

CREATING STITCHES, STEP 1: Use your right hand to bring the needle toward you and under both thumb strands, then swing the tip of the needle toward you again and down into the loop on your thumb, then swing the needle up and away from you, around the outside and over top of the first finger strand, catching the nearest finger strand (Figure 2).

CREATING STITCHES, STEP 2: Bring the needle back down through the thumb loop (Figure 3) and to the front, turning your thumb slightly to make room for the needle to pass through. Pull your thumb out of the thumb loop (Figure 4), then pull the two strands to snug the stitch on the needle (Figure 5).

Reposition your hand and repeat from Step 1 for each additional stitch.

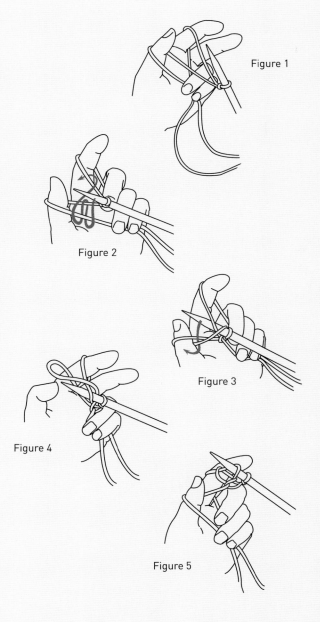

Figure 1

Figure 2

Figure 3

Figure 4

Figure 5

GUSSET DECREASES

Stitches are picked up along the edges of the heel flap for the gussets that join the heel stitches to the instep stitches. Many knitters avoid knitting socks from the top down because they're unsure of how to pick up stitches for the gussets without holes forming at the boundary between the heel and instep stitches.

There are three reasons why holes can form at the tops of the gussets—the uppermost gusset stitches are picked up too far down from the instep, the edge stitches between the heel and instep have stretched, or an "extra" stitch is picked up in the wrong place between the heel and instep stitches. All of these possibilities are easily eliminated.

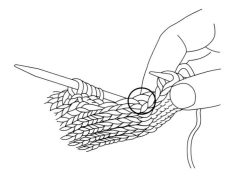

Pick up the first stitch in the "corner" tucked in beside the line of heel decreases.

Beginning in the "corner," insert the needle tip under *both strands* of the first edge stitch (the slipped selvedge stitch of the heel flap), wrap the yarn around the needle knitwise, then pull the new stitch through. Repeat this for every slipped edge stitch along the heel flap.

The next step is critical when it comes to preventing holes at the tops of the gussets.

Don't pick up a stitch here—this creates a hole!

Many knitters pick up an extra stitch in the "corner" between the instep and heel flap stitches as shown above.

To do so, they knit into the horizontal strand that runs between the instep and heel stitches, which effectively creates a yarnover hole. Even if the lifted strand is twisted, a hole is still formed because the new stitch forces apart the adjacent two columns of stitches.

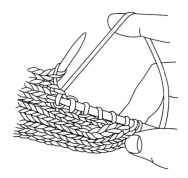

Pick up 2 extra stitches into the leg along the same column (shown as a straight line) used to pick up the other gusset stitches.

You can prevent the hole from forming by avoiding the corner altogether. The trick is to pick up 2 more stitches *in the same column of stitches* as the others. This places these two stitches *above* the separation between the heel flap and instep, which snugs the last gusset stitch next to the instep stitches, covers the stitches that might have stretched out, and places the last picked-up stitches farther into the fabric of the heel flap, all of which avert a hole.

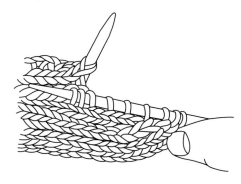

The 2 "extra" stitches are picked up into the leg of the sock.

Pick up the 2 "extra" gusset stitches in line with the previous pick-ups, but up into the leg of the sock to cover the potential stretched-out stitches. To pick up these stitches, insert the needle through the fabric into the inside of the sock; pick up the second of these stitches just above the row where you separated the heel and instep.

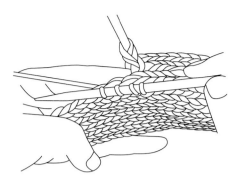

Pick up the extra 2 stitches into the leg on the other side of the heel flap.

Tidy SSK Decrease Lines

If you find that the ssk decrease line doesn't align as well as the k2tog decrease line along the gusset (or toe) decreases, try the trick I learned from Cat Bordhi. On the round following the decrease round, work the stitch above the ssk decrease through the back loop to shift the angle of the decreased stitch so that it aligns better with the decrease on the previous round.

Pick up 2 extra stitches along the other side of the heel flap as well. But, because you'll be working in the opposite direction, begin by picking up the extra stitches above the edge of the heel flap as shown above, then pick up 1 stitch in each chain selvedge stitch along the heel flap as usual.

Count the edge gusset stitches on the heel flap to determine where to begin picking up.

It can be difficult to determine exactly where to begin picking up the extra stitches on the second gusset. I find it helps to count the chain edge stitches, beginning at the heel-turn end of the heel flap, then follow the same line to pick up the first 2 stitches.

After the gusset stitches are all picked up, work 1 round even, working the picked-up stitches through the back loops to remove any possible slack. The gusset decreases begin on the following round—1 stitch is decreased at each gusset every other round until the original number of cast-on stitches is reached.

FOOT

The foot is worked on the same number of stitches as the cuff and leg if you're using the Half & Half Toe shape (see page 176). The length of the foot depends on the sock size. In general, if there are 50 or fewer stitches in the sock foot,

then the foot is worked until the sock measures 1½ inches (3.8 cm) less than the desired total finished length; if there are more than 50 stitches, the foot is worked until the sock measures 2 inches (5 cm) less than the desired total finished length. See Chapter 1 for more on sock foot lengths.

TOE

The toes in this book follow traditional "wedge" construction in which the shaping is worked on the two sides of the foot. Each shaping round decreases 4 stitches per round, 1 stitch each at each end of each of instep and sole. The decreases are positioned 1 stitch in from the end of the instep and sole stitches so that there are 2 "plain" stitches between the shaping stitches to form the wedge at each side. Of course, you can choose to work a wider or narrower wedge by changing the number of stitches between the decreases at the sides of the foot.

The top-down toe is shaped with decreases that are worked every other round until about 50 percent of the necessary decreases have been made, then decreases are worked every round until 8 or 10 stitches remain (depending on whether or not the number of stitches in the foot is divisible by 4). If there is an odd number of stitches in the foot, you'll decrease to 7 or 9 stitches.

For example, for a sock that has 64 stitches (which is divisible by 4), we'll decrease to 8 stitches. In other words, we'll decrease 56 stitches.

64 stitches – 8 stitches = 56 stitches to decrease

Because 4 stitches are decreased in each decrease round, we'll work a total of 14 decrease rounds.

56 stitches ÷ 4 = 14 decrease rounds

Sample Socks Based on the Basic Top-Down Instructions on page 40

Sample 1:
Woman's medium in fingering-weight yarn

This version is knitted with fingering-weight yarn at a sturdy gauge of 8 stitches per inch (2.5 cm).

FINISHED CIRCUMFERENCE
7½" (19 cm).

YARN
Hand Maiden Casbah (81% merino, 9% cashmere, 10% nylon; 355 yd [325 m]/115 grams): Cedar; 1 skein.

NEEDLES
U.S. size 1.5 (2.5 mm).

GAUGE
8 stitches = 1" (2.5 cm) in stockinette stitch, worked in rounds.

NUMBER OF LEG/FOOT STITCHES:
60.

DESIGN DETAILS
2" (5 cm) of k1, p1 ribbing at cuff; 7" (18 cm) leg length; 8½" (21.5 cm) foot length.

Sample 2:
Woman's medium in worsted-weight yarn

This version is knitted in worsted-weight yarn at a tighter-than-normal gauge of 6 stitches per inch (2.5 cm).

FINISHED CIRCUMFERENCE
7½" (19 cm).

YARN
Anzula For Better Or Worsted (80% superwash merino, 10% cashmere, 10% nylon; 200 yd [183 m]/100 g): Persimmon, 1 skein.

NEEDLES
U.S. size 5 (3.75 mm).

GAUGE
6 stitches = 1" (2.5 cm) in stockinette stitch, worked in rounds.

NUMBER OF LEG/FOOT STITCHES
44.

DESIGN DETAILS
2" (5 cm) of k1, p1 ribbing at cuff; 7" (18 cm) leg length; 8½" (21.5 cm) foot length.

To give the tip of the toe a nice rounded shape, we'll alternate a plain round between a decrease round for the first half of these decrease rounds (7 decrease rounds), then we'll omit the plain rounds and work consecutive decrease rounds for the remaining 7 decrease rounds to end up with 8 stitches.

I don't use the Kitchener stitch to graft the tip of a top-down toe. This is for two reasons—the Kitchener stitch is fiddly and often intimidating, and, more importantly, it isn't necessary for a nicely shaped toe. I prefer to cinch the final 8 or 10 stitches by drawing a tail of the working yarn through them and pulling tight—just as I would for the top of a hat. It's quicker and simpler.

Let's dispel a myth—the pointy toes that top-down sock knitters often complain about on non-grafted toes is *not* a result of the type of closure. The shape of a toe is a function of the rate of decrease and the number of decreases, which determines the number of stitches that remain at the end of the toe. The shaping I've used in the templates and patterns in this book creates a nice curve that fits the natural rounded shape of the toes.

Sample 3:
Woman's medium in fingering-weight yarn

This version is knitted from leftover bits of fingering-weight sock yarn from various other projects. The same yarn is used for the heels and toes for a unified look.

FINISHED CIRCUMFERENCE
7½" (19 cm).

YARN
Heel and toes: Austermann Step Classic (75% superwash wool, 25% nylon; 459 yd [420 m]/100 g): Black, small amount (leftovers would be sufficient).

Feet and legs: Small amounts each of a random assortment of fingering-weight sock yarns.

NEEDLES
U.S. size 1.5 (2.5 mm).

GAUGE
8 stitches = 1" (2.5 cm) in stockinette stitch, worked in rounds.

NUMBER OF LEG/FOOT STITCHES
60.

DESIGN DETAILS
2" (5 cm) of k2, p1 ribbing at cuff; 7" (18 cm) leg length; 9" (23 cm) foot length.

If You Prefer to Graft

If you enjoy grafting the toes of your socks, by all means, do so. But to ensure a good look and fit (see the toe section on page 37), stop after the first half of the decrease rounds (alternating a decrease round with a plain round) have been worked, or about one-third of the foot stitches remain, which will be sooner than my patterns instruct.

For example, if there are 60 stitches in the foot, stop the toe decreases when 20 stitches remain.

For another example, if there are 40 stitches in the foot, stop the toe decreases when 16 stitches remain.

40 ÷ 3 = 14.33, which we'll round to 16 stitches (a number that results from subtracting a multiple of 4 stitches from 40)

Stopping the decrease earlier creates a wider, flatter toe top, which produces a more attractive and more natural shape when combined with the straight-across grafted closure. It's also the best shape for when there's not a big difference in length between the shortest and longest toes.

A BASIC TOP-DOWN SOCK PATTERN

These generic instructions are for a sock that's worked from the top down with an unshaped leg, which permits a comfortable fit for a calf- or ankle-length leg; samples are shown at right.

The band heel begins with a heel flap, then short-rows are worked to produce a nice square shape. Stitches are picked up along the sides of the heel flap, then gussets are created by working decreases at the sides of the instep. The toe is finished with my favorite "no graft" technique.

Make a photocopy of this page and use the appropriate table on pages 42–45 to fill in the appropriate numbers for your size and gauge.

Cuff

Using a flexible method, such as long-tail or twisted German (see pages 34 and 35), cast on _____ (**Sock Stitches**).

Distribute stitches across needles as you prefer, and join for working in the round, being careful not to twist the stitches.

Note or mark the beginning of the round (see page 23).

Work in k1, p1 ribbing for about 2" (5 cm).

Leg

Continue even in stockinette stitch until the sock leg is the desired length (see page 15 for the table of Leg Lengths). Alternatively, work in ribbing for the entire length of the leg.

Heel Flap

Slip _____ (**Heel Stitches**) onto one needle to work for heel. The remaining stitches (the same number as the **Heel Stitches**) will be worked later for the instep.

Work back and forth in rows as follows.

HEEL FLAP ROW 1: (RS) Knit _____ (**Heel Stitches**), turn work.

HEEL FLAP ROW 2: (WS) Slip 1 purlwise with yarn in front, purl to end of heel stitches, turn work.

HEEL FLAP ROW 3: (RS) Slip 1 knitwise with yarn in back, knit to end of heel stitches, turn work.

HEEL FLAP ROW 4: (WS) Slip 1 purlwise with yarn in front, purl to end of heel stitches, turn work.

Repeat **Heel Flap Rows 3 and 4** until _____ (**Heel Rows**) have been worked.

Heel Turn

Beginning with a right-side row, short-rows are used to form the cup shape of the heel.

HEEL TURN ROW 1: (RS) Knit _____ (**HT1**), ssk, turn work.

HEEL TURN ROW 2: (WS) Sl 1 purlwise with yarn in front, purl _____ (**HT2**), p2tog, turn work.

HEEL TURN ROW 3: (RS) Sl 1 purlwise with yarn in back, knit _____ (**HT2**), ssk, turn work.

HEEL TURN ROW 4: (WS) Sl 1 purlwise with yarn in front, purl _____ (**HT2**), p2tog, turn work.

Repeat **Heel Turn Rows 3 and 4** until all heel stitches have been worked, ending having worked a wrong-side row— _____ (**HT2**) + 2 stitches remain.

With RS facing, knit remaining heel stitches.

Gusset Decreases

Gusset Pick-Up Round: With RS facing and working under both legs of each slipped selvedge stitch, pick up and knit _____ (**Gusset Stitches per Side**) along the first side of the heel flap, picking up the last 2 stitches above the break between the heel and instep stitches, as described on page 36.

Work across the instep stitches (maintaining the rib pattern from the leg, if desired).

With RS still facing, pick up and knit _____ (**Gusset Stitches per Side**) along the other side of the heel flap, picking up the first 2 stitches above the break between the heel and instep stitches as before, then use the same needle to knit half of the remaining heel stitches again— _____ (**Total Sock Stitches Plus Gussets**) stitches total.

The rounds now begin in the center of the heel stitches (if you're using double-pointed needles, this will be the boundary between two needles; if you're using circular needles or the magic-loop method, this will be in the center of a needle. Place a marker to denote the start of the rounds.

GUSSET ROUND 1: Knit to the end of the heel stitches, knit all picked-up stitches through the back loop to twist them, work across instep stitches in pattern as desired, knit all picked-up stitches through the back loop, knit to end of round.

GUSSET ROUND 2: (decrease round) Knit to 3 stitches before start of instep, k2tog, k1; work across instep stitches; k1, ssk, knit to end of round—2 Gusset Stitches decreased.

GUSSET ROUND 3: Knit.

Repeat **Gusset Rounds 2 and 3** until _____ (**Sock Stitches**) remain.

Foot

The foot length depends on the number of stitches initially cast on.

If you began with 50 or fewer cast-on stitches, work even (maintaining stitch pattern on instep stitches if desired) until piece measures 1½" (3.8 cm) less than _____ the desired finished sock foot length (see pages 12–14).

If you began with more than 50 cast-on stitches, work even (maintaining stitch pattern on instep stitches if desired) until piece measures 2" (5 cm) less than _____ the desired finished sock foot length.

Toe

TOE ROUND 1: (decrease round) Knit to 3 stitches before instep, k2tog, k2, ssk, knit to 3 stitches before end of instep, k2tog, k2, ssk, knit to end of round—4 stitches decreased.

TOE ROUND 2: Knit even.

Repeat these 2 rounds _____ (**TD1**) times— _____ (**First Toe Decrease Count**) stitches remain.

Repeat Toe Round 1 every round (i.e., decrease every round) _____ (**TD2**) times—8 stitches remain if you cast on a multiple of 4 stitches; 10 stitches remain if you cast on other than a multiple of 4 stitches.

Finishing

Cut yarn, leaving an 8" (20.5 cm) tail. Thread tail on a tapestry needle, draw through remaining stitches, pull tight to close hole, and secure to wrong side.

Weave in loose ends.

Block as desired (see page 18).

STITCH AND ROW NUMBERS FOR THE BASIC TOP-DOWN SOCK PATTERN ON PAGE 40

Find the block of numbers that corresponds to your desired finished sock circumference along the left edge of the table on the following four pages, then follow the column of numbers that corresponds to your gauge (measured in

TOP-DOWN SOCK STITCH AND ROW/ROUND NUMBERS

FINISHED SOCK CIRCUMFERENCE		GAUGE: STITCHES PER INCH								
		4	5	5½	6	6½	7	7½	8	9
5" (12.5 cm)	Sock Stitches	20	24	28	30	32	34	38	40	44
	Heel Stitches	10	12	14	15	16	17	19	20	22
	Heel Rows	8	10	12	12	14	14	16	16	18
	HT1	7	8	9	10	11	11	13	13	15
	HT2	3	4	4	5	6	5	7	6	8
	Gusset Stitches per Side	6	7	8	8	9	9	10	10	11
	Stitches After Gusset Pick-Up	28	32	36	38	42	42	48	48	54
	TD1	2	2	3	3	3	4	4	4	5
	First Toe Decrease Count	12	16	16	18	20	18	22	24	24
	TD 2	1	2	2	2	3	3	4	4	4
5½" (14 cm)	Sock Stitches	22	28	30	32	36	38	40	44	50
	Heel Stitches	11	14	15	16	18	19	20	22	25
	Heel Rows	10	12	12	14	16	16	16	18	20
	HT1	7	9	10	11	12	13	13	15	17
	HT2	3	4	5	6	6	7	6	8	9
	Gusset Stitches per Side	7	8	8	9	10	10	10	11	12
	Stitches After Gusset Pick-Up	30	36	38	42	46	48	48	54	60
	TD1	2	3	3	3	4	4	4	5	5
	First Toe Decrease Count	14	16	18	20	20	22	24	24	30
	TD 2	1	2	2	3	3	3	4	4	5
6" (15 cm)	Sock Stitches	24	30	32	36	38	42	44	48	54
	Heel Stitches	12	15	16	18	19	21	22	24	27
	Heel Rows	10	12	14	16	16	18	18	20	22
	HT1	8	10	11	12	13	14	15	16	18
	HT2	4	5	6	6	7	7	8	8	9
	Gusset Stitches per Side	7	8	9	10	10	11	11	12	13
	Stitches After Gusset Pick-Up	32	38	42	46	48	52	54	58	64
	TD1	2	3	3	4	4	4	5	5	6
	First Toe Decrease Count	16	18	20	20	22	26	24	28	30
	TD2	2	2	3	3	3	4	4	5	5

stitches per inch). For example, if you want to knit a sock with a 6 inch (15 cm) circumference at 5 stitches to the inch, you'd follow the second column of numbers in the third block, which begins with 30 sock stitches.

TOP-DOWN SOCK STITCH AND ROW/ROUND NUMBERS, CONT.

FINISHED SOCK CIRCUMFERENCE		GAUGE: STITCHES PER INCH								
		4	5	5½	6	6½	7	7½	8	9
6½" (16.5 cm)	Sock Stitches	26	32	36	38	42	46	48	52	58
	Heel Stitches	13	16	18	19	21	23	24	26	29
	Heel Rows	12	14	16	16	18	20	20	22	24
	HT1	9	11	12	13	14	15	16	17	19
	HT2	5	6	6	7	7	7	8	8	9
	Gusset Stitches per Side	8	9	10	10	11	12	12	13	14
	Stitches After Gusset Pick-Up	36	42	46	48	52	56	58	62	68
	TD1	2	3	4	4	4	5	5	6	6
	First Toe Decrease Count	18	20	20	22	26	26	28	28	34
	TD2	2	3	3	3	4	4	5	5	6
7" (18 cm)	Sock Stitches	28	34	38	42	46	48	52	56	62
	Heel Stitches	14	17	19	21	23	24	26	28	31
	Heel Rows	12	14	16	18	20	20	22	24	26
	HT1	9	11	13	14	15	16	17	19	21
	HT2	4	5	7	7	7	8	8	10	11
	Gusset Stitches Per Side	8	9	10	11	12	12	13	14	15
	Stitches After Gusset Pick-Up	36	42	48	52	56	58	62	68	74
	TD1	3	3	4	4	5	5	6	6	7
	First Toe Decrease Count	16	22	22	26	26	28	28	32	34
	TD2	2	3	3	4	4	5	5	6	6
7½" (19 cm)	Sock Stitches	30	38	40	44	48	52	56	60	68
	Heel Stitches	15	19	20	22	24	26	28	30	34
	Heel Rows	12	16	16	18	20	22	24	26	28
	HT1	10	13	13	15	16	17	19	20	23
	HT2	5	7	6	8	8	8	10	10	12
	Gusset Stitches Per Side	8	10	10	11	12	13	14	15	16
	Stitches After Gusset Pick-Up	38	48	48	54	58	62	68	72	80
	TD1	3	4	4	5	5	6	6	7	8
	First Toe Decrease Count	18	22	24	24	28	28	32	32	36
	TD2	2	3	4	4	5	5	6	6	7

TOP-DOWN SOCK STITCH AND ROW/ROUND NUMBERS, CONT.

FINISHED SOCK CIRCUMFERENCE		GAUGE: STITCHES PER INCH								
		4	5	5½	6	6½	7	7½	8	9
8" (20.5 cm)	Sock Stitches	32	40	44	48	52	56	60	64	72
	Heel Stitches	16	20	22	24	26	28	30	32	36
	Heel Rows	14	16	18	20	22	24	24	26	30
	HT1	11	13	15	16	17	19	20	21	24
	HT2	6	6	8	8	8	10	10	10	12
	Gusset Stitcher per Side	9	10	11	12	13	14	14	15	17
	Stitches After Gusset Pick-Up	42	48	54	58	62	68	70	74	84
	TD1	3	4	5	5	6	6	7	7	8
	First Toe Decrease Count	20	24	24	28	28	32	32	36	40
	TD2	3	4	4	5	5	6	6	7	8
8½" (21.5 cm)	Sock Stitches	34	42	46	50	54	60	64	68	76
	Heel Stitches	17	21	23	25	27	30	32	34	38
	Heel Rows	14	18	20	20	22	24	26	28	32
	HT1	11	14	15	17	18	20	21	23	25
	HT2	5	7	7	9	9	10	10	12	12
	Gusset Stitches per Side	9	11	12	12	13	14	15	16	18
	Stitches After Gusset Pick-Up	42	52	56	60	64	70	74	80	88
	TD1	3	4	5	5	6	7	7	8	9
	First Toe Decrease Count	22	26	26	30	30	32	36	36	40
	TD2	3	4	4	5	5	6	7	7	8
9" (23 cm)	Sock Stitches	36	44	50	54	58	62	68	72	80
	Heel Stitches	18	22	25	27	29	31	34	36	40
	Heel Rows	16	18	20	22	24	26	28	30	32
	HT1	12	15	17	18	19	21	23	24	27
	HT2	6	8	9	9	9	11	12	12	14
	Gusset Stitches per Side	10	11	12	13	14	15	16	17	18
	Stitches After Gusset Pick-Up	46	54	60	64	68	74	80	84	92
	TD1	4	5	5	6	6	7	8	8	9
	First Toe Decrease Count	20	24	30	30	34	34	36	40	44
	TD2	3	4	5	5	6	6	7	8	9

TOP-DOWN SOCK STITCH AND ROW/ROUND NUMBERS, CONT.

FINISHED SOCK CIRCUMFERENCE	GAUGE: STITCHES PER INCH								
	4	5	5½	6	6½	7	7½	8	9
9½" **(24 cm)** Sock Stitches	38	48	52	56	62	66	70	76	86
Heel Stitches	19	24	26	28	31	33	35	38	43
Heel Rows	16	20	22	24	26	28	30	32	34
HT1	13	16	17	19	21	22	23	25	29
HT2	7	8	8	10	11	11	11	12	15
Gusset Stitches per Side	10	12	13	14	15	16	17	18	19
Stitches After Gusset Pick-Up	48	58	62	68	74	78	82	88	98
TD1	4	5	6	6	7	7	8	9	10
First Toe Decrease Count	22	28	28	32	34	38	38	40	46
TD2	3	5	5	6	6	7	7	8	9
10" **(25.5 cm)** Sock Stitches	40	50	54	60	64	70	74	80	90
Heel Stitches	20	25	27	30	32	35	37	40	45
Heel Rows	16	20	22	24	26	28	30	32	36
HT1	13	17	18	20	21	23	25	27	30
HT2	6	9	9	10	10	11	13	14	15
Gusset Stitches per Side	10	12	13	14	15	16	17	18	20
Stitches After Gusset Pick-Up	48	60	64	70	74	80	86	92	102
TD1	4	5	6	7	7	8	8	9	10
First Toe Decrease Count	24	30	30	32	36	38	42	44	50
TD2	4	5	5	6	7	7	8	9	10
10½" **(26.5 cm)** Sock Stitches	42	52	58	62	68	74	78	84	94
Heel Stitches	21	26	29	31	34	37	39	42	47
Heel Rows	18	22	24	26	28	30	32	34	38
HT1	14	17	19	21	23	25	26	28	31
HT2	7	8	9	11	12	13	13	14	15
Gusset Stitches per Side	11	13	14	15	16	17	18	19	21
Stitches After Gusset Pick-Up	52	62	68	74	80	86	90	96	106
TD1	4	6	6	7	8	8	9	10	11
First Toe Decrease Count	26	28	34	34	36	42	42	44	50
TD2	4	5	6	6	7	8	8	9	10

Calculating the Numbers in the Top-Down Sock Tables

The ten variables in the tables on pages 42–45 were calculated according to the following formulas. If you're knitting for a foot that doesn't conform to the measurements or if you're working at a gauge that isn't specified on the tables, you can use these formulas to calculate the numbers you need for the pattern.

To calculate these formulas, you'll need the key measurements determined in Chapter 1, along with your gauge, measured in stitches per inch.

Note that for top-down socks, you don't necessarily need to work all the way through a set of formulas to get the numbers for your size. If your calculated Sock Stitches matches that for one of the other sizes, you can simply follow all of the numbers for that size.

Sock Stitches = (Gauge in Stitches per Inch × Foot Circumference) × 0.9

Because all of the socks are based on an even number of stitches (to allow for k1, p1 ribbing at the cuff), round the calculated number to the nearest even number.

For example, if you're knitting a sock for a foot with a 10 inch (25.5 cm) circumference at a gauge of 7 stitches per inch (2.5 cm), your Sock Stitches number will be 63, which you'll round to 64.

$$(7 \text{ stitches per inch} \times 10") \times 0.9 =$$
$$70 \text{ stitches} \times .9 = 63 \text{ stitches; round to } 64$$

To allow for k1, p1 ribbing, round to an even number. In this case, we'll round up to 64 stitches. Find this Sock Stitches number in the table on page 45, then use those numbers.

Heel Stitches = Sock Stitches ÷ 2

For example, if there are 64 Sock Stitches, you'll work the heel on 32 stitches.

Heel Rows = Heel Stitches × 0.8

For example, if there are 32 Heel Stitches, the heel will be worked for 25.6 rows. Always round up to the nearest even number.

$$32 \text{ stitches} \times 0.8 = 25.6 \text{ stitches; round up to } 26$$

If your stitch gauge/row gauge ratio is significantly different from the expected 3:4 ratio (see the sidebar on page 28), calculate the heel rows slightly differently.

Heel Rows = (Sock Circumference × Rounds per Inch) × 0.3

For example, if the sock circumference is 8 inches and the you're getting 9 rounds to the inch, you'll work the heel for

$$(8" \times 9 \text{ rounds per inch}) \times 0.3$$
$$72 \text{ rounds} \times 0.3$$
$$21.6 \text{ rounds; round up to } 22 \text{ rows}$$

HT1 = 2/3 Heel Stitches

HT2 = 1/3 Heel Stitches

If your Heel Stitches number is evenly divisible by 3, then HT1 is two-thirds of that value and HT1 is one-third of that value.

What you're actually doing with this heel turn is dividing the stitches into thirds as closely as possible; once the set-up row is complete, you'll work back and forth over the center third of the stitches.

For example if there are 27 Heel Stitches, HT1, is 18 and HT2 is 9.

$$27 \text{ stitches} \div 3 = 9 \text{ stitches}$$
$$HT1 = 2 \times 9 \text{ stitches} = 18 \text{ stitches}$$
$$HT2 = 1 \times 9 \text{ stitches} = 9 \text{ stitches}$$

If your Heel Stitches number doesn't divide evenly by 3, it will divide so that two numbers are the same and one is different. HT1 will be the two non-matching numbers added together and HT2 will be the unique number.

For example, 32 Heel Stitches divided by 3 gives us 11, 11, and 10 stitches. HT1 is the sum of two non-matching numbers; HT2 is the unique number.

$$32 \text{ stitches} \div 3 = 11 \text{ stitches} + 11 \text{ stitches} + 10 \text{ stitches}$$

$$HT1 = 11 \text{ stitches} + 10 \text{ stitches} = 21 \text{ stitches}$$

$$HT2 = 10 \text{ stitches}$$

Gusset Stitches = (Heel Rows ÷ 2) + 2

The number of gusset stitches on each side of the foot is equal to half the total number of Heel Rows, plus 2.

For example if there are 26 Heel Rows, there will be 15 Gusset Stitches at each side.

$$(26 \text{ rows} \div 2) + 2 = 13 + 2 =$$
$$15 \text{ gusset stitches at each side}$$

The total number of stitches after the gusset pick-up is a function of the instep stitches plus the remaining Heel Stitches plus the Gusset Stitches on each side.

Instep Stitches + remaining Heel Stitches + Gusset Stitches = (Sock Stitches ÷ 2) + (HT2 + 2) + (2 × Gusset Stitches Per Side)

For example, if there are 64 Sock Stitches and 15 Gusset Stitches are picked up at each side, there will be a total of 74 stitches.

$$32 + 12 + (2 \times 15) = 74$$

TD1 = (Sock Stitches − final stitch count) ÷ 8

The number of repeats in the initial Toe Decrease shaping (alternating a decrease round with an even round) is equal to the number of stitches decreased divided by 8.

TD1 and TD2 each represent half the total number of decrease rounds in the toe. If there is an odd number of decrease rounds, TD1 is rounded up and TD2 is rounded down.

The final stitch count will be 8 if Sock Stitches is evenly divisible by 4; the final stitch count will be 10 if Sock Stitches is not evenly divisible by 4.

For example, if there are 64 sock stitches (a number divisible by 4), the final stitch count will be 8.

$$(64 − 8) \div 8$$

$$56 \div 8 = 7$$

If necessary, round up to the nearest whole number.

First Toe Decrease Count = Sock Stitches − (4 × TD1)

The number of stitches that remain after the initial toe decreases equals 4 times the number of times the decrease round is worked.

For example, if the shaping is worked 7 times, there will be 36 stitches after the first set of shaping decreases.

$$64 − (4 \times 7)$$

$$64 − 28 = 36$$

TD2 = (Sock Stitches − final stitch count) ÷ 8

The number of repeats in the second set of toe decreases (decreasing every round) is equal to the number of stitches decreased divided by 8.

If your Sock Stitches number divides evenly by 4, then the final stitch count is 8; otherwise it will be 10.

For example,

$$(36 − 8) \div 8$$

$$28 \div 8 = 3.5$$

If necessary, round down to the nearest whole number (see TD1 at left for more information).

The Toe-Up Sock

The standard toe-up sock instructions that follow include a wedge toe and a square heel that includes a heel flap and gussets. It looks much the same as the top-down sock, but it is worked in the opposite direction. The sock begins with a special cast-on at the tip of the toe that sets up the stitches for working in rounds. Stitches are increased at each side of the toe every other round until the desired number of foot stitches is achieved. The foot is worked even for the specified length, then stitches are increased at each side of the foot to form the gussets. The center heel stitches are worked in short-rows to turn the heel, then the heel flap is worked at the same time as the gusset stitches are decreased, ending at the ankle with the same number of stitches as were worked for the foot. The leg is worked in stockinette stitch to 2 inches (5 cm) short of the desired total length, then ribbing is worked for the cuff, which ends with a flexible bind-off.

Let's look at each part in detail.

TOE

The toe-up sock shaping in this book begins with a special cast-on (see sidebar at right) that sets up the stitches for working in rounds. Typically, about 30 percent of the number of stitches needed for the foot are cast on.

The toe is shaped by traditional "wedge" construction in which the shaping is worked on the two sides of the foot. In general, a shaping round is alternated with the plain stockinette-stitch round until the desired number of foot stitches is achieved. Each shaping round increases 4 stitches per round, 1 stitch each at each end of the instep and sole. The increases are positioned 1 stitch in from each end of the instep and sole stitches so that there are 2 "plain" stitches between the shaping stitches to form the wedge at each side. (Of course, you can choose to work a wider or narrower wedge by changing the number of stitches between the increases at the sides of the foot.)

For example, if we want 64 stitches for the foot, we'll cast on 20 stitches.

$$64 \div 3 = 21.3; \text{ which we'll round to} \\ \text{the nearest even number; } 22$$

But we can't end up with 64 stitches if we increase from 22 stitches in multiples of 4 stitches. In other words, the number of stitches increased isn't evenly divisible by 4.

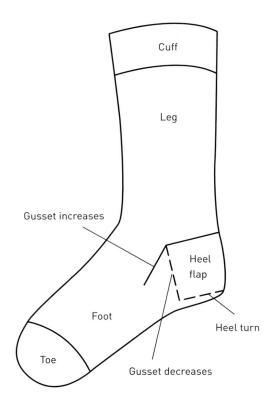

Anatomy of a toe-up sock.

$$64 - 22 = 42 \\ \text{and} \\ 42 \div 4 = 10.5 \text{ increases}$$

We need to either round up to 11 increases (begin with 20 stitches) or round down to 10 increases (begin with 24 stitches).

$$64 - 20 = 44; 44 \div 4 = 11 \\ \text{or} \\ 64 - 24 = 40; 40 \div 4 = 10$$

FOOT

The foot is worked even in rounds until the piece measures the specified distance from the tip of the toe.

GUSSET INCREASES

Increases are worked at each side of the foot to provide the extra fabric needed to span the gap between the heel and instep stitches. These gusset increases are grouped with the bottom-of-foot, or sole, stitches.

Judy's Magic Cast-On

Judy Becker first published her magic cast-on technique in the Spring 2006 issue of Knitty.com and revolutionized the way we cast on for toe-up socks. Until then, the tip of the toe had to begin with an unstable figure-eight cast-on or a tricky Turkish cast-on. Proposed as a "more humane" way to cast-on for a toe-up sock, Judy's method is very easy once you get the hang of it.

If you're using double-pointed or two circular needles, you'll need two needles to get started. If you're using a single circular needle, you'll hold the two tips together and treat them as two needles.

SET-UP, STEP 1: Leaving a tail about ¼" (6 mm) long per stitch to be cast on, drape the yarn over one needle, then hold a second needle parallel to and below the first and on top of the yarn tail (**Figure 1**).

SET-UP, STEP 2: Bring the tail to the back and the ball yarn to the front, then place the thumb and index finger of your left hand between the two strands so that the tail is over your index finger and the ball yarn is over your thumb (**Figure 2**). This forms the first stitch on the top needle.

*Continue to hold the two needles parallel and loop the finger yarn over the lower needle by bringing the lower needle over the top of the finger yarn (**Figure 3**), then bringing the finger yarn up from below the lower needle, over the top of this needle, then to the back between the two needles.

Point the needles downward, bring the bottom needle past the thumb yarn, then bring the thumb yarn to the front between the two needles and over the top needle (**Figure 4**).

Repeat from * until you have the desired number of stitches on each needle (**Figure 5**).

Remove both yarn ends from your left hand, rotate the needles like the hands of a clock so that the bottom needle is now on top, both strands of yarn are at the needle tip, and the last stitch cast on is on the top (**Figure 6**).

Notice that this stitch isn't anchored on the needle—twist the two yarn strands around each other to secure this stitch.

Using the working needle, knit the stitches on the top needle (**Figure 7**). If you're using double-pointed needles, use an empty one; if you're using the magic-loop method, pull out the lower needle and work with that; if you're using two circular needles, work with the needle that's holding these stitches.

Rotate the two needles 180° again to work the stitches that were on the bottom needle. If you're using double-pointed needles, work the first half of these stitches with one empty needle, then work the second half of these stitches with another; if you're using the magic-loop method, pull out the lower needle and work with that; if you're using two circular needles, work with the needle that's holding these stitches. This completes the first round.

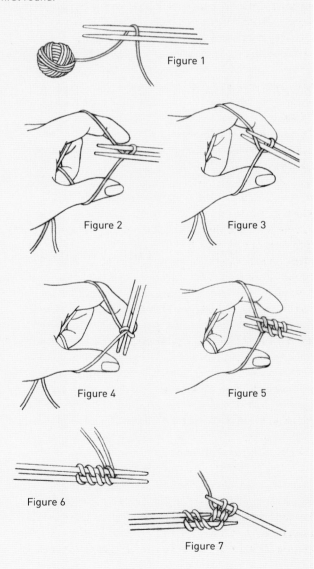

Figure 1

Figure 2

Figure 3

Figure 4

Figure 5

Figure 6

Figure 7

HEEL TURN

The back of the heel is shaped with short-rows that are worked on the stitches that formed the bottom of the foot (excluding the stitches increased for the gussets).

HEEL FLAP

The heel flap is worked in short-rows and is created at the same time that gusset stitches are decreased. Each short-row decreases 1 gusset stitch, alternating between the two gussets on right- and wrong-side rows. The gusset stitches are decreased until the same number of stitches remains that was worked for the foot.

Holes often develop at the boundary between the instep, or front-of-leg, stitches and the heel, or back-of-leg, stitches when the stitches are rejoined for working in rounds. This is due to a quirk in the geometry of a toe-up sock. If all of the heel flap/gusset decreases are completed when working in rows, the back of the leg would essentially be a row or two "taller" than the front of the leg. This length difference causes a gap, which appears as a hole. To mitigate this, the instructions in this book specify resuming working in rounds when 1 gusset stitch remains to be decreased on each side. This ensures the same number of rows—or rounds—are on the front of the leg as are on the back of the leg.

If a gap is still evident, you can eliminate it in the first round or two of the leg by working 2 stitches together across the gap as described below and illustrated at right.

When you have worked the last stitch of the instep, use the left needle tip to lift the left leg of the stitch 2 rows below the stitch just worked and place this lifted leg onto the left needle tip (**Figure 1**), in front of the back-of-leg stitches. Then knit this lifted leg together with the first back-of-leg stitch as k2tog (**Figure 2**). Work to 1 stitch before the end of the back-of-leg stitches, then slip this last stitch knitwise to the right needle (**Figure 3**). Use the right needle tip to lift the right leg of the stitch directly below the next stitch on the left needle (that is, the first stitch of the instep; **Figure 4**). Insert the tip of the left needle into these 2 stitches and knit them together through their back loops (**Figure 5**) as for an ssk decrease.

These increase/decrease pairs might distort the fabric a tiny bit, but because it's positioned directly above the heel flap decreases, it's not distracting. And the hole will disappear!

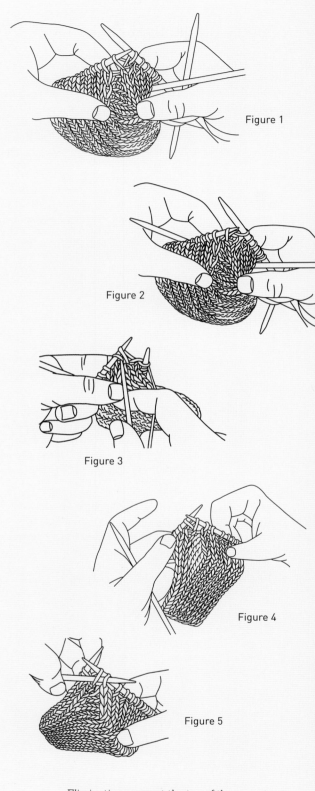

Eliminating a gap at the top of the gusset.

LEG

The leg is worked in stockinette stitch on the same number of stitches as were used to work the foot, ending about 2 inches (5 cm) short of the desired total leg length (see sock leg lengths on page 15).

CUFF

The cuff is worked in ribbing to ensure a snug fit. The instructions on page 55 specify an even number of stitches, which allows for k1, p1 (single) ribbing on the cuff (or all along the leg). If you'd prefer to use k2, p2 (double) ribbing, you'll need a number of stitches that's evenly divisible by 4. If the size/gauge you've chosen is not a multiple of 4, simply increase or decrease up to 2 stitches as necessary to obtain the necessary number of stitches for the ribbing.

Typically, ribbing is worked for just the last 2 inches (5 cm), but it can extend all the way from the heel (and along the top of the instep) if you prefer.

A stretchy bind-off (see page 52) is essential for a toe-up sock to have the flexibility to pull on and off over the heel.

The Lindisfarne Sock, page 124.

Stretchy Bind-Offs

A toe-up sock requires a stretchy bind-off. My two favorites are the Russian lace bind-off and Jeny's surprisingly stretchy bind-off. The Russian method is excellent for most purposes; Jeny's is a bit trickier to work, but it is definitely the stretchier of the two.

Russian Lace Bind-Off

Also called the decrease bind-off, this method provides a very simple and elegant way to get a nice, stretchy edge. Because the edge tends to flare when relaxed, this method is best when the resulting edge will be blocked or stretched. I use it at the cuffs of toe-up socks, as well as shawls that are to be stretched with blocking. This method produces a tidy "chain" along the bind-off edge because each stitch is effectively worked twice—the extra yarn at the base of each stitch makes a more prominent edge.

To work this bind-off, knit 1 stitch, knit 1 stitch (2 stitches on the right needle tip), *insert the tip of the left needle into the fronts of these 2 stitches from left to right (as if for a ssk decrease; **Figure 1**) then knit them together through their back loops, knit 1 stitch (**Figure 2**).

Repeat from * for each stitch to be bound off.

Jeny's Surprisingly Stretchy Bind-Off

Jeny Staiman's bind-off is, indeed, surprisingly stretchy! It's particularly well-suited to ribbing, as it buckles and bends with the ribbing. As with the Russian lace method, this technique is best used when the resulting edge will be stretched. Basically, you'll work a yarnover before each stitch, then pull that yarnover over the just-worked stitch to "collar" that stitch before proceeding to the next stitch.

If the stitch you are to work is a knit stitch, then the yarnover should be worked in reverse, bringing the yarn up from the back, then over the right needle toward you (**Figure 1**). Knit the stitch, then pull the yarnover over the stitch (**Figure 2**) to collar it.

If the stitch you are to work is a purl stitch, then the yarnover should be worked as normal, bringing the yarn up from the front, then over the right needle away from you (**Figure 3**). Purl the stitch, then pull the yarnover over the stitch (**Figure 4**) to collar it.

*Collar the next stitch according to its nature (**Figure 5**), then pass the previous stitch over the collared stitch and off the needle (**Figure 6**).

Repeat from * for each stitch to bind off.

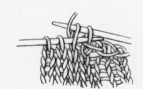

Figure 1

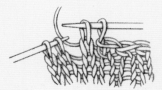

Figure 2

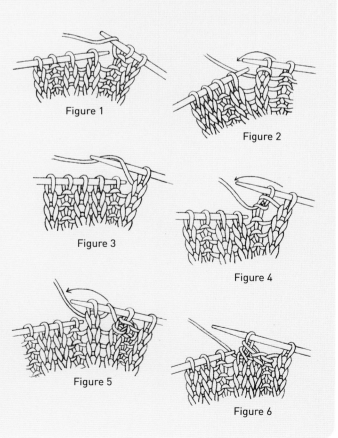

Figure 1

Figure 2

Figure 3

Figure 4

Figure 5

Figure 6

Sample Socks Based on the Basic Toe-Up Instructions on Page 54

Sample 1: Woman's medium slipper in bulky-weight yarn

This short version is knitted in bulky-weight yarn at a 4 stitches per inch (2.5 cm). The cuff turns down.

FINISHED CIRCUMFERENCE
7½" (19 cm).

YARN
Space Cadet Creations Elara (100% superwash merino wool; 120 yd [110 m]/100 g): Dark Skies, 1 skein (very little left over).

NEEDLES
U.S. size 8 (5 mm).

GAUGE
4 stitches = 1" (2.5 cm) in stockinette stitch, worked in rounds.

NUMBER OF LEG/FOOT STITCHES
30.

DESIGN DETAILS
1½" (3.8 cm) of k1, p1 ribbing for cuff and leg (worn turned down); 9" (23 cm) foot length.

Sample 2: Man's medium in fingering-weight yarn

This version is knitted with fingering-weight yarn at a sturdy gauge of 9 stitches per inch (2.5 cm).

FINISHED CIRCUMFERENCE
7" (18 cm).

YARN
Rowan Fine Art (45% wool, 20% mohair, 25% polyamide, 10% silk; 437 yd [400 m]/100 g): #307 Pheasant, 1 skein.

NEEDLES
U.S. size 1½ (2.5 mm).

GAUGE
9 stitches = 1" (2.5 cm) in stockinette stitch, worked in rounds.

NUMBER OF LEG/FOOT STITCHES
64.

DESIGN DETAILS
2" (5 cm) of k1, p1 ribbing for cuff; 7½" (19 cm) leg length; 10" (25.5 cm) foot length.

Sample 3: Child's medium in worsted-weight yarn

This version is knitted in worsted-weight yarn in a child's size.

FINISHED CIRCUMFERENCE
6½" (16.5 cm).

YARN
Drops Big Fabel (75% wool, 25% polyamide; 164 yd [150 m]/100 g): #522, 1 ball (very little left over).

NEEDLES
U.S. size 6 (4 mm).

GAUGE
5 stitches = 1" (2.5 cm) in stockinette stitch, worked in rounds.

NUMBER OF LEG/FOOT STITCHES
32.

DESIGN DETAILS
2" (5 cm) of k1, p1 ribbing at cuff; 5" (12.5 cm) leg length; 7½" (19 cm) foot length.

A BASIC TOE-UP SOCK PATTERN

These generic instructions are for a sock that's worked from the toe up, beginning with a clever cast-on that sets up the wedge toe. Gusset increases are worked on the foot, then the heel is worked in two steps—first, short-rows are worked to shape the cup, then decreases are worked to decrease the gusset stitches while forming the flap at the back of the heel. The leg is unshaped, which permits a comfortable fit for a calf- or ankle-length leg. The leg is finished with a flexible bind-off.

Make a photocopy of this page and use the table on pages 56–58 to fill in the appropriate numbers for your size and gauge.

Toe
Using Judy's magic method (see page 49), cast on _____ (**Cast-On Stitches**), so that half of the stitches are on each of two needles.

Knit 1 round even, distributing stitches as follows, depending on your needle choice.

FOUR DOUBLE-POINTED NEEDLES: Distribute the stitches so that the first half of the stitches are all on one needle and the second half are divided between two needles.

FIVE DOUBLE-POINTED NEEDLES: Distribute the stitches so that the first half of the stitches are divided between two needles and the second half of the stitches are divided between two other needles.

TWO CIRCULAR NEEDLES: Distribute the stitches so that half are on each needle.

MAGIC-LOOP METHOD: Distribute the stitches so that half are on each needle tip.

SHORT CIRCULAR NEEDLE: There are too few stitches at the tip of a toe-up sock to work on a short circular needle. You'll need to start the toe using another method and then change to the short circular needle once the sock has reached its full circumference.

Place one pin or marker in the fabric to indicate the start of the round and a second to indicate the halfway point of the round.

ROUND 1: (increase round) K1, M1 (see Glossary), knit to 1 st before center of round, M1, k2, M1, knit to 1 st before end of round, M1, k1—4 stitches increased.

ROUND 2: Knit even.

Repeat Rounds 1 and 2 until there are _____ (**Sock Stitches**).

Note: The first half of the round forms the instep; the second half forms the sole. The heel is worked on the sole stitches. Arrange the stitches, if necessary, so that the sole stitches are grouped together.

Foot
Work even in rounds until sock measures _____ (**Heel/Gusset Length**) less than _____ (finished sock foot length as given on pages 12–14), measured from cast-on at tip of toe.

Gusset Increases
Note: Keep the increased gusset stitches grouped with the sole stitches; markers are placed around the heel stitches, and the increases worked at the edges of the sole stitches.

SET-UP ROUND: Knit instep sts; M1R (see Glossary), place marker for heel, knit to end of round, place second heel marker, M1L (see Glossary)—2 gusset stitches increased.

ROUND 2: Knit.

ROUND 3: Knit instep sts; M1R, knit to end of round, M1L—2 gusset stitches increased.

ROUND 4: Knit.

Repeat Rounds 3 and 4 until you've increased _____ (**Gusset Stitches per Side**) at each side of the marked heel stitches— _____ (**Total Sock Plus Gusset Stitches**) total.

Heel Turn

The heel is worked back and forth in short-rows (see Glossary) on _____ (**Heel Stitches**) stitches between the heel markers, which correspond to half of the initial _____ (**Sock Stitches**).

HEEL TURN ROW 1: (RS) Knit to 1 stitch before second marker, wrap the next stitch (see Glossary), turn work.

HEEL TURN ROW 2: (WS) Purl to 1 stitch before marker, wrap next stitch, turn work.

HEEL TURN ROW 3: (RS) Knit to 1 stitch before last wrapped stitch, wrap next stitch, turn work.

HEEL TURN ROW 4: (WS) Purl to 1 stitch before last wrapped stitch, wrap next stitch, turn work.

Repeat Heel Rows 3 and 4 until _____ (**Heel Base Stitches**) remain unwrapped in the center of the heel stitches, ending with a wrong-side row.

Remove the heel markers.

Heel Flap

Decrease the gusset stitches while working the heel flap as follows.

HEEL FLAP ROW 1: (RS) Knit to first wrapped stitch, *knit the wrapped stitch together with its wrap (see Glossary); repeat from * until 1 wrapped stitch remains, work the remaining wrapped stitch (together with its wrap) and the first gusset stitch together as ssk, turn work—1 gusset stitch decreased.

HEEL FLAP ROW 2: (WS) Slip 1 purlwise with yarn in front, purl to first wrapped stitch, *purl the wrapped stitch together with its wrap; repeat from * until 1 wrapped stitch remains, work the remaining wrapped stitch (together with its wrap) and the first gusset stitch together as p2tog, turn work—1 gusset stitch decreased.

Working back and forth on the center heel stitches, always stopping 1 stitch before the gusset, continue to work _____ (**Heel Stitches - 2**) between the initial slipped stitch and the gusset decrease each row as follows.

HEEL FLAP ROW 3: (RS) Slip 1 purlwise with yarn in back, knit to 1 stitch before gusset stitches, ssk, turn work—1 gusset stitch decreased.

HEEL FLAP ROW 4: (WS) Slip 1 purlwise with yarn in front, purl to 1 st before gusset stitches, p2tog, turn work—1 gusset stitch decreased.

Repeat Rows 3 and 4 until all but 2 gusset stitches have been decreased (one on each side), ending with a right-side row— _____ (**Leg Start Stitches**) stitches remain—the final 2 gusset stitches will be decreased during the first round of the leg to keep the top of the heel tidy and to prevent holes from forming.

Leg

With right side still facing, rejoin for working in rounds as follows.

SET-UP ROUND: Slip 1 purlwise with yarn in back, knit to 1 stitch before first gusset stitch, ssk; knit across instep sts; k2tog, knit to end of sole sts—2 gusset stitches decreased; _____ (**Sock Stitches**) remain.

Continue in stockinette until leg measures about 2" (5 cm) less than desired total length (see pages 12–14 for sock leg length tables).

Cuff

Work in to k1, p1 ribbing for 2" (5 cm). Alternatively, work in ribbing for the entire length of the leg.

Using a stretchy method (see page 52), bind off all stitches.

Finishing

Cut yarn. Weave in loose ends. Block as desired (see page 18).

Stitch and Row Numbers for the Basic Toe-Up Sock Pattern

Find the block of numbers that corresponds to your desired finished sock circumference along the left edge of the table on the following pages, then follow the column of numbers that corresponds to your gauge (measured in

TOE-UP SOCK STITCH AND ROW/ROUND NUMBERS

FINISHED SOCK CIRCUMFERENCE		GAUGE: STITCHES PER INCH								
		4	5	5½	6	6½	7	7½	8	9
5" (12.5 cm)	Sock Stitches	20	24	28	30	32	34	38	40	44
	Cast-On Stitches	8	8	8	10	12	14	14	16	16
	Heel/Gusset Length (in inches)	2¾	2¾	2¾	2¾	2½	2½	2¾	2½	2¾
	Gusset Stitches per Side	4	5	6	6	6	7	8	8	9
	Stitch Count Before Heel Turn	28	34	40	42	44	48	54	56	62
	Heel Stitches	10	12	14	15	16	17	19	20	22
	Heel Base Stitches	4	4	6	5	6	7	7	8	8
	Leg Start Stitches	22	26	30	32	34	36	40	42	46
5½" (14 cm)	Sock Stitches	22	28	30	32	36	38	40	44	50
	Cast-On Stitches	6	8	10	12	12	14	16	16	18
	Heel/Gusset Length (in inches)	2¾	3	3	2¾	3	3	2¾	3	3
	Gusset Stitches per Side	4	6	6	6	7	8	8	9	10
	Stitch Count Before Heel Turn	30	40	42	44	50	54	56	62	70
	Heel Stitches	11	14	15	16	18	19	20	22	25
	Heel Base Stitches	5	6	5	6	6	7	8	8	9
	Leg Start Stitches	24	30	32	34	38	40	42	46	52
6" (15 cm)	Sock Stitches	24	30	32	36	38	42	44	48	54
	Cast-On Stitches	8	10	12	12	14	14	16	16	18
	Heel/Gusset Length (in inches)	3½	3¼	3	3¼	3¼	3¼	3¼	3½	3¼
	Gusset Stitches per Side	5	6	6	7	8	8	9	10	11
	Stitch Count Before Heel Turn	34	42	44	50	54	58	62	68	76
	Heel Stitches	12	15	16	18	19	21	22	24	27
	Heel Base Stitches	4	5	6	6	7	7	8	8	9
	Leg Start Stitches	26	32	34	38	40	44	46	50	56
6½" (16.5 cm)	Sock Stitches	26	32	36	38	42	46	48	52	58
	Cast-On Stitches	10	12	12	14	14	14	16	16	18
	Heel/Gusset Length (in inches)	3½	3¼	3½	3½	3½	3¾	3½	3½	3¾
	Gusset Stitches per Side	5	6	7	8	8	9	10	10	12
	Stitch Count Before Heel Turn	36	44	50	54	58	64	68	72	82
	Heel Stitches	13	16	18	19	21	23	24	26	29
	Heel Base Stitches	5	6	6	7	7	7	8	8	9
	Leg Start Stitches	28	34	38	40	44	48	50	54	60

stitches per inch). For example, if you want to knit a sock with a 6-inch (15 cm) circumference at 5 stitches to the inch, you'd follow the second column of number in the third block, which begins with 30 sock stitches.

TOE-UP SOCK STITCH AND ROW/ROUND NUMBERS, CONT.

FINISHED SOCK CIRCUMFERENCE		GAUGE: STITCHES PER INCH								
		4	5	5½	6	6½	7	7½	8	9
7" (18 cm)	Sock Stitches	28	34	38	42	46	48	52	56	62
	Cast-On Stitches	8	10	14	14	14	16	16	20	22
	Heel/Gusset Length (in inches)	4	4	3¾	3¾	4	3¾	3¾	3/34	3¾
	Gusset Stitches per Side	6	7	8	8	9	10	10	11	12
	Stitch Count Before Heel Turn	40	48	54	58	64	68	72	78	86
	Heel Stitches	14	17	19	21	23	24	26	28	31
	Heel Base Stitches	4	5	7	7	7	8	8	10	11
	Leg Start Stitches	30	36	40	44	48	50	54	58	64
7½" (19 cm)	Sock Stitches	30	38	40	44	48	52	56	60	68
	Cast-On Stitches	10	14	12	16	16	16	20	20	24
	Heel/Gusset Length (in inches)	4¼	4½	4	4¼	4¼	4	4¼	4	4¼
	Gusset Stitches per Side	6	8	8	9	10	10	11	12	14
	Stitch Count Before Heel Turn	42	54	56	62	68	72	78	84	96
	Heel Stitches	15	19	20	22	24	26	28	30	34
	Heel Base Stitches	5	7	6	8	8	8	10	10	12
	Leg Start Stitches	32	40	42	46	50	54	58	62	70
8" (20.5 cm)	Sock Stitches	32	40	44	48	52	56	60	64	72
	Cast-On Stitches	12	12	16	16	16	20	20	20	24
	Heel/Gusset Length (in inches)	4½	4½	4¾	4½	4½	4½	4½	4½	4½
	Gusset Stitches per Side	6	8	9	10	10	11	12	13	14
	Stitch Count Before Heel Turn	44	56	62	68	72	78	84	90	100
	Heel Stitches	16	20	22	24	26	28	30	32	36
	Heel Base Stitches	6	6	8	8	8	10	10	10	12
	Leg Start Stitches	34	42	46	50	54	58	62	66	74
8½" (21.5 cm)	Sock Stitches	34	42	46	50	54	60	64	68	76
	Cast-On Stitches	10	14	14	18	18	20	20	24	24
	Heel/Gusset Length (in inches)	5	4½	4¾	4¾	4¾	4¾	4¾	4¾	4¾
	Gusset Stitches per Side	7	8	9	10	11	12	13	14	15
	Stitch Count Before Heel Turn	48	58	64	70	76	84	90	96	106
	Heel Stitches	17	21	23	25	27	30	32	34	38
	Heel Base Stitches	5	7	7	9	9	10	10	12	12
	Leg Start Stitches	36	44	48	52	56	62	66	70	78

FINISHED SOCK CIRCUMFERENCE		GAUGE: STITCHES PER INCH								
		4	5	5½	6	6½	7	7½	8	9
9" **(23 cm)**	Sock Stitches	36	44	50	54	58	62	68	72	80
	Cast-On Stitches	12	16	18	18	18	22	24	24	28
	Heel/Gusset Length (in inches)	5	5	5	5	5	5	5	5	5
	Gusset Stitches per Side	7	9	10	11	12	12	14	14	16
	Stitch Count Before Heel Turn	50	62	70	76	82	86	96	100	112
	Heel Stitches	18	22	25	27	29	31	34	36	40
	Heel Base Stitches	6	8	9	9	9	11	12	12	14
	Leg Start Stitches	38	46	52	56	60	64	70	74	82
9½" **(24 cm)**	Sock Stitches	38	48	52	56	62	66	70	76	86
	Cast-On Stitches	14	16	16	20	22	22	22	24	30
	Heel/Gusset Length (in inches)	5½	5½	5¼	5¼	5½	5	5¼	5	5¼
	Gusset Stitches per Side	8	10	10	11	12	13	14	15	17
	Stitch Count Before Heel Turn	54	68	72	78	86	92	98	106	120
	Heel Stitches	19	24	26	28	31	33	35	38	43
	Heel Base Stitches	7	8	8	10	11	11	11	12	15
	Leg Start Stitches	40	50	54	58	64	68	72	78	88
10" **(25.5 cm)**	Sock Stitches	40	50	54	60	64	70	74	80	90
	Cast-On Stitches	12	18	18	20	20	22	26	28	30
	Heel/Gusset Length (in inches)	5½	5¾	5½	5½	5½	5½	5½	5½	5½
	Gusset Stitches per Side	8	10	11	12	13	14	15	16	18
	Stitch Count Before Heel Turn	56	70	76	84	90	98	104	112	126
	Heel Stitches	20	25	27	30	32	35	37	40	45
	Heel Base Stitches	6	9	9	10	10	11	13	14	15
	Leg Start Stitches	42	52	56	62	66	72	76	82	92
10½" **(26.5 cm)**	Sock Stitches	42	52	58	62	68	74	78	84	94
	Cast-On Stitches	14	16	18	22	24	26	26	28	30
	Heel/Gusset Length (in inches)	5¾	5¾	6	5¾	6	6	5¾	5¾	5¾
	Gusset Stitches per Side	8	10	12	12	14	15	16	17	19
	Stitch Count Before Heel Turn	58	72	82	86	96	104	110	118	132
	Heel Stitches	21	26	29	31	34	37	39	42	47
	Heel Base Stitches	7	8	9	11	12	13	13	14	15
	Leg Start Stitches	44	54	60	64	70	76	80	86	96

The Fitzcarraldo Knee Sock, page 178.

Calculating the Numbers in the Toe-Up Sock Table

The eight variables in the table on pages 56–58 were calculated according to the following formulas. You can use the formulas to calculate the numbers you need if you're knitting for a foot that doesn't conform to the measurements or if you're working at a gauge that isn't specified on the tables.

To calculate these formulas, you'll need the key measurements determined in Chapter 1, along with your gauge, measured in stitches per inch.

Sock Stitches = (Gauge in Stitches per Inch × Foot Circumference) × 0.9

Because all the socks are based on an even number of stitches (to allow for k1, p1 ribbing at the cuff), round the calculated number to the nearest even number.

For example, if you're knitting a sock for a foot with a 9 inch (23 cm) circumference at a gauge of 7.5 stitches per inch (2.5 cm), your Sock Stitches number will be 60.75, which you'll round to 60.

$$(7.5 \text{ stitches per inch} \times 9") \times .9 = 67.5 \text{ stitches} \times .9 = 60.75 \text{ stitches; round to } 60$$

Find this Sock Stitches number in the Toe-Up Sock table on page 58, then follow those numbers for the gusset stitches, the heel stitches, and the heel base stitches, but check the heel and gusset length by your own calculations. *Note: If your calculated Sock Stitches match those for one of the other sizes, you may be able to follow the other numbers for that size, but you should check the heel and gusset length calculation by hand.*

Cast-On Stitches = About ⅓ of Sock Stitches

There are two requirements for the Cast-On Stitches number. If the Sock Stitches is an even number, the Cast-On Stitches has to be an even number; if the Sock Stitches is an odd number, the Cast-On Stitches has to be an odd number. In addition, the difference between the Sock Stitches and the Cast-On Stitches must be divisible by 4 (increases from the cast-on to the full number of sock stitches occur in groups of 4). If the number is not divisible by 4, add or subtract 2 from the Cast-On Number. If you're making the socks for a foot with wide toes, add 2; if the foot has pointier toes, subtract 2.

For example, if the Sock Stitches number is 60, the Cast-On Stitches number is 20.

$$60 \text{ stitches} \div 3 = 20 \text{ stitches}$$

To confirm that you'll be able to increase from 20 to 60 in groups of 4, subtract the Cast-On Stitches from Sock Stitches and divide by 4.

$$60 \text{ stitches} - 20 \text{ stitches} = 40 \text{ stitches}$$

$$40 \text{ stitches} \div 4 = 10 \text{ stitches}$$

In this example, the calculated Cast-On Stitches will work because 10 is a whole number.

But what if your Sock Stitches number was 62? In this case, the Cast-On Stitches number would be 20.6.

$$62 \text{ stitches} \div 3 = 20.6 \text{ stitches}$$

You'll first have to round this to a whole number. If we round down to 20, we'll have to increase 42 stitches between the Cast-On Stitches and the full Sock Stitches.

$$62 \text{ stitches} - 20 \text{ stitches} = 42 \text{ stitches}$$

But this number isn't divisible by 4, so we won't be able to achieve 62 stitches by working the increases in groups of 4.

$$42 \text{ stitches} \div 4 = 10.5 \text{ stitches}$$

In this case, we'll have to adjust the Cast-On Stitches by adding or subtracting 2 stitches.

If you're knitting socks for a foot with wide toes, add 2 stitches for Cast-On Stitches of 22; if you're knitting socks for a foot with narrow toes, subtract 2 stitches for Cast-On Stitches of 18.

Gusset Stitches Per Side = Sock Stitches × 0.2

Round up to the nearest whole number if necessary.

For example, if there are 60 Sock Stitches, there will be 12 Gusset Stitches Per Side.

$$60 \text{ stitches} \times 0.2 = 12 \text{ Gusset Stitches Per Side}$$

**Total Sock Stitches + Gusset Stitches =
Sock Stitches + (2 × Gusset Stitches Per Side)**

The number of stitches when the gusset stitches have been increased equals the original number of sock stitches plus twice the number of gusset stitches that were increased on one side.

For example, if there are 60 Sock Stitches and 12 Gusset Stitches increased on each side, there will be a total of 84 stitches.

$$60 + (2 \times 12) = 84$$

Heel Stitches = Sock Stitches ÷ 2

For example, if there are 60 Sock Stitches, you'll work the heel on 30 stitches.

$$60 \text{ stitches} \div 2 = 30 \text{ stitches}$$

Heel Base Stitches = About ⅓ of Heel Stitches

This calculated number must be a whole number, which must also be an even number if Heel Stitches is an even number; it must be an odd number if Heel Stitches is an odd number.

For example, if there are 60 Sock Stitches, there will be 30 Heel Stitches and 10 Heel Base Stitches.

$$30 \text{ stitches} \div 3 = 10 \text{ stitches}$$

Both numbers are even, so the number will work.

If, for example, there were 31 Heel Stitches, there would be 10.3 calculated Heel Base Stitches, which will have to be rounded to a whole number.

$$31 \text{ stitches} \div 3 = 10.3 \text{ stitches}$$

Because Heel Stitches is an odd number, we'll need to round this up to 11, which is the nearest odd number.

**Length of Heel and Gusset = [(Gusset Stitches × 2) +
(Heel Stitches – Heel Base Stitches)] ÷ Rounds per Inch**

In this calculation, (Gusset Stitches × 2) is the number of rounds in the gusset, and (Heel Stitches – Heel Base Stitches) is the number of rows in the heel. When the two are added together, we have the total number of rows/rounds worked for that section of the sock. We have to divide that number by the number of rounds per inch (2.5 cm) to determine the length in inches.

For example, if we have 12 Gusset Stitches, we'll have 24 rounds in the gusset.

$$12 \text{ Gusset Stitches} \times 2 = 24 \text{ rounds in the gusset}$$

If we have 30 Heel Stitches and 10 Heel Base Stitches, we'll have a total of 20 rows in the heel.

$$30 \text{ heel stitches} - 10 \text{ heel base stitches} =$$
$$20 \text{ rows in the heel flap}$$

We add these numbers together to get the total number of rows/rounds in this section.

$$24 \text{ rounds} + 20 \text{ rows} = 44 \text{ rounds/rows}$$

Finally, we divide this number by the number of rounds per inch (2.5 cm) to determine how many inches are involved in those 44 rows/rounds. Let's say our round gauge is 10 rounds per inch (2.5 cm).

$$44 \text{ rounds/rows} \div 10 \text{ rounds per inch} = 4.4"$$

This tells us that the length of the heel plus the gusset is 4.4" (11.2 cm).

Leg Start Stitches = Sock Stitches + 2

The number of stitches at the beginning of the leg is 2 more than the number of Sock Stitches. This is because the final gusset decreases are worked in the first round of the leg.

For example, if we begin with 60 Sock Stitches, there will be 62 stitches at the start of the leg.

$$60 + 2 = 62$$

Chapter 4
On Adding Stitch Patterns

Up to this point, we've only discussed "plain" socks. In other words, the socks are all worked in stockinette stitch with some ribbing at the cuff.

The same guidelines and formulas can be used when a stitch or color pattern stitch is added, but some of the rules change if the stitch pattern gauge is significantly different than the "plain" stockinette-stitch gauge. In general, ribbing and knit-purl patterns can be treated the same as stockinette, but lace, cables, and colorwork patterns will affect the gauge. We'll look at all of these types of patterns in this chapter.

For practical purposes, the sole stitches are always worked in stockinette, regardless of the stitch pattern that's added to the leg or instep. This is for a very good reason—anything other than stockinette can feel uncomfortable underfoot.

The Princess Sole

Typical sock designs place the knit side of the stockinette sole facing out and the purl side facing in. Although a densely knitted stockinette fabric should feel good this way, some knitters contend that the sock is more comfortable if the knit side is on the inside. This actually makes very good sense—the smoother side of the fabric is against the foot. You can work this "inside out" sole on any sock in this book—simply purl the sole stitches instead of knitting them.

If you're working a plain stockinette foot, a quick cheat makes this very simple—work the heel and foot inside out, so you don't have to make any changes to the heel or gusset. For a top-down sock, work an extra heel flap row so that you end with a right-side row—you'll be facing the inside of the sock. Work the heel turn instructions as specified, but treat the inside of the leg as the "right" side. Stop after the final (WS) decrease heel row; skip that final even row on the heel stitches and start picking up stitches immediately. Pick up the gusset stitches purlwise along the edges of the heel flap, purling the sole stitches and knitting the instep stitches all the way to the sole.

For a toe-up sock, purl the instep stitches purlwise (see Glossary) from the onset, including the instep side of the toe, working purlwise increases. Work the gusset and heel turn as set. After the last wrap and turn, reverse the right and wrong sides by purling the first rows of the heel flap (including hiding the wraps) and knitting the second row of the heel flap. From there, work with the purl side of the sole as the right side of the heel flap. When the gusset decreases are complete, you'll be positioned at the start of the instep with the right side facing. At that point, resume working in the round.

If you want to add a pattern to the instep, it's easiest to work the heel turn and sole inside out, rather than attempting to turn the instep patterns the other way around. The simplest solution is to work the heel turn in stockinette as usual. For a top-down sock, start working in reverse stockinette at the gusset pick-up, purling all the gusset and sole stitches and working p2tog for the gusset decreases. (If you want to get fancy, use the right-leaning p2tog instead of k2tog and the left-leaning p2tog-tbl instead of ssk, but I find that the difference isn't necessarily worth the effort.) For a toe-up sock, work purlwise increases—I like the backward-loop cast-on (see Glossary) for this.

You can get a bit fancier and reverse the heel turns without much additional effort. For a toe-up sock, you'll work the wraps and turns and hide the wraps the same way, but just remember that you'll be purling on right-side rows and knitting on wrong-side rows. For a top-down sock, reverse the heel turn—purl the right-side rows and knit the wrong-side rows—and substitute k2tog for the p2tog decrease and substitute p2tog tbl for the ssk decrease.

Adding Ribbed Patterns

It's a good idea to work 1 inch to 2 inches (2.5 to 5 cm) of ribbing at the top of the sock leg to help it stay up. But in addition to the cuff, you can add ribbed patterns as a design element along the entire leg (and onto the instep). The advantage to ribbed patterns is that they have more

elasticity than stockinette stitch and therefore can hug the leg and foot a little better.

Although ribbing compresses horizontally, and therefore looks "smaller" than stockinette stitch, for the purposes of sock design and fit, you can and should treat them the same. In its natural—the elusive "slightly stretched"— state, the gauge of a ribbed fabric matches the gauge of stockinette stitch worked on with the same yarn and needles. Although they look narrower, ribbed fabrics can be stretched out to the same degree as a stockinette fabric.

Note that the fewer the stitches in the rib repeat—for example k1, p1 rather than k3, p3—the more the fabric "buckles" or compresses and the "stretchier" it seems. For example, k1, p1 ribbing will contract to a narrower width than k3, p3 ribbing, but the two will stretch to the same width.

Your instinct might be that a ribbed fabric stretches out more than a stockinette fabric. But that's all an illusion— stockinette fabric simply looks more distorted than ribbing when extremely stretched. This is why we tend to think of stockinette fabrics as less stretchy than ribbed fabrics— they don't look as good when stretched. Try it for yourself with a sock that has a ribbed cuff and a stockinette leg. You'll be able to pull the two fabrics equally wide, but the ribbed portion will look better than the stockinette portion.

Looks Can Be Deceiving

It's worthwhile to distinguish between fabrics that are tighter or smaller and those fabrics that simply look tighter or smaller. Consider a 30-stitch swatch, knitted with the same yarn and needles throughout, that begins with a section of stockinette stitch followed by a section of ribbing and a section of a cabled pattern.

The ribbing and cabled patterns will be narrower than the stockinette section because both of these patterns cause the fabric to contract widthwise. The ribbing only looks narrower—the juxtaposition of knit and purl stitches causes compression—but it will stretch to the same width as the stockinette section. The cable pattern, however, is truly narrower—it cannot be stretched to the same width as the stockinette section.

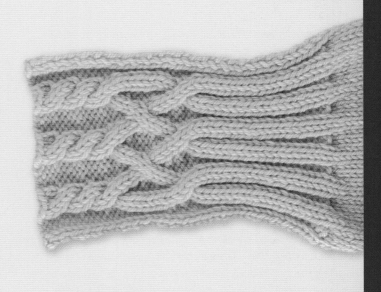

When calculating the gauge of ribbed patterns, therefore, you can use the stockinette-stitch gauge (worked with the same yarn and needles of course). This is good news! It means you can substitute a ribbed pattern for plain stockinette stitch in any sock pattern without having to make any adjustment to the size or the stitch counts and without facing the challenge of measuring the gauge of ribbing. It also means that you can extend the ribbed pattern in the cuff along the full length of the sock leg of your sock (and even on the instep) without any additional calculations.

The only adjustment you might need to make is to ensure that you have the correct number of stitches to accommodate your pattern multiple. For example, if your ribbing is a 5-stitch repeat, such as k3, p2, you'll need to work on a number of stitches that is divisible by 5. In this case, simply round down to the closest multiple of 5 stitches. If the foot will be worked in stockinette stitch, simply work the number of increases or decreases required to get back to the original number of stitches when you transition between the leg and the foot—in the last leg round if working from the top down; in the first leg round if working from the toe up. (Of course, if you're working the leg in stockinette, work the increases/decreases in the transition between the cuff and leg.)

If you want to continue the ribbed pattern along the instep, you might have to adjust the number of stitches at the split between the instep and sole as well. More on that later.

Ribbing provides a simple solution for minor fit adjustments. For example, if you're knitting a sock for average calves and average feet, but with skinnier-than-average ankles, consider working ribbing all the way down the leg. The fabric won't need to stretch as much for the narrower ankles where the ribbing will remain compressed and cling better than plain stockinette stitch.

If you don't like the look of a fully ribbed leg (it can be distracting in a busy variegated or self-striping yarn), you can get the fit benefit by adding a bit of ribbing in a select area. For example, if you work about 25 percent of the stitches in k1, p1 ribbing centered over the heel, you'll get the extra "cling" of the ribbing along the back of the leg while maintaining the attractive look of stockinette across the front of the leg. For a balanced and centered ribbing, begin and end the ribbed section with purl stitches. For

Swatching for Twisted Ribbing

To work a gauge swatch for twisted ribbing, cast on about 50 percent more stitches than you would expect for stockinette so that the swatch will be at least 4 inches (10 cm) wide. For example, for a fingering-weight sock yarn that would be knitted at a gauge of 30 stitches to 4 inches (10 cm) in stockinette, work the twisted ribbing swatch on about 45 stitches.

Work the twisted ribbing pattern for at least 4 inches (10 cm) to get a good sense of how much it pulls in. Then wash the swatch as usual. Once dry, flatten it out slightly to remove the buckle, but don't stretch it before measuring the gauge. See page 68 (Swatching For A Patterned Sock) for more details.

The twisted ribbing in The Secrets & Lies Sock (see page 102) helped tighten the lace pattern for a snug fit.

k1, p1 ribbing, this means you'll want to work the ribbed section on an odd number of stitches. For k2, p2 ribbing, you'll want to work the ribbed section on a number of stitches that is a multiple of 4 stitches plus 2.

TWISTED RIBBING

Twisted ribbing—ribbed patterns in which the knit stitches are worked through the back loop (it's less common to work the purl stitches through the back loop, though it can be done)—will change the character of the fabric. The fabric will be less compressed and the twisted stitches will be tighter and have less stretch. If you plan to work a large section of a sock in twisted ribbing, you'll need to check your gauge as described in the sidebar at left and adjust your numbers if necessary.

If you're working a fully ribbed leg, consider working the cuff in the twisted version of the ribbing. It visually distinguishes the cuff by pulling it in a bit more, and it creates a bit more snugness at the top of the leg. If you don't like the look of twisted ribbing, you can get the same effect by working only the purl stitches through the back loop instead of the knit stitches.

I used a twisted ribbing for the Secrets & Lies Sock (see page 102) to improve the fit, as well as for cosmetic reasons. Because lace fabrics stretch out more than stockinette, I wanted the ribbed portion to be tighter. I gave a unified look to the design by continuing the twisted ribbing from the pattern repeat in the leg into the cuff.

I also used a twisted purl stitch in the Oh, Valencia! Sock (see page 88) to create a smaller pattern repeat and in the Fitzcarraldo Knee Sock (see page 178) to harmonize with the pattern on the leg. Because twisted ribbings are a bit tighter than a standard ribbing, they help ensure that the socks stay up on the legs.

Adding Knit/Purl Patterns

Patterns made up of non-ribbed combinations of knit and purl stitches, such as brocade, embossed, and zigzag patterns, also behave like stockinette stitch from a gauge and stretch perspective. No adjustments to the basic patterns are needed if you want to use these stitch patterns in your sock.

Accommodating Repeats
HEEL VERSUS INSTEP STITCHES

Although all of the formulas and tables in this book assume that the heel is worked on precisely half the stitches for the leg or foot, there are times when this rule can be broken. It's perfectly fine to adjust the number of stitches (either by adding or subtracting a few stitches) in the instep to accommodate a stitch pattern.

When designing a sock with a pattern stitch, my objective is a symmetrical pattern that's centered on the instep. In the case of a ribbing-based pattern, I like to begin and end the instep with a purl rib.

In some cases (the Basic Ribbed Sock on page 76, for example) I divide the stitches so that the complete instep pattern is positioned on the instep stitches. In other cases (the Marpleridge Sock on page 82 and the Secrets & Lies Sock on page 102, for example) I "borrow" 1 or 2 stitches from the top of each gusset to complete the instep pattern. In general, my choice is driven by the stitch counts. I always try to keep the number of instep stitches as close as possible to the number of heel stitches. A difference of 1 or 2 stitches between the two doesn't affect the fit significantly, but if the difference is any bigger, I prefer to "borrow" from the sole to complete the pattern on the instep. To do this, I simply work the necessary number of stitches at the edges of the sole in the pattern, rather than in stockinette stitch.

When "borrowing" heel or gusset stitches, the results are most attractive and easiest to keep track of if the same number of stitches is borrowed from each side. This will ensure that the instep pattern is centered.

If there won't be the same number of stitches for the instep and heel, I prefer to have the instep wider for the simple reason that I think it's better to have more pattern than less. But again, if the difference between the two is only a couple of stitches, it's not going to be visible either way. But a difference of more than about ½ inch (1.3 cm) in width between the heel flap width and the instep will affect the fit, and other adjustments should be made.

The adjustments depend on whether the sock is worked from the top down or from the toe up.

Top-Down Socks

For a sock worked from the top down, the number of rows in the heel flap should be based on 50 percent of the number of stitches in the full sock circumference, not the adjusted heel width. This will ensure that the length of the heel flap is proportionate to the full circumference.

Also, the center group of stitches in the heel turn should be based on 50 percent of the sock stitches. For example, the heel of a 60-stitch sock would normally be worked on 30 stitches. These 30 stitches would be divided in thirds for the heel turn, so that there would be 10 stitches in the center group and 10 stitches in each side group (i.e., 10, 10, and 10). If, for example, you adjust the heel to 26 stitches to accommodate a particularly wide instep pattern, you'll still want to work the center section of the heel turn on 10 stitches—divide the stitches as 8, 10, and 8. If the heel flap were wider, such as 34 stitches instead of 30, divide the stitches as 12, 10, and 12.

Remember from the formulas in Chapter 3 that HT2 is the center third of the stitches; in this case, 10. HT1 is the remaining two-thirds of the stitches; in this case, 16 (8 + 8).

If the heel flap is narrower than usual, the edges will sit slightly farther back on the foot, which also places the gusset pick-up stitches farther back. This isn't an issue when it comes to fit, but you'll need to spread out the gusset decreases over more rounds to accommodate the difference. If you complete the gusset decreases too early, the sock may feel tight around the arch of your foot. To compensate, simply work some additional even rounds between the gusset decrease rounds. For example, if your heel flap is less than about one-third of the sock stitches, work 2 even rounds between each gusset decrease round.

If, on the other hand, the heel flap is wider than normal, you run the risk of completing the gusset decreases too late and creating a sock that may feel too loose. In this case, you'll want to omit some of the even rounds between the gusset decrease rounds to compensate. If your heel flap is more than two-thirds of the sock stitches, omit about half of the even rounds while working the gusset decreases.

Of course, there are practical limitations to these adjustments. There must be at least 4 or 5 stitches on each side of the center section to create a reasonable shape in the heel turn.

Finally, you must remember to readjust the division between the instep and sole stitches so that there is the same number in each before you begin decreasing for the toe—otherwise the toe won't be symmetrical.

Toe-Up Socks

For a sock worked from the toe up, the adjustments begin once you've increased to the desired number of stitches for the foot. Divide the instep and sole stitches as necessary to accommodate the instep pattern, then work the gusset and heel on the adjusted number of stitches.

You'll want to keep the gusset stitch count proportionate to the full circumference, but the fit won't be affected if these gusset stitches are positioned a little more to the top or bottom of the foot. As long as the overall circumference is achieved, the position of the increased stitches doesn't matter.

As with top-down sock, if you work a heel on a significantly different number of stitches than specified in the table, leave the Heel Base Stitches (the number of stitches left unwrapped) the same as for a stockinette-stitch sock. You'll need enough wrapped stitches on each side to create a good shape in the heel turn—at least 3 or 4 wrapped stitches on each side of the center section.

LEG VERSUS FOOT STITCHES

The leg and foot don't have to have the same number of stitches either, especially if you need to adjust the number of stitches in the leg to accommodate a pattern stitch. Of course, the toe shaping is tidier (whether you're working top down or toe up) if there is an even number of stitches on the foot, but some stitch patterns might require an odd number of stitches for the leg.

For example, a 5-stitch ribbing pattern—such as k3, p2— might require 55 stitches for the leg. But the foot will be easier if it's worked on an even number of stitches, such as 56. There's no reason that you can't use both numbers, as the necessary stitch-count adjustments can be made in a couple of places.

Small adjustments are easily worked at the top of the heel flap. When working from the top down, the adjustment is made in the first row of the heel flap; when working from the toe up, the adjustment is made in the last row of the heel flap (which corresponds to the first round of the leg). For the top-down Harcourt Sock on page 132, for example, I worked shaping at the top of the heel flap to accommodate the difference between the lace pattern and the stockinette gauges. For the toe-up Lindisfarne Sock on

The Lindisfarne Sock, page 124.

page 124, I worked shaping in the first row of the heel flap to set up the right stitch count for the leg.

If the difference is just a single stitch, I've indulged in a quick and dirty "cheat" when working top-down socks. I adjust the stitch count on the sole by working one more gusset decrease on just one side of the heel. The decrease is well hidden among the others, and no one will know that there isn't the same number of decreases on each side.

HEEL FLAP POSITION

For convenience, the heel flap begins at the start of the round for most of the socks in this book, but it doesn't have to. If you want to align the heel flap with a particular part of the leg patterning, simply work to that point before starting the first row of the flap. For example, I designed the Wellington Road Sock on page 138 so that the left and right socks were mirror images when it comes to the position of the cable panel in relation to the heel. The legs for the two socks are worked the same, but the position of the heel determines the placement of the cable on the two socks.

For a toe-up sock, the position of the heel and heel flap is defined by the division between the instep and sole

stitches—it will always be aligned with the sole stitches. Any changes have to be planned for during the shaping of the toe.

LARGE REPEATS

Up to this point, all of the discussion on accommodating pattern repeats has assumed relatively small repeats of no more than 6 stitches. Such small repeats provide a lot of options when it comes to adjusting stitch counts and allow for relatively easy "fudging" of the numbers in the tables. For example, a 6-stitch pattern repeat fits evenly into 24, 30, 36, 42, 48, 54, 60, 66, 72, 78, 84, and 90 stitches. Chances are that one of these numbers is close to the number of stitches you need for your circumference at your gauge, in which case you can use the adjustments previously discussed.

In many of these cases, the available number of stitches is "close enough" to the stitch count you require and will result in less than ½ inch (1.3 cm) difference in the finished circumference. You can round up, which will result in a slightly looser leg, but you can compensate for that by tightening up the ribbing—work a twisted ribbing or work the ribbing on smaller needles.

Larger pattern repeats, however, can pose larger challenges. For example, a 12-stitch repeat fits evenly into 24, 36, 48, 60, 72, and 84 stitches. These fewer options mean that the nearest multiple that works with the pattern may be significantly different than the number of stitches you need.

For example, if you want to knit a sock that measures 7½" inches (19 cm) in circumference at 7½ stitches per inch (2.5 cm), you'll want 56 stitches.

7.5" × 7.5 stitches per inch = 56 stitches

If you want to add a 12-stitch repeat evenly, the closest possibility is 60 stitches, which is 4 stitches more than your target amount. At a gauge of 7.5 stitches per inch (2.5 cm), these 4 stitches will add more than ½ inch (1.3 cm) in the overall circumference, and the finished sock will be bigger than you may want. In these cases, you'll want to make adjustments to the fabric, pattern stitch, or gauge. The following case studies explain how.

Gauge-Affecting Pattern Stitches

Lace, cables, and colorwork patterns will all affect the gauge of a fabric. That is, a fabric worked in one of these patterns will have a different gauge than the same yarn worked on the same needles in stockinette stitch. If you want to use one of these patterns in a sock, you'll need to make some adjustments.

SWATCHING FOR A PATTERNED SOCK

The first step is to knit a gauge swatch (in the round; see page 27) that's at least 5 inches (12.5 cm) in circumference so you can measure 2 inches or 3 inches (5 or 7.5 cm) in width. Be sure to include at least two or three full pattern repeats, which might necessitate an even larger swatch, if the pattern repeats over a large number of stitches. For example, when swatching the 18-stitch pattern repeat for the Secrets & Lies Sock (see page 102), I cast on enough stitches for three full repeats.

The next step is to wash the swatch so that the gauge you measure will be the gauge the sock will assume once it's been washed. Soak the swatch for at least 20 minutes, squeeze out the excess moisture, and lay it flat to dry. For lace patterns, stretch and pin the swatch when it's still wet to open up the pattern.

Finally, measure the gauge of the dry swatch. Be sure to remove the pins from the lace patterns before measuring so that the pattern can relax, but stretch it widthwise by hand to simulate the stretch in the fabric.

A SIMPLE PATTERNED SOCK: THE FORMULAS

The formulas used to calculate the stitch counts for socks knitted in patterns that affect the gauge are a little different than those used for "plain" socks knitted entirely in stockinette stitch (or stitch patterns that behave like stockinette). As an example, let's consider a sock that has a ribbed cuff, a simple lace pattern around the leg and along the instep, and a stockinette-stitch heel, sole, and toe, such as the Harcourt Sock on page 132.

To begin, you'll need to knit two separate gauge swatches —one in stockinette stitch for the heel, sole, and toe and another in the pattern stitch for the leg and instep. You'll use these gauges when calculating the stitch counts (or using the numbers in the tables).

Begin by calculating the numbers for the basic sock at the stockinette gauge. Assuming an allover patterned leg, you'll then need to calculate the leg stitch count at the pattern stitch gauge. If the pattern continues along the instep, you'll also need to calculate the stitch count for the instep, adjusting the number of sole stitches accordingly if necessary.

The stockinette gauge is used in the formulas for the base sock and heel stitch counts, which are the same as those presented in Chapter 3. Here, I've added the word "stockinette" to clarify that these formulas are based on the stockinette-stitch gauge.

Base Sock Stitches = (Stockinette Gauge in Stitches per Inch × Foot Circumference) × 0.9

Base Heel Stitches = Stockinette Sock Stitches ÷ 2

You'll use the formulas or the tables to get the gusset and heel numbers. The adjusted stitch counts for the leg and foot have to take into account the gauge of the pattern stitch. Keep in mind that an ease adjustment might be required, the amount of which depends on the fabric—for a fabric with little stretch, such as stranded colorwork, you'll need to work the sock larger than for a sock worked in a fabric that has a lot of stretch, such as lace.

Patterned Leg Stitches = (Ankle Circumference × Ease Adjustment) × Pattern Gauge in Stitches per Inch)

The ease adjustment will be between 0.9 and 1 (based on the fabric; see table at top right). The finished sock leg circumference is a simple product of the foot circumference and the ease adjustment.

Finished Leg Circumference = Foot Circumference × Ease Adjustment

As with the basic stockinette sock patterns, if the ease adjustment is 0.9, the finished sock circumference is about 10 percent smaller than the actual foot circumference; if the ease adjustment is 1, the finished sock circumference is equal to the actual foot circumference.

TYPICAL EASE ADJUSTMENT

FABRIC	EASE ADJUSTMENT
Stockinette/Knit/Purl	0.9
Cables	1
Stranded Colorwork	1
Lace	1

Because the sole half of the foot is worked in stockinette and the instep half is worked in pattern, separate calculations are needed. The number of sole stitches is still the same as the number of heel stitches (at the stockinette-stitch gauge), and can be determined from the tables or the formulas.

Sole Stitches = Heel Stitches

You can also calculate this separately as for a stockinette-stitch sock.

(Half of Foot Circumference × .9) × Stockinette Gauge in Stitches per Inch

The number of stitches for the patterned instep is calculated separately, based on the pattern gauge. Just as for the leg, we also have to include the proper amount of ease adjustment.

Instep Stitches = (Half of Foot Circumference × Ease Adjustment) × Pattern Gauge in Stitches per Inch

The total number of the stiches for the foot is the sum of the sole and instep stitches.

Foot Stitches = Sole Stitches + Instep Stitches

Of course, you can adjust the split between the sole and instep stitches to accommodate a pattern repeat on the instep. But keep in mind that if you do so, you'll need to ensure that the finished foot is still the desired circumference. Because the instep and sole have different gauges, you have to account for these differences when "borrowing" stitches from the sole.

For example, let's say that the stockinette gauge is 8 stitches per inch (2.5 cm), the pattern gauge is 6 stitches per inch (2.5 cm), and that you need to add 3 stitches

to the instep to accommodate the stitch pattern. At our gauge of 6 stitches per inch, these 3 stitches will represent ½ inch (1.3 cm) in width on the instep.

$$3 \text{ stitches} \div 6 \text{ stitches per inch} = 0.5"$$

However, it will take 4 of the sole stitches to represent the same ½ inch (1.3 cm).

$$0.5" \times 8 \text{ stitches per inch} = 4 \text{ stitches}$$

Therefore, in order to add 3 stitches to the instep, you'll remove 4 stitches from the sole for a net reduction of 1 stitch in the foot circumference. Use the following formula to check your calculations.

Foot Circumference = (Instep Stitches ÷ Pattern Gauge in Stitches per Inch) + (Sole Stitches ÷ Stockinette Gauge in Stitches per Inch)

For example, let's say we want to knit a sock for a 9-inch (23 cm) foot circumference and that our stockinette gauge is 8 stitches per inch (2.5 cm), and our pattern gauge is a stretchy 6 stitches per inch (2.5 cm).

Our target finished circumference will be 8.1 inches (20.6 cm).

$$9" \times 0.9 = 8.1" \ (20.6 \text{ cm})$$

The Harcourt Sock, page 132.

Therefore, base number of stitches for the sock leg will be this circumference multiplied by the stockinette gauge.

$$8.1" \times 8 \text{ stitches per inch} = 64 \text{ stitches}$$

The heel and sole will be worked on half of that number of stitches.

$$64 \div 2 = 32 \text{ stitches}$$

Assuming we're working the sock from the top down, we can take the heel and gusset numbers directly from the table on page 44 (use the table on page 58 for a toe-up version).

If our pattern stitch is stretchy, we'll allow for the usual 10 percent negative ease, which means that the number of pattern leg stitches is 48.

$$9" \times 0.9 \times 6 \text{ stitches per inch} = 48 \text{ stitches}$$

The number of pattern stitches for the instep will be half of the total pattern stitches.

$$48 \text{ stitches} \div 2 = 24 \text{ stitches}$$

If we want to work from the top down, we'll cast on 64 stitches, work the cuff in a ribbing pattern, then decrease to 48 stitches and work the leg in the pattern stitch. At the first row of the heel flap, we'll increase the first 24 stitches to 32 stitches for the heel, which will be worked in stockinette stitch. When the heel and instep stitches are reunited for the foot, there will be 66 stitches —24 instep stitches worked in pattern and 42 sole stitches (12 left over from the heel turn and 15 gusset stitches on each side), which we'll work in stockinette; 24 instep stitches, which we'll work in pattern stitch. Just before

Simple Recipe for a Patterned Sock

Once you've checked your gauge and calculated your numbers, use these recipes to create your own patterned sock.

Top-Down Sock

Cast-On and Cuff: Cast on stitches according to the stockinette gauge and work cuff ribbing as desired.

Leg: Work an adjustment round, increasing or decreasing as necessary to achieve the necessary number of leg stitches. Work the leg in pattern as desired.

Heel: On half of the leg stitches, work increases or decreases as necessary to achieve the necessary number of heel stitches. Work the heel in stockinette stitch according to the table on pages 42–45, or using the formulas as necessary.

Foot: Work the instep stitches in pattern and the sole stitches in stockinette. On the last round, work increases or decreases as necessary to achieve the necessary number of stitches for a stockinette-stitch toe.

Toe: Making sure that there is the same number of stitches on the top of the foot as the bottom of the foot, decrease the toe as usual.

Note: If you work the entire foot in stockinette stitch instead of continuing the leg pattern on the instep, simply adjust to the necessary foot stitches on the last round of the leg and work the heel, foot, and toe as usual.

Toe-Up Sock

Cast-On and Toe: Cast on stitches according to the stockinette gauge and work the toe as usual.

Foot: Work increases or decreases as required on the instep half of the round to achieve the necessary number of stitches for the instep. Work the instep stitches in pattern and the sole stitches in stockinette.

Gusset and Heel: Work the gusset and heel according to the table on pages 56–58. On the last row of the heel flap, work increases or decreases as necessary to achieve the necessary total number of leg stitches.

Leg: Work the leg in pattern as desired. On the last round, work increases or decreases as necessary to achieve the necessary number of cuff stitches.

Cuff: Work the cuff as usual.

Note: If you work the entire foot in stockinette stitch instead of beginning the leg pattern on the instep, simply work to the end of the foot as usual, then adjust to the necessary number of leg stitches on the first round of the leg.

the toe decreases, we'll increase the instep stitches from 24 to 32 stitches to restore the foot to the full stitch count of 64 stitches.

Let's say that to align the pattern stitch on the instep, we need a multiple of 6 stitches plus 3. We'll need to "borrow" 3 stitches from the sole to accommodate this adjustment. But because 3 stitches amounts to ½ inch (1.3 cm) at the pattern gauge, we have to adjust the number of sole stitches accordingly. At the stockinette-stitch gauge, ½ inch (1.3 cm) corresponds to 4 stitches. Therefore, we'll work the instep on 27 stitches (24 + 3), and the sole on 28 stitches (32 − 4).

Adding Stranded-Colorwork Patterns

Stranded-colorwork patterns (often referred to as Fair Isle; see box at right) involve two or more colors in a row or round of knitting. Although they require a bit more work, stranded-colorwork patterns are immensely practical. They produce a fabric with double thickness—one layer of the knitted stitches and another layer of the stranded "unworked" yarn)—that's warmer and longer wearing than its single-color counterpart. The sole of a sock worked in an allover colorwork pattern is more comfortable, too—the stranded yarn provides a nice squishy fabric underfoot. The only downside is that the thicker fabric can make shoes feel tighter.

In general, stranded-colorwork patterns have two significant effects on knitted fabric—they tighten the gauge by about 25 percent, and they eliminate some of the inherent stretch in the stitches. The two examples of stranded-colorwork socks in this book were knitted with yarns that typically knit up at 8 stitches per inch (2.5 cm). But in both cases, the gauge in the stranded-colorwork pattern is 10 stitches per inch (2.5 cm). This is because the floats of unworked stitches across the back of the fabric pull in the knitted stitches. This is of particular concern in the heel and gusset area—there must be sufficient give for the sock to stretch onto the foot.

When knitting socks (or other projects, for that matter) in stranded-colorwork patterns, I typically work on needles one size larger than I would use to knit the same yarn in stockinette stitch. Although it's possible to use sufficiently

In Terms of Terms

"Fair Isle" is to "colorwork" as "Kleenex" is to "facial tissue." Although we often use the terms interchangeably, they do have slightly different meanings.

The general technique of creating knitting patterns by alternating two colors across a row or round is called "stranded colorwork." The unused color is *stranded* across the back of the *colorwork* pattern. In the strictest sense, "Fair Isle" refers only to the stranded-colorwork technique and patterns developed on the tiny Shetland island of the same name. Over the years, the two terms have come to be used interchangeably.

large needles to match the single-color stockinette gauge of the same yarn, I only recommended doing so for small sections of colorwork. Increasing the needle size will loosen the stitches and produce a fabric that's more easily abraded—and loose stranded-colorwork fabrics can look sloppy.

The way that stitch counts are determined for stranded-colorwork socks depends on the placement of the colorwork design. There are three main options—a plain sock with a small, isolated section of colorwork, a sock with a patterned leg and plain foot, and a sock with patterned leg and patterned foot. Let's take a closer look at each situation.

ISOLATED COLORWORK STRIPE

If there's only a small section of stranded colorwork—a 2-inch (5 cm) band around the leg, for example—the calculations are reasonably straightforward. You'll base the stitch counts on the stockinette-stitch gauge and make adjustments for the colorwork section. The objective is to make the colorwork stripe the same circumference as the rest of the leg. There are two adjustments that can help—using larger needles as described above or increasing the stitch count in the colorwork section.

For example, if the sock is 9 inches (23 cm) in circumference and the stockinette gauge is 8 stitches per inch (2.5 cm), there will be 72 stitches for the leg.

9" × 8 stitches per inch = 72 stitches

If the gauge for the colorwork pattern is 10 stitches per inch (2.5 cm), it follows that you'll need 90 stitches for the same 9-inch (23 cm) circumference.

$$9" \times 10 \text{ stitches per inch} = 90 \text{ stitches}$$

Therefore, you can simply increase to 90 stitches in the first colorwork round, then decrease back to 72 stitches in the last round. This means that you'll want to choose a colorwork repeat that fits evenly into 90 stitches. Patterns that repeat over 2, 3, 6, 9, 10, or 15 stitches would all work.

Once the colorwork section is complete, it's a good idea to confirm that the fabric has sufficient stretch by slipping it on your foot and up over your heel. Unless you're using two circular needles or the magic-loop method, you'll need to transfer at least some of the stitches onto waste yarn or additional needles to prevent dropped stitches while you do this. If you can't ease the colorwork section around your heel, you won't be able to get the sock on when you've finished knitting it.

PATTERN ON THE LEG ONLY

If you want to work the entire leg in a stranded-colorwork pattern, you'll need to allow for more ease in the calculations. Because stranded colorwork doesn't have significant stretch, you'll want to knit the leg to match the actual leg circumference. In other words, there is zero ease for the leg.

Leg Stitches = Ankle Circumference × Pattern Gauge in Stitches per Inch

The stockinette foot, however, will be calculated as usual with about 10 percent negative ease. At the transition between the leg and heel, simply decrease the appropriate number of stitches if working from the top down or increase the appropriate number of stitches if working from the toe up.

Again, when you're partway along the leg, it's a good idea to confirm that the fabric will stretch over your heel— I once worked a pair of allover colorwork socks that I was never able to wear. I could have saved myself a lot of time, yarn, and heartache if I'd tried on the first sock when the leg was just partly finished instead of waiting until the pair was complete.

PATTERN THROUGHOUT

If you want to work the stranded-colorwork pattern throughout the foot as well as the leg, you'll also have to adjust the number of foot stitches to account for the decreased stretch. As for the patterned leg, you'll want zero ease in the foot so the number of stitches should fit the actual foot circumference.

Sock Stitches = Foot Circumference × Pattern Gauge in Stitches per Inch

Whether you're working from the top down or from the toe up, you'll need to measure both your stitch and round gauge. Although you can expect your stitch gauge to be tighter than you'd get when working the same yarn single-stranded, the round gauge generally doesn't change nearly as much. In fact, stranded-colorwork patterns typically have the same stitch and round gauges—that is, there is the same number of stitches per inch (2.5 cm) as rounds per inch (2.5 cm). For example, the Carpita Sock on page 116 has a gauge of 10 stitches and 10.5 rounds per inch (2.5 cm).

This means that you'll have to consider heel adjustments a little differently. The formulas and tables assume a standard 3:4 ratio of stitch gauge to row/round gauge (that is, the width of 3 stitches is about the same as the height of 4 rows), which holds true for stockinette stitch and most stockinette-based fabrics (including ribbing), but not for stranded colorwork.

The proper heel adjustment depends on whether the sock is worked from the top down or from the toe up. For a top-down sock, use the usual rules for the heel stitches and the numbers for the turn, but don't use numbers in the table for the heel flap rows—doing so will make the heel flap too long and produce the wrong number of gusset stitches.

Instead, the number of rows in the heel flap is a function of the row/round gauge and the foot circumference.

Heel Flap Rows = [(Round Gauge × 0.75) × (Foot Circumference × 0.5)] × 0.8

Let's break this complicated formula down into its components.

The round gauge is multiplied by the 3:4 ratio typical for stitch versus row gauge to give us an estimate of the stockinette-stitch gauge.

The foot circumference multiplied by 0.5 gives us the width of the heel flap.

We then multiply that number by 0.8 (as usual) to calculate the number of rows in the heel flap.

If you'd rather, you can simply multiply the round gauge by 0.75 to determine the stitch gauge to use in the table on pages 42–45. From that, just look up the number of heel flap rows.

The number of stitches in each gusset is proportionate to the stitch gauge and therefore can be taken from the same tables. But because there are proportionately fewer rows in the heel flap, you can't simply pick up 1 stitch for every slipped edge stitch—you'll have to pick up 2 stitches in a few of them. This is easiest to do if 2 stitches are picked up in the two different yarns. I alternated colors of the picked-up stitches in the Carpita Sock so that I could do just this.

As when working stranded-colorwork patterns in isolated bands or on just the leg, you'll want to try on the sock as you go—particularly once you're past the heel and the gusset decreases have been started—to make sure the fabric will stretch over your heel and feel comfortable on your leg and foot. If it feels tight around the heel, add a few more rows to the heel flap and pick up more gusset stitches, maintaining a ratio of about 4 gusset stitches for every 5 rows in the heel flap.

Two adjustments are needed for a stranded-colorwork heel worked in this direction—the length of the gusset/heel section and the relationship between the number of stitches in the gusset and the number of rows in the heel flap.

Use the following formula to calculate the length of the gusset and heel—you can't get the proper information from the tables in Chapter 3.

Length of Heel and Gusset − [(Gusset Stitches × 2) + (Heel Stitches − Heel Base Stitches)] ÷ Gauge in Rounds per Inch

Because the number of gusset stitches, heel stitches, and heel base stitches are proportionate to the actual number of stitches in the sock, you can use the standard formula on pages 60 and 61 or use the numbers in the table on pages 56–58.

When working from the toe up for a "plain" sock, the depth of the heel flap (i.e., the number of rows/rounds) is determined by the number of gusset stitches. But if you were to use the same relationship in stranded colorwork, the heel flap would end up too long. Therefore, the number of rows you'll want to work in a stranded-colorwork heel flap depends on both the number of stitches in the stranded-colorwork foot and the number of gusset stitches for the same sock knitted in single-color stockinette.

Number of Rows in Heel Flap = 2 × Gusset Stitches in Equivalent Plain Sock

There will also be more gusset stitches in the colorwork sock than in the plain sock. Typically, the number of gusset stitches determines the number of heel flap rows. You don't want to change the heel flap length, so you'll need to work some double decreases in the heel flap (working sssk and p3tog decreases on some rows instead of the usual ssk and p2tog decreases; see Glossary for decreases) so that the heel flap is the appropriate length for the round gauge.

Number of Double Heel Flap Decreases on Each Side = Gusset Stitches in Colorwork Sock − Gusset Stitches in Plain Sock

You'll work those double decrease rows in the first rows of the heel flap.

As with stranded-colorwork socks worked from the top down, I prefer to hold both strands together when working the edge stitches of the heel flap. Although the double-stranded stitches are visible in the finished sock, they produce a tidier, less gappy fabric.

Adding Lace Patterns

Although lace patterns are commonly worked on a stockinette-stitch background (see the Harcourt Sock on page 132), lace fabric behaves differently than plain stockinette stitch. Because lace patterns look best when stretched (for a shawl or garment, this is achieved through blocking), you'll want to plan for the fabric to fully stretch around the leg of a sock.

Therefore, you want to use an ease adjustment of 1 in the calculations and measure the gauge on a fully blocked, fully stretched swatch. Don't skimp on this step—be sure to knit a swatch in the lace pattern, wash it, stretch the damp swatch to its full stretch, then pin it in place. When it's completely dry, remove the pins and use your hands to stretch it widthwise to encourage it settle into its true stretched width before you measure the gauge.

The gauge of a lace fabric is typically looser than that of the same yarn worked in stockinette stitch on the same needles. This means that you'll likely need fewer stitches for the lace portion of a sock than the same portion worked in stockinette. For example, the stockinette gauge in the Harcourt Sock is 8 stitches per inch (2.5 cm), while the lace gauge in the same sock is 7 stitches per inch (2.5 cm).

Adding Cable Patterns

Cable patterns have two significant effects on knitted fabric—they compress the fabric widthwise (which affects the gauge), and they greatly reduce the amount of stretch. The more cable turns there are in a round and the more often those cables are turned, the tighter and less stretchy the fabric will be.

To accommodate this, cabled socks should be worked with zero ease—use the actual foot/leg circumferences for finished sock circumference.

Cable Leg Stitches = Leg Circumference × Cable Gauge in Stitches per Inch (2.5 cm)

For example, if your leg circumference is 9 inches (23 cm), and your cable gauge is 10 stitches per inch (2.5 cm), you'll work the leg on 90 stitches.

$$9. \times 10 \text{ stitches/inch} = 90 \text{ stitches}$$

Don't be surprised if this number seems large—the cable crossing effectively remove stitches so it takes more stitches to achieve the same circumference as stockinette. For example, a 6-stitch cable is only 3 stitches wide at the cable cross, and the cable reduces the stretch in the fabric.

As with stranded colorwork, cable patterns affect the stitch gauge but not the number of rows or rounds per inch—the vertical gauge is the same as if you're working stockinette. If you're working a cabled heel flap from the top down, you'll work the same number of rows as you would for an equivalent stockinette sock. Be sure to change to stockinette stitch for the heel turn and adjust for the different number of stitches in the cabled heel flap. The Wellington Road Sock on page 138 and The Man of Aran Sock on page 146 offer two ways to solve this problem.

In general, the foot is worked with half of the stitches in the cable pattern for the instep and the other half of the stitches in stockinette for the sole, with adjustments made to accommodate the stitch pattern as described on pages 65–67.

The Man of Aran Sock, page 146.

The BASIC RIBBED Sock

| | | | | | | | | | | | | | | | | | | | | | | | | | | | | | | | | | | | | | | | | | | | | | | | | |

FINISHED SIZE
Ankle/foot circumference, lightly stretched: 7 (7½, 8, 8½, 9)" (18 [19, 20.5, 21.5, 23] cm).

Leg length: Adjustable to fit.

Foot length: Adjustable to fit; finished length should be about ½" (1.3 cm) shorter than actual foot length.

Sock shown measures 7½" (19 cm) ankle/foot circumference.

YARN
CYCA #1, Super Fine.

Shown here: Indigodragonfly Merino Nylon Sock (80% superwash merino, 20% nylon; 390 yd [357 m]/100 g): Not All Mathletes are Created Equallaterally, 1 skein.

NEEDLES
Size U.S. 1.5 (2.5 mm): set of 4 double-pointed (dpn), two circular (cir) or one long cir, as you prefer (see page 20).

NOTIONS
Markers (m); tapestry needle.

GAUGE
32 sts and 48 rnds = 4" (10 cm) in (k3, p1) ribbing worked in rnds, lightly stretched.

32 sts and 48 rnds = 4" (10 cm) in St st worked in rnds.

This handsome ribbed sock is suitable for both men and women. It's interesting, but not too challenging, to knit. This is a good choice for variegated yarns because the subtle ribbing doesn't complete with (or get overwhelmed by) the color changes. Instructions are provided for working this simple sock from the top down as well as from the toe up. Try both directions!

Notes

+ This pattern works for any sock yarn that specifies a gauge of 28 to 30 stitches in 4" (10 cm).

+ The following instructions are based on the Basic Patterns on pages 40 and 55 worked at a gauge of 8 stitches per inch (2.5 cm), with finished sizes of 7 (7½, 8, 8½, 9)" (18 [19, 20.5, 21.5, 23] cm) foot circumferences.

+ Choose a size based on foot circumference, allowing for the usual 10 percent negative ease.

THE BASIC RIBBED SOCK

The Basic Ribbed Sock incorporates a simple 4-stitch ribbed pattern (k3, p1) throughout the leg. Because this stitch pattern doesn't affect the gauge, I was able to follow the numbers in the tables in Chapter 3. I worked the sock at a gauge of 8 stitches per inch (2.5 cm), which meant that all of the numbers were divisible by 4. For balance, I wanted the ribbed pattern on the instep to begin and end with a single purl stitch. This meant that there had to be a multiple of 4 stitches plus 1 extra (purl) stitch across the instep.

When dividing for the heel, therefore, the heel flap had to begin and end with k3, which resulted in a multiple of 4 stitches plus 3 extra knit stitches in the heel flap. But doing so meant that there couldn't be the same number of stitches on the instep as on the heel flap. To determine where to best split for the heel, I first had to decide on how many repeats of the 4-stitch pattern would be across the entire circumference. My choices were 14 repeats (56 stitches), 15 repeats (60 stitches), 16 repeats (64 stitches), 17 repeats (68 stitches), 18 repeats (72 stitches), and so on.

For those sizes that have an even number of repeats (14, 16, or 18 repeats for a total of 56, 64, or 72 stitches, for example), the division is simple—an equal number of repeats (7, 8, or 9, respectively) will be on the instep and heel. To adjust for the pattern alignment, a single (purl) stitch needs to be taken from the heel and added to the instep. For a 56-stitch sock, for example, there would be 29 stitches for the instep and 27 stitches for the heel (instead of 28 stitches on each). For a 64-stitch sock, there would be 33 stitches on the instep and 31 stitches on the heel (instead of 32 on each). For a 72-stitch sock, there would be 37 stitches on the instep and 35 stitches on the heel (instead of 36 stitches on each).

56 total stitches = 29 instep stitches + 27 heel stitches

64 total stitches = 33 instep stitches + 31 instep stitches

72 total stitches = 37 instep stitches + 35 heel stitches

Because the difference is only 1 stitch each on the instep and sole, there won't be a noticeable effect on the fit. I used the number of stitches in the heel flap when working the formulas for the heel flap length, heel turn, and gusset numbers. If there was a size in the table that had the same number of stitches in the heel flap, I simply followed those numbers instead of doing my own calculations.

For those sizes that have an odd number of repeats (15 or 17 repeats for a total of 60 or 68 stitches, for example), the math changes slightly. If there can't be the same number of stitches on the instep and heel, I prefer to put the "extra" repeat on the instep—I always think a larger patterned area makes for a nicer looking sock. If the sock has 60 stitches, there will be 15 pattern repeats. If 8 of those repeats are assigned to the instep, there will be 32 instep stitches. Adding the purl stitch for balance will give a total of 33 instep stitches, which leaves 27 stitches for the heel.

60 total stitches = 33 instep stitches + 27 heel stitches

This 3-stitch difference from the table numbers of the instep and heel stitches isn't enough to change the fit of the sock. I do make one change in my calculations, though—the number of heel flap rows and gusset stitches based on 50 percent of the sock stitches (30 stitches in this case), not based on the adjusted number of heel stitches. This ensures that the gusset circumference and heel flap depth are proportionate to the full sock circumference.

TOP-DOWN VERSION

Cuff

CO 56 (60, 64, 68, 72) sts. Distribute sts across the needles as you prefer and join for working in rnds, being careful not to twist sts.

Work in k1, p1 ribbing until piece measures 1½" (3.8 cm) from CO.

Leg

Work in k3, p1 ribbing until piece measures 7 (7, 8, 8, 8)" (18 [18, 20.5, 20.5, 20.5] cm) from CO, or desired length to top of heel.

Heel

HEEL FLAP

The heel flap is worked back and forth on half of the leg sts.

ROW 1: (RS) Work 27 (31, 31, 35, 35) sts in ribbing as set; place rem 29 (29, 33, 33, 37) sts onto a spare needle or holder to work later for instep (these sts beg and end with p1).

Beg with a WS row, work 27 (31, 31, 35, 35) heel sts (these sts beg and end with k3) back and forth in rows as foll.

ROW 2: (WS) Sl 1, k2, [p1, k3] 6 (7, 7, 8, 8) times.

ROW 3: (RS) Sl 1, p2, [k1, p3] 6 (7, 7, 8, 8) times.

ROW 4: Sl 1, k2, [p1, k3] 6 (7, 7, 8, 8) times.

Rep Rows 3 and 4 until a total of 24 (26, 26, 28, 30) rows have been worked, ending with a WS row.

TURN HEEL

Work short-rows as foll.

Although there is a slight difference in the tip of the toe-up version (left) and the top-down version (right), the fit is the same.

ROW 1: (RS) K18 (21, 21, 23, 23), ssk, turn work.

ROW 2: (WS) Sl 1, p9 (11, 11, 11, 11), p2tog, turn work.

ROW 3: Sl 1, k9 (11, 11, 11, 11), ssk (1 st each side of gap), turn work.

ROW 4: Sl 1, p9 (11, 11, 11, 11), p2tog (1 st each side of gap), turn work.

Rep Rows 3 and 4 until all sts have been worked, ending with a WS row—11 (13, 13, 13, 13) sts rem.

Gusset

K11 (13, 13, 13, 13) heel sts, then with the same needle, pick up and knit 14 (15, 15, 16, 17) sts along selvedge edge at the side of the heel flap, using slipped sts as a guide (see page 36). With a new needle, work in rib patt as set across 29 (29, 33, 33, 37) instep sts. With another new needle, pick up and knit 14 (15, 15, 16, 17) sts along the selvedge edge at the other side of the heel flap, using slipped sts as a guide, then work the first 6 (7, 7, 7, 7) sts from the first needle again—68 (72, 76, 78, 84) sts total; 19 (21, 21, 22, 23) sts between the start of the rnd and the start of the instep, 29 (29, 33, 33, 37) instep sts, and 20 (22, 22, 23, 24) sts between the end of the instep and the end of the rnd.

Rnd begins at center of heel. If you're working on two cir needles or using the magic-loop method, place a marker in this position.

From here on, the 29 (29, 33, 33, 37) instep sts will be worked in rib patt as set; the gusset and sole sts will be worked in St st (knit every rnd).

SET-UP RND: K5 (6, 6, 6, 6), k14 (15, 15, 16, 17) through back loop (tbl), work instep sts in patt as set, k14 (15, 15, 16, 17) tbl, knit to end of rnd.

DEC RND: Knit to 2 sts before instep, k2tog, work instep sts in patt, ssk, knit to end of rnd—2 sts dec'd.

Work 1 rnd even, maintaining patt on instep.

Rep the last 2 rnds 5 (5, 5, 4, 5) more times—56 (60, 64, 68, 72) sts rem.

Foot

Work even in patt as set until foot measures 1½ (1¾, 1¾, 2, 2)" (3.8 [4.5, 4.5, 5, 5] cm) less than desired finished sock foot length.

Toe

Rearrange sts if necessary so that there are 28 (30, 32, 34, 36) sts on each needle for the sole and instep. Cont in St st as foll.

DEC RND: Knit to 3 sts before start of instep, k2tog, k2, ssk; knit to 3 sts before end of instep, k2tog, k2, ssk, knit to end of rnd—4 sts dec'd.

Knit 1 rnd even.

Rep the last 2 rnds 5 (6, 6, 7, 7) more times—32 (32, 36, 36, 40) sts rem.

Rep dec rnd every rnd 6 (6, 7, 7, 8) times—8 sts rem.

Cut yarn, leaving an 8" (20.5 cm) tail. Thread tail on a tapestry needle, draw through rem sts, pull tight to close hole, and secure on WS.

Finishing

Weave in loose ends. Block as desired (see page 18).

Toe-up version

Toe

Using Judy's magic method (see page 49), CO 20 (20, 24, 24, 24) sts—10 (10, 12, 12, 12) sts each on two needles.

RND 1: Work as foll, depending on the type of needle(s) used.

FOR DPN: K5 (5, 6, 6, 6) with one needle, k5 (5, 6, 6, 6) with a second needle, k10 (10, 12, 12, 12) sts with a third needle.

FOR TWO CIR OR MAGIC LOOP: K10 (10, 12, 12, 12) with one needle, k10 (10, 12, 12, 12) with a second needle.

Place a safety pin or marker in the toe to indicate beg of rnd and a second one to indicate the center of the rnd.

INC RND: K1, M1R (see Glossary), knit to 1 st before center of rnd, M1L (see Glossary), k2, M1R, knit to 1 st before end of rnd, M1L, k1— 4 sts inc'd.

Knit 1 rnd even.

Rep the last 2 rnds 8 (9, 9, 10, 11) more times—56 (60, 64, 68, 72) sts total.

Foot

SET-UP RND: P1, [k3, p1] 7 (7, 8, 8, 9) times, knit to end of rnd.

Rearrange sts if necessary so that the 29 (29, 33, 33, 37) sts worked in ribbing form the instep and the rem 27 (31, 31, 35, 35) sts form the sole.

Cont even in patt as set until foot measures 3¼ (3¾, 3¾, 4¼, 4¼)" (8.5 [9.5, 9.5, 11, 11] cm) less than desired finished sock length.

Gusset

Rearrange sts if necessary so that the sole sts are on one needle. Work the gusset incs at each end of the needle holding the sole sts.

RND 1: Work instep sts in patt as set, M1R, place marker (pm) for beg of heel, knit to end of rnd, pm for end of heel, M1L—2 sts inc'd.

RND 2: Work instep sts in patt as set, knit to end of rnd.

RND 3: Work instep sts in patt as set, 1R, knit to end of rnd, M1L—2 sts inc'd.

RND 4: Work instep sts in patt as set, knit to end of rnd.

Rep the last 2 rnds 9 (10, 11, 12, 12) more times—78 (84, 90, 96, 100) sts total.

Heel
TURN HEEL
Work short-rows (see Glossary) as foll.

ROW 1: (RS) Work instep in patt as set, knit to 1 st before second heel m, wrap next st and turn work (w&t).

ROW 2: (WS) Purl to 1 st before m, w&t.

Working only on the heel sts, cont as foll.

ROW 3: (RS) Knit to 1 st before last wrapped st, w&t.

ROW 4: (WS) Purl to 1 st before last wrapped st, w&t.

Rep Rows 3 and 4 until 9 (11, 11, 11, 11) sts rem unwrapped in the middle, ending with a WS row.

Remove heel markers.

HEEL FLAP
Work the heel flap and dec gusset sts as foll.

ROW 1: (RS) Knit to first wrapped st, *knit the wrapped st tog with its wrap; rep from * until 1 wrapped st rem, ssk (final st tog with its wrap and the first gusset st), turn work."

ROW 2: (WS) Sl 1, purl to first wrapped st, *purl the wrapped st tog with its wrap; rep from * until 1 wrapped st rem, p2tog (final st tog with its wrap and the first gusset st), turn work.

ROW 3: Sl 1, k2, [p1, k3] 5 (6, 6, 7, 7) times, p1, k2, ssk, turn work.

ROW 4: Sl 1, p2, k1, [p3, k1] 5 (6, 6, 7, 7) times, p2, p2tog, turn work.

Rep Rows 3 and 4 until only 1 gusset st rem on each side, ending with a WS row—58 (62, 66, 70, 74) sts rem.

Leg

Rejoin for working in rnds, working the final gusset decs in the first rnd as foll.

RND 1: Sl 1, k2, [p1, k3] 5 (6, 6, 7, 7) times, p1, k2, ssk, work instep sts in patt as set—57 (61, 65, 69, 73) sts rem.

RND 2: K2tog, work in patt as set to end of rnd—56 (60, 64, 68, 72) sts rem.

Work even in patt as set until leg measures 5½ (5½, 6½, 6½, 6½)" (14 [14, 16.5, 16.5, 16.5] cm) or 1½" (3.8 cm) less than desired total length.

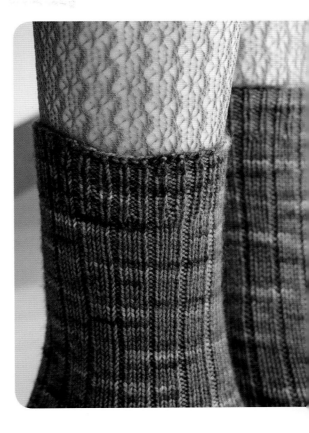

Cuff
SET-UP RND: *K1, p1; rep from *.

Cont in ribbing as set for 1½" (3.8 cm).

Use a stretchy method (see page 52) to BO all sts.

Finishing

Weave in loose ends. Block as desired (see page 18).

The MARPLERIDGE Sock

FINISHED SIZE

Ankle/foot circumference, lightly stretched: 7 (7½, 8, 8½, 9)" (18 [19, 20.5, 21.5, 23] cm).

Leg length: Adjustable to fit.

Foot length: Adjustable to fit; finished length should be about ½" (1.3 cm) shorter than actual foot length.

Sock shown measures 7½" (19 cm) ankle/foot circumference.

YARN

CYCA #1, Super Fine.

Shown here: Regia 4-ply (75% superwash wool, 25% nylon; 230 yd [210 m]/50 g): #02137 Jeans Marl, 2 balls.

NEEDLES

Size U.S. 1.5 (2.5 mm): set of 4 double-pointed (dpn), two circular (cir) or one long cir, as you prefer (see page 20).

NOTIONS

Markers (m); tapestry needle.

GAUGE

32 sts and 48 rnds = 4" (10 cm) in ridge rib patt worked in rnds, lightly stretched.

32 sts and 48 rnds = 4" (10 cm) in St st worked in rnds.

Manly, but not boring, these socks offer a change from the usual stockinette-stitch legs. The traditional stitch pattern used here looks great in a heathered or slightly variegated yarn—I've chosen a classic denim shade for wide appeal. Instructions are provided for working the sock from the top down and from the toe up. Knit one of each!

Notes

+ This pattern works for any sock yarn that specifies a gauge of 30 to 32 stitches in 4" (10 cm).

+ The instructions that follow are based on the Basic Patterns (see pages 40 and 54) worked at a gauge of 8 stitches per inch (2.5 cm), with finished sizes of 7 (7½, 8, 8½, 9)" (18 [19, 20.5, 21.5, 23] cm).

+ The calculations are based on the stockinette-stitch gauge, which is essentially the same gauge as the stitch pattern (with a bit of stretching).

+ Choose a size based on foot circumference, allowing for the usual 10 percent negative ease.

THE MARPLERIDGE SOCK

The Marpleridge Sock is quite similar to the Basic Ribbed Sock on page 76. It's also worked at a gauge of 8 stitches per inch (2.5 cm) and follows the numbers in the tables in Chapter 3. But, in this case, the stitch pattern is a variation of k2, p2 ribbing.

For a balanced look, I wanted the instep patterning to begin and end with p2, which meant that there should be a multiple of 4 stitches plus 2 extra (purl) stitches across the instep. The math is a little trickier because there's a bigger difference between the heel and instep stitches, but I could be clever about it. I got the extra 2 instep stitches by "borrowing" 2 stitches from the sole. Then I realized that if the instep started and ended with p1, I could make up the second purl stitch on each side at the top of the sole. This meant that I'd need a multiple of 4 stitches for the instep, which could be made tidy if I arranged it in the necessary multiple of the k2, p2 repeat, plus k2, p1 at one edge and p1 at the other edge.

Again, the specifics depend on whether there's an even or odd number of 4-stitch repeats in the full sock circumference. For those sizes that have an even number of repeats (14, 16, or 18 repeats for a total of 56, 64, or 72 stitches respectively), there will be an equal number of repeats (7, 8, or 9, respectively) each for the heel and instep, resulting in a multiple of 4 stitches (28, 32, or 36, respectively) stitches in each. In these cases, the numbers in the tables can be used without adjustment.

For those sizes that have an odd number of repeats (15 or 17 repeats for a total of 60 or 68 stitches), I assign the "extra" repeat to the instep. For a 60-stitch sock, there will be 32 stitches for the instep and 28 stitches for the heel. For a 68-stitch sock, there will be 36 stitches for the instep and 32 stitches for the heel. As with the Basic Ribbed Sock on page 76, a 2-stitch difference in the width of the heel flap doesn't change the fit significantly. But to ensure that the heel flap and gussets are the proper length, those numbers are based on 50 percent of the sock stitches (30 or 34, for example).

To align the pattern, the top stitch of the heel/sole stitches (i.e., the stitch closest to the instep on each side) is worked in the instep pattern (purled). Therefore, for a toe-up sock, the gusset and heel turn are worked within the stockinette portion of the sole (ignoring the first and last purl stitch). For a top-down sock, purl the top stitch of each gusset. Although the heel flap might be a couple of stitches narrower than normal for a sock of the same circumference, it's not a big enough difference to affect the overall fit.

At first glance, it might seem odd to choose this "break the repeat" approach on the instep, beginning and ending the instep with incomplete repeats and p1 (as opposed to simply adding an extra stitch to the repeat, as for the Basic Ribbed Sock on page 76), but it makes the math simpler. This approach makes it easier to break the pattern between the instep and the heel. In each case, I need a multiple of four stitches for both the instep and heel. For the sizes that have an even number of multiples of 4 stitches (56, 64, or 72 total stitches, for example), the heel and instep are worked on exactly half of the stitches. In these cases, you can follow the numbers in the tables instead of having to recalculate.

I didn't use this method of "borrowing" a stitch from the top of the gusset for the Basic Ribbed Sock on page 76 because only 1 stitch was needed, which would have put 1 less stitch in one gusset. Although from a fit perspective, a 1-stitch difference isn't significant, it can make it harder to keep track of the patterns and stitch counts.

TOP-DOWN VERSION

Cuff

CO 56 (60, 64, 68, 72) sts. Distribute sts across needles as you prefer and join for working in rnds, being careful not to twist sts.

Work in k2, p2 ribbing until piece measures 2" (5 cm) from CO.

Leg

Beg with Rnd 1, work ridge rib patt for mult of 4 sts (see Stitch Guide) until piece measures 7 (7, 8, 8, 8)" (18 [18, 20.5, 20.5, 20.5] cm) from CO, or desired length to top of heel, ending with Rnd 1 of patt.

Heel
HEEL FLAP

The heel is worked back and forth in St st over 28 (28, 32, 32, 36) sts, beg and ending in the center of the 2-st purl rib (the instep also begs and ends in the center of the purl rib); place rem 28 (32, 32, 36, 36) sts onto a spare needle or holder to work later for instep (these sts beg and end in the middle of the 2-st purl rib). The second purl st is created from the top of the gusset sts so that the instep on the foot is a multiple of 4 sts + 2, beg and ending with the 2-st purl rib.

ROW 1: (RS) K28 (28, 32, 32, 36), turn work.

ROW 2: (WS) Sl 1, p27 (27, 31, 31, 35).

ROW 3: Sl 1, k27 (27, 31, 31, 35).

ROW 4: Sl 1, p27 (27, 31, 31, 35).

Rep Rows 3 and 4 until a total of 24 (26, 26, 28, 30) rows have been worked.

TURN HEEL

Work short-rows as foll.

ROW 1: (RS) K19 (19, 21, 21, 24), ssk, turn work.

ROW 2: (WS) Sl 1, p10 (10 10, 10, 12), p2tog, turn work.

ROW 3: Sl 1, k10 (10 10, 10, 12), ssk (1 st each side of gap), turn work.

ROW 4: Sl 1, p10 (10 10, 10, 12), p2tog (1 st each side of gap), turn work.

Rep Rows 3 and 4 until all sts have been worked, ending with a WS row—12 (12, 12, 12, 14) sts rem.

Gusset

K12 (12, 12, 12, 14) heel sts, then with the same needle, pick up and knit 14 (15, 15, 16, 17) sts along selvedge edge at the side of the heel flap, using slipped sts as a guide (see page 36). With a new needle, work in ridge rib patt as set across 28 (32, 32, 36, 36) instep sts (beg and end in the middle of the 2-st purl rib). With another new needle, pick up and knit 14 (15, 15, 16, 17) sts along selvedge edge at other side of heel flap, using slipped sts as a guide, then work the first 6 (6, 6, 6, 7) sts from the first needle again—68 (74, 74, 80, 84) sts total; 20 (21, 21, 22, 24) sts on each side between the start of the rnd and the start of the instep; 28 (32, 32, 36, 36) instep sts.

Rnd begins at center of heel. If you're working on two cir needles or using the magic-loop method, place a marker in this position.

From here on, the 28 (32, 32, 36, 36) instep sts will be worked in rib patt;

RIDGE RIB (MULT OF 4 STS)

RND 1: Purl.

RNDS 2 AND 3: *K2, p2; rep from *.

RND 4: Knit.

Rep Rnds 1–4 for patt.

RIDGE RIB (MULT OF 4 STS + 2)

Rnd 1: Purl.

Rnds 2 and 3: P2, *k2, p2; rep from *.

Rnd 4: Knit.

Rep Rnds 1–4 for patt.

gusset and sole sts will be worked in St st (knit every rnd).

SET-UP RND: K6 (6, 6, 6, 7), k13 (14, 14, 14, 15, 16) through back loop (tbl), p1, work 28 (32, 32, 36, 36) instep sts in patt as set, p1, k13 (14, 14, 15, 16) tbl, knit to end of rnd.

Note: The top 2 gusset sts (worked as p1 in the previous rnd) will be incorporated into the instep so that the instep patt begs and ends with a 2-st purl rib. Rearrange sts as you wish.

DEC RND: Knit to 2 sts before instep, k2tog, work 30 (34, 34, 38, 38) instep sts in patt, ssk, knit to end of rnd—2 sts dec'd.

Work 1 rnd even, maintaining patt on instep.

Rep the last 2 rnds 5 (6, 4, 5, 5) more times—56 (60, 64, 68, 72) sts rem.

Foot

Work even in patt at set until foot measures 1½ (1¾, 1¾, 2, 2)" (3.8 [4.5, 4.5, 5, 5] cm) less than desired finished sock foot length ending with Rnd 1 of ridge rib patt.

Toe

Rearrange sts if necessary so that there are 28 (30, 32, 34, 36) sts each for the sole and instep. Cont in St st as foll.

DEC RND: Knit to 3 sts before start of instep, k2tog, k2, ssk; knit to 3 sts before end of instep, k2tog, k2, ssk, knit to end of rnd—4 sts dec'd.

Knit 1 rnd even.

toe up   top down

Rep the last 2 rnds 5 (6, 6, 7, 7) more times—32 (32, 36, 36, 40) sts rem.

Rep dec rnd every rnd 6 (6, 7, 7, 8) times—8 sts rem.

Cut yarn, leaving an 8" (20.5 cm) tail. Thread tail on a tapestry needle, draw through rem sts, pull tight to close hole, and secure on WS.

Finishing

Weave in loose ends. Block as desired (see page 18).

|||||||||||||||||||||||||||||||||||||

TOE-UP VERSION

Toe

Using Judy's magic method (see page 49), CO 20 (20, 24, 24, 24) sts—10 (10, 12, 12, 12) sts each on two needles.

RND 1: Work as foll, depending on the type of needle(s) used.

FOR DPN: K5 (5, 6, 6, 6) with one needle, k5 (5, 6, 6, 6) with a second needle, k10 (10, 12, 12, 12) with a third needle.

FOR TWO CIR OR MAGIC LOOP: K10 (10, 12, 12, 12) with one needle, k10 (10, 12, 12, 12) with a second needle.

Place a safety pin or marker in the toe to indicate beg of rnd and a second to indicate the center of the rnd.

INC RND: K1, M1R (see Glossary), knit to 1 st before center of rnd, M1L (see Glossary), k2, M1R, knit to 1 st before end of rnd, M1L, k1—4 sts inc'd.

Knit 1 rnd even.

Rep the last 2 rnds 8 (9, 9, 10, 11) more times—56 (60, 64, 68, 72) sts total.

Foot

SET-UP: K27 (28, 31, 32, 35)—this is the new start of rnd.

SET-UP RND: Work ridge rib patt for a mult of 4 sts + 2 (see Stitch Guide) over 30 (34, 34, 38, 38) instep sts; knit to end of rnd for sole.

Work even in patt as set until foot measures 3¼ (3¼, 3¾, 4, 4¼)" (8.5 [8.5, 9.5, 10, 11] cm) less than desired finished sock foot length.

Gusset

Rearrange sts if necessary so that the sole sts are on one needle. Work the gusset incs at each end of the needle holding the sole sts.

RND 1: Work instep sts in patt as set, M1R, place marker (pm) for beg of heel, knit to end of rnd, pm for end of heel, M1L—2 sts inc'd.

RND 2: Work instep sts in patt as set, knit to end of rnd.

RND 3: Work instep sts in patt as set, M1R, knit to end of rnd, M1L—2 sts inc'd.

RND 4: Work instep sts in patt as set, knit to end of rnd.

Rep the last 2 rnds 9 (10, 11, 12, 12) more times—78 (84, 90, 96, 100) sts total.

Heel
TURN HEEL
Work short-rows (see Glossary) as foll.

ROW 1: (RS) Work instep in patt as set, knit to 1 st before second heel m, wrap next st and turn work (w&t).

ROW 2: (WS) Purl to 1 st before m, w&t.

Working only on the heel sts, cont as foll.

ROW 3: (RS) Knit to st before last wrapped st, w&t.

ROW 4: (WS) Purl to st before last wrapped st, w&t.

Rep Rows 3 and 4 until 8 (10, 10, 10, 12) sts rem unwrapped in the middle, ending with a WS row.

Remove heel markers.

HEEL FLAP
Work the heel flap and dec gusset sts as foll.

ROW 1: (RS) Knit to first wrapped st, *knit the wrapped st tog with its wrap; rep from * until 1 wrapped st rem, ssk (final st tog with its wrap and the first gusset st), turn work.

ROW 2: (WS) Sl 1, purl to first wrapped st, *purl the wrapped st tog with its wrap; rep from * until 1 wrapped st rem, p2tog (final st tog with its wrap and the first gusset st), turn work.

ROW 3: (RS) Sl 1, k24 (24, 28, 28, 32), ssk, turn work.

ROW 4: (WS) Sl 1, p24 (24, 28, 28, 32), p2tog, turn work.

Rep Rows 3 and 4 until only 1 gusset st rem on each side, ending with a WS row—58 (62, 66, 70, 74) sts rem.

Leg
Rejoin for working in rnds, working the final gusset decs in the first rnd as foll.

RND 1: Sl 1, k24 (24, 28, 28, 32), ssk, work instep sts in patt as set—57 (61, 65, 69, 73) sts rem.

RND 2: K2tog, work instep sts in patt as set, knit to end of rnd—56 (60, 64, 68, 72) sts rem.

Cont in patt as set until Rnd 4 of the instep patt is complete.

NEXT RND: Work Rnd 1 of ridge rib patt for a mult of 4 sts across all sts.

Cont even in patt as set until leg measures 5 (5, 6, 6, 6)" (12.5 [12.5, 15, 15, 15] cm) or 2" (5 cm) less than desired total length.

Cuff
Work in k2, p2 ribbing for 2" (5 cm).

Use a stretchy method (see page 52) to BO all sts.

Finishing
Weave in loose ends. Block as desired (see page 18).

The OH, VaLeNCIa! Sock

FINISHED SIZE

Ankle circumference, lightly stretched: 7¼ (7½, 8¾, 9)" (18.5 [19, 22, 23] cm).

Foot circumference, lightly stretched: 7 (7½, 8, 8½)" (18 [19, 20.5, 21.5] cm).

Leg length: 7" (18 cm) shown; adjustable to fit.

Foot length: Adjustable to fit; finished length should be about ½" (1.3 cm) shorter than actual foot length.

Sock shown measures 7½" (19 cm) foot circumference.

YARN

CYCA #1, Super Fine.

Shown here: Sweet Georgia Yarns BFL Sock (80% superwash Bluefaced Leicester wool, 20% nylon; 400 yd [366 m]/115 g): Pumpkin, 1 skein.

NEEDLES

Size U.S. 1.5 (2.5 mm): set of 4 double-pointed (dpn), two circular (cir) or one long cir, as you prefer (see page 20).

NOTIONS

Marker (m); tapestry needle.

GAUGE

32 sts and 44 rnds = 4" (10 cm) in St st worked in rnds.

29½ sts and 44 rnds = 4" (10 cm) in lace patt (for second and fourth sizes) worked in rnds, blocked but unstretched; stretches easily to 24 sts = 4" (10 cm).

This top-down sock is worked in a traditional Estonian leaf lace. It's a little more visually complex than the Harcourt Sock on page 132, but no more difficult to knit. The addition of purl stitches makes a lace pattern look more sophisticated while improving the fit. They also provide a nice little trick for grading—working the purl stitches through the back loop tightens up the fabric without requiring changes in the stitch count, and it's undetectable in the look of the finished sock.

Notes

+ This pattern works for any sock yarn that specifies a gauge of 30 to 32 stitches in 4" (10 cm).

+ The following instructions are based on the Basic Pattern on page 40 worked at a gauge of 8 stitches per inch (2.5 cm), with finished sizes of 7 (7½, 8, 8½)" (18 [19, 20.5, 21.5] cm).

+ Choose size based on foot circumference, allowing for the usual 10 percent negative ease.

THE OH, VALENCIA! SOCK

The Oh, Valencia! Sock is an example of how to adjust the knitted fabric to accommodate a 12-stitch pattern repeat. Worked at a gauge of 8 stitches per inch (2.5 cm), the sock circumference is limited to 48 or 60 stitches (5 or 6 pattern repeats), for a finished circumference of 7½ inches and 8½ inches (19 and 21.5 cm). In order to provide multiple sizes, I decided to create two slightly different versions of the pattern to adjust the width of the pattern repeat. In one version, the purl ribs are worked as normal; in the other version, the purl ribs are worked through their back loops. Working the purl rib stitches through the back loop tightens up the gauge and allows for four finished sizes—48 stitches with twisted purls, 48 stitches with standard purls, 60 stitches with twisted purls, and 60 stitches with standard purls, for finished circumferences of 7 inches, 7½ inches, 8 inches, and 8½ inches (18, 19, 20.5, and 21.5 cm), respectively.

The cuff is worked on the number of stitches appropriate for the stockinette gauge. Decreases are worked at the boundary between the cuff and leg to adjust the stitch count as necessary for each size. This requires that increases are worked at the transition from the patterned leg to plain stockinette stitch in the heel and toe. The leg of the two larger sizes is worked on an odd number of pattern repeats. At the heel, I chose to divide the stitches evenly to maintain an equal number of stitches in the sole and instep, which resulted in an extra half of a pattern repeat on the instep. In this case, the inherent symmetry of the pattern makes this work very nicely.

Cuff

CO 56 (56, 65, 70) sts. Distribute across needles as you prefer and join for working in rnds, being careful not to twist sts.

Cont for your size as foll.

First, second, and fourth sizes only
SET-UP RND: *[K1, p1] 2 times, k1, p2; rep from *.

Third size only
SET-UP RND: *[K1, p1] 5 times, k1, p2; rep from *.

All sizes
Cont in ribbing as set until piece measures 1½ (1½, 2, 2)" (3.8 [3.8, 5, 5] cm) from CO.

Cont for your size as foll.

First, second, and fourth sizes only
NEXT RND: *[K1, p1] 2 times, k1, p2tog; rep from *—48 (48, 60) sts rem.

Third size only
NEXT RND: *[K1, p1] 5 times, k1, p2tog; rep from *—60 sts rem.

Leg

SET-UP RND: Work Row 1 of Lace chart (see page 92) for your size 4 (4, 5, 5) times around.

Work through Row 12 of chart, then rep Rows 1–12 four more times—5 full patt reps.

Note: To adjust leg length, work more or fewer pattern rounds as desired. It looks best if you end with Rnd 6 or 12 of patt, but it's not critical.

Heel
HEEL FLAP
The heel flap is worked back and forth on half of the leg sts. Sts are inc'd on the first row to bring the st count to the number required for the St st gauge.

Cont for your size as foll.

First size only
ROW 1: (RS) [K4, M1 (see Glossary)] 5 times, k3—23 sts inc'd to 28 sts.

Second size only
ROW 1: (RS) [K3, M1 (see Glossary)] 7 times, k2—23 sts inc'd to 30 sts.

Third size only
ROW 1: (RS) [K7, M1 (see Glossary)] 3 times, k8—29 sts inc'd to 32 sts.

Fourth size only
ROW 1: (RS) [K5, M1 (see Glossary)] 5 times, k4—29 sts inc'd to 34 sts.

All sizes
Place rem 25 (25, 31, 31) sts on spare needle to be worked later for instep.

Turn work so that WS is facing and work 28 (30, 32, 34) heel sts back and forth in rows as foll.

Lace chart, 1st and 3rd sizes

(chart, rows labeled 1, 3, 5, 7, 9, 11)

Lace chart, 2nd and 4th sizes

(chart, rows labeled 1, 3, 5, 7, 9, 11)

Legend:

- ☐ knit
- • purl
- ℛ p tbl
- ○ yo
- ＼ ssk
- ／ k2tog

ROW 2: (WS) Sl 1, p27 (29, 31, 33).

ROW 3: Sl 1, k27 (29, 31, 33).

ROW 4: Sl 1, p27 (29, 31, 33).

Rep Rows 3 and 4 until a total of 24 (26, 28, 30) rows have been worked, ending with a WS row.

TURN HEEL

Work short-rows as foll.

ROW 1: (RS) K19 (20, 21, 23) ssk, turn work.

ROW 2: (WS) Sl 1, p10 (10, 10, 12), p2tog, turn work.

ROW 3: Sl 1, k10 (10, 10, 12), ssk (1 st each side of gap), turn work.

ROW 4: Sl 1, p10 (10, 10, 12), p2tog (1 st each side of gap), turn work.

Rep Rows 3 and 4 until all sts have been worked, ending with a WS row—12 (12, 12, 14) sts rem.

Gusset

From here on, work the 25 (25, 31, 31) instep sts as established for your size as foll.

First and second sizes only

P1, work 2 full reps of Lace chart.

Third and fourth sizes only

Work sts 6–12 of Lace chart, then work 2 full reps.

All sizes

K12 (12, 12, 14) heel sts, with same needle, pick up and knit 14 (15, 16, 17) sts along selvedge edge at the side of the heel flap using slipped sts as a guide (see page 36). With a new needle, work 25 (25, 31, 31) instep sts as set. With another new needle, pick up and knit 14 (15, 16, 17) sts along selvedge edge at other side of heel flap, then work the first 6 (6, 6, 7) sts from the first needle again—65 (67, 75, 79) sts total; 20 (21, 22, 24) sts between the start of rnd and instep on each side, 25 (25, 31, 31) instep sts.

Rnd begins at center of heel. If you're working on two cir needles or using the magic-loop method, place a marker in this position.

From here on in, the 25 (25, 31, 31) instep sts will be worked as set; the gusset and sole sts will be worked in St st (knit every rnd).

SET-UP RND: K6 (6, 6, 7), k14 (15, 16, 17) through back loop (tbl), work instep sts in patt as set, k14 (15, 16, 17) tbl, knit to end of rnd.

DEC RND: Knit to 2 sts before instep, k2tog, work instep sts patt as set, ssk, knit to end of rnd—2 sts dec'd.

Work 1 rnd even, maintaining patt on instep.

Rep the last 2 rnds 5 (5, 5, 6) more times—53 (55, 63, 65) sts rem; 28 (30, 32, 34) sole sts.

Foot

Work even in patt as set until foot measures 1½ (2, 2, 2¼)" (3.8 [5, 5, 5.5] cm) less than desired finished sock length. It looks best if you end with Rnd 6 or 12 of patt, but it's not critical.

Toe

Work for your size as foll.

First size only

SET-UP RND: Knit to instep, [k6, M1] 3 times, knit to end of rnd—56 sts; 28 sts each on sole and instep.

Second size only

SET-UP RND: Knit to instep, [k4, M1] 5 times, knit to end of rnd—60 sts; 30 sts each on sole and instep.

Third size only

SET-UP RND: K31 (to midpoint of instep), M1, knit to end of rnd—64 sts; 32 sts each on sole and instep.

Fourth size only

SET-UP RND: Knit to instep, [k8, M1] 3 times, knit to end of rnd—68 sts; 34 sts each on sole and instep.

All sizes

DEC RND: Knit to 3 sts before instep, k2tog, k1; k1, ssk, knit to 3 sts before end of instep, k2tog, k1; k1, ssk, knit to end of rnd—4 sts dec'd.

Knit 1 rnd even.

Rep the last 2 rnds 5 (6, 6, 7) more times—32 (32, 36, 36) sts rem.

Rep dec rnd 6 (6, 7, 7) times— 8 sts rem.

Cut yarn, leaving an 8" (20.5 cm) tail. Thread tail on a tapestry needle, draw through rem sts, and pull tight to close hole.

Finishing

Weave in loose ends. Block as desired (see page 18).

The WELLESLEY Sock

‖|‖|‖|‖| ‖ | ‖ | ‖ | ‖ | ‖ | ‖ | ‖ | ‖ | ‖ | ‖ | ‖ | ‖ | ‖ | ‖ |‖|‖|‖‖

FINISHED SIZE

Ankle/foot circumference, lightly stretched: 7 (7½, 8, 8½, 9, 9½, 10)" (18 [19, 20.5, 21.5, 23, 24, 25.5] cm).

Leg length: Adjustable to fit.

Foot length: Adjustable to fit; finished length should be about ½" (1.3 cm) shorter than actual foot length.

Sock shown measures 9" (23 cm).

YARN

CYCA #1, Super Fine.

Shown here: Brown Sheep Wildfoote (75% washable wool, 25% nylon; 215 yd [197 m]/50 g): #SY40 Gunsmoke, 2 (2, 2, 3, 3, 3, 3) balls.

NEEDLES

Size U.S. 1.5 (2.5 mm): set of 4 double-pointed (dpn), two circular (cir) or one long cir, as you prefer (see page 20).

NOTIONS

Cable needle (cn); markers (m); tapestry needle.

GAUGE

32 sts and 44 rnds = 4" (10 cm) in St st worked in rnds.

42 sts and 44 rnds = 4" (10 cm) in cable and rib patt worked in rnds, unstretched.

Handsome, classic, and perfect—this is just what a sock should be. Although I've knitted this pair in a sensible gray, they'd be just as wonderful in a bright color. In addition to providing instructions for working in both directions, I've reversed the cable turns on the second sock. You can make both socks the same, of course, but they're more interesting to knit— and wear—this way. The cable and rib combo pulls in for a nice snug fit that's ideal for legs that are slightly skinnier than "normal."

Notes

+ This pattern works for any sock yarn that specifies a gauge of 30 to 32 stitches in 4" (10 cm).

+ The following instructions are based on the Basic Patterns on pages 40 and 54 worked at a gauge of 8 stitches per inch (2.5 cm) with finished sizes of 7 (7½, 8, 8½, 9, 9½, 10)" (18 [19, 20.5, 21.5, 23, 24, 25.5] cm).

+ Choose size based on foot circumference, allowing for the usual 10 percent negative ease.

THE WELLESLEY SOCK

The Wellesley Sock is an example of how a stitch pattern can be adjusted to accommodate multiple sizes. Although this sock looks relatively simple, I used three techniques to generate the different sizes—adjusted stitch numbers, adjusted pattern repeats, and different stitch counts for the leg and foot.

The stitch pattern repeats over 8 stitches, which limits the possible stitch counts to multiples of 8 for the leg. At a gauge of 8 stitches per inch, the sizes were limited to 7 inches, 8 inches, 9 inches, and 10 inches (18, 20.5, 23, and 25.5 cm) circumferences. To allow for additional sizes at ½ inch (1.3 cm) increments, I designed a similar pattern that repeats over 10 stitches (each purl rib consists of 2 stitches instead of just 1). Although the difference is slightly visible in the different sizes, the wider purl rib doesn't change the overall integrity or intent of the pattern stitches.

The balanced pattern on the instep begins and ends with the same element of the cable pattern. This means that for some sizes the instep begins and ends with a purl rib next to a cable rib; for other sizes the instep begins and ends with a purl rib next to a knit rib. Again, the different sizes are slightly different, but the basic look of the design is retained throughout.

By balancing the pattern on the instep, I limited the number of stitches that could be included in the instep, which, in turn, meant that adjustments had to be made to the heel. For the first three sizes, the heel flap is narrower than standard for the same gauge. I've compensated for that by adjusting the heel turn—I kept the same number of stitches in the center portion (the stitches of the band for the top-down sock; the unwrapped stitches for the toe-up sock) specified in

the tables in Chapter 3, which meant that there were slightly fewer stitches in the outer two portions.

For the top-down version, the adjusted proportions of the heel turn results in fewer decrease rounds. This, combined with the narrower heel flap, positions the sides of the heel farther back on the foot than usual. To compensate, I slowed the gusset decreases so that more rounds would be worked to fill in the gap. For the toe-up sock, I designated more than the usual one-third of heel stitches in the unwrapped portion at the center of the heel, which means fewer rows in the heel turn, which requires that you start a little later than usual.

I indulged in one final "cheat"—the two largest sizes have the same number of stitches in the leg and heel, but there are more stitches in the heel flap and gussets of the larger size, as well as a larger foot.

top down   *toe up*

TOP-DOWN VERSION

Leg

CO 56 (60, 64, 70, 72, 80, 80) sts. Distribute sts across needles as you prefer and join for working in rnds, being careful not to twist sts.

Beg with Rnd 1, work the appropriate Leg chart (see pages 98 and 99) for your size until piece measures 7 (7½, 8, 8, 8, 8½, 8½)" (18 [19, 20.5, 20.5, 20.5, 21.5, 21.5] cm) or desired length to top of heel. Make note of last patt rnd worked so patt can cont on instep.

Heel
HEEL FLAP

The heel flap is worked back and forth in St st over 26 (24, 26, 34, 34, 42, 42) sts; rem 30 (36, 38, 36, 38, 38, 38) sts will be worked later for instep. For the sizes using an 8-st rep, the beg and end of the heel flap aligns with a knit rib; for the sizes using a 10-st rep, the beg and end of the heel flap aligns with the center of a purl rib. For all sizes, this arranges the instep sts so that they begin and end with a single purl st beside a cable column.

ROW 1: (RS) K2, p 0 (1, 0, 1, 0, 0, 0) turn work.

ROW 2: (WS): Sl 1, p25 (23, 25, 33, 33, 41, 41), turn work.

ROW 3: Sl 1, k25 (23, 25, 33, 33, 41, 41).

ROW 4: Sl 1, p25 (23, 25, 33, 33, 41, 41).

Rep Rows 3 and 4 until a total of 24 (26, 26, 28, 30, 32, 34) rows have been worked, ending with a WS row.

TURN HEEL

Work short-rows as foll.

ROW 1: (RS) K17 (17, 18, 23, 23, 28, 28), ssk, turn work.

ROW 2: (WS) Sl 1, p8 (10, 10, 12, 12, 14, 14), p2tog, turn work.

ROW 3: Sl 1, k8 (10, 10, 12, 12, 14, 14), ssk (1 st each side of gap), turn work.

ROW 4: Sl 1, p8 (10, 10, 12, 12, 14, 14), p2tog (1 st each side of gap), turn work.

Rep Rows 3 and 4 until all sts have been worked, ending with a WS row—10 (12, 12, 14, 14, 16, 16) sts rem.

Gusset

K10 (12, 12, 14, 14, 16, 16) heel sts, then with the same needle, pick up and knit 14 (15, 15, 16, 17, 18, 19) sts along selvedge edge at the side of the heel flap using slipped sts as a guide (see page 36). With a new needle, work 30 (36, 38, 36, 38, 38, 38) instep sts in patt as set. With another new needle, pick up and knit 14 (15, 15, 16, 17, 18, 19) sts along selvedge edge at other side of heel flap, using slipped sts as a guide, then work first 5 (6, 6, 7, 7, 8, 8) sts from the first needle again—68 (78, 80, 82, 86, 90, 92) sts total; 19 (21, 21, 23, 24, 26, 26) sts on each side between the start of the rnd and the start of the instep, 30 (36, 38, 36, 38, 38, 38) instep sts.

Rnd begins at center of heel. If you're working on two cir needles or using the magic-loop method, place a marker in this position.

From here on, the instep sts will be worked in the cable and rib patt as set, beg and end with p1; the gusset and sole sts will be worked in St st.

SET-UP RND: K5 (6, 6, 7, 7, 8, 8), k14 (15, 15, 16, 17, 18, 19) through back loops (tbl), work across instep in patt as set, k14 (15, 15, 16, 17, 18, 19) tbl, knit to end of rnd.

DEC RND: Knit to 2 sts before instep, k2tog, work instep sts in patt as set, ssk, knit to end of rnd—2 sts dec'd.

Work 1 (2, 2, 1, 1, 1, 1) rnd(s) even in patt as set.

Rep the last 2 (3, 3, 2, 2, 2, 2) rnds 5 (2, 2, 6, 6, 6, 5) more times—56 (72, 74, 68, 72, 76, 80) sts rem.

Second and third sizes only

[Rep dec rnd one, then work 1 rnd even] 6 (5) times—(60, 64) sts rem.

All sizes

Proceed to Foot.

Foot

SET-UP RND: Knit to instep, work instep sts in patt as set, knit to end of rnd.

Cont even in patt as set until foot measures 1¾ (1¾, 2, 2, 2¼, 2¼, 2½)" (4.5 [4.5, 5, 5, 5.5, 5.5, 6.5] cm) less than desired finished sock foot length.

Toe

Rearrange sts if necessary so that there are 28 (30, 32, 34, 36, 38, 40) sts each for sole and instep.

DEC RND: Knit to 3 sts before beg of instep, k2tog, k2, ssk, knit to 3 sts before end of instep, k2tog, k2, ssk, knit to end of rnd—4 sts dec'd.

Knit 1 rnd even.

Right Leg chart
1st, 3rd, 5th, 6th, and 7th sizes

8-st repeat

Right Leg chart
2nd and 4th sizes
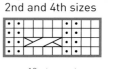
10-st repeat

Right Instep
1st, 3rd, 5th, 6th, and 7th sizes
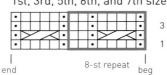
end 8-st repeat beg

☐ knit

⊡ purl

⧄ 2/2RC

⧅ 2/2LC

▢ pattern repeat

Right Instep
2nd and 4th sizes
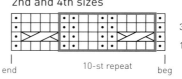
end 10-st repeat beg

Rep the last 2 rnds 5 (6, 6, 7, 7, 8, 8) more times—32 (32, 36, 36, 40, 40, 44) sts rem.

Rep dec rnd every rnd 6 (6, 7, 7, 8, 8, 9) times—8 sts rem.

Cut yarn, leaving an 8" (20.5 cm) tail. Thread tail on a tapestry needle, draw through rem sts, pull tight to close hole, and secure on WS.

Finishing

Weave in loose ends.Block as desired (see page 18).

||||||||||||||||||||||||||||||||||||||

TOE-UP VERSION
Toe

Using Judy's magic method (see page 49), CO 20 (20, 20, 24, 24, 24, 28) sts—10 (10, 10, 12, 12, 12, 14) sts each on two needles.

RND 1: Work as foll, depending on the type of needle(s) used.

FOR DPN: K5 (5, 5, 6, 6, 6, 7) with one needle, k5 (5, 5, 6, 6, 6, 7) with a second needle, k10 (10, 10, 12, 12, 12, 14) with a third needle.

FOR TWO CIR OR MAGIC LOOP: K10 (10, 10, 12, 12, 12, 14) with one needle, k10 (10, 10, 12, 12, 12, 14) with a second needle.

Place a safety pin or marker in the toe to indicate beg of the rnd and a second one to indicate the center of the rnd.

INC RND: K1, M1R (see Glossary), knit to 1 st before center of rnd, M1L (see Glossary), k2, M1R, knit to

1 st before end of rnd, M1L, k1—4 sts inc'd.

Knit 1 rnd even.

Rep the last 2 rnds 8 (9, 10, 10, 11, 12, 12) more times, ending with an inc rnd—56 (60, 64, 68, 72, 76, 80) sts total.

Set up for start of instep for your size as foll.

First (second, third, fourth, fifth) sizes only
SET-UP RND: Knit to last 1 (3, 3, 1, 1) st(s).

Sixth size only
SET-UP RND: Knit.

Seventh size only
SET-UP RND: Knit to end of rnd, then knit the first st of the next rnd.

All sizes
This is the start of instep—the first 30 (36, 38, 36, 38, 38, 38) sts form the instep; rem 26 (24, 26, 32, 34, 38, 42) sts form the sole.

Rearrange the sts on your needles or place markers as necessary.

Foot
SET-UP RND: Work 30 (36, 38, 36, 38, 38, 38) sts according to appropriate Instep chart, knit to end of rnd.

Cont in patt as set until foot measures 3¾ (3½, 3¾, 4½, 4½, 5, 5½)" (9.5 [9, 9.5, 11.5, 11.5, 12.5, 14] cm) less than desired finished sock foot length.

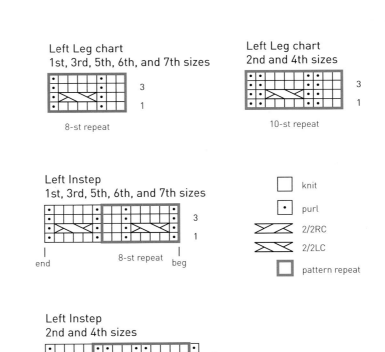

Left Leg chart
1st, 3rd, 5th, 6th, and 7th sizes
8-st repeat

Left Leg chart
2nd and 4th sizes
10-st repeat

Left Instep
1st, 3rd, 5th, 6th, and 7th sizes
end   8-st repeat   beg

Left Instep
2nd and 4th sizes
end   10-st repeat   beg

knit
purl
2/2RC
2/2LC
pattern repeat

top down

toe up

Gusset

Rearrange sts if necessary so that the sole sts are on one needle. Work the gusset incs at each end of the needle holding the sole sts.

RND 1: Work instep sts in patt as set, M1R, place marker (pm) for beg of heel, knit to end of rnd, pm for end of heel, M1L—2 sts inc'd.

RND 2: Work instep sts in patt as set, knit to end of rnd.

RND 3: Work instep sts in patt as set, M1R, knit to end of rnd, M1L— 2 sts inc'd.

RND 4: Work instep sts in patt as set, knit to end of rnd.

Rep the last 2 rnds 9 (10, 11, 12, 12, 13, 14) more times—78 (84, 90, 96, 100, 106, 112) sts total.

Heel
TURN HEEL
Work short-rows (see Glossary) as foll.

ROW 1: (RS) Work instep sts in patt as set, knit to 1 st before second heel m, wrap next st and turn work (w&t). Make note of the patt rnd just completed.

ROW 2: (WS) Purl to 1 st before m, w&t.

Working only on the heel sts, cont as foll.

ROW 3: (RS) Knit to st before last wrapped st, w&t.

ROW 4: (WS) Purl to st before last wrapped st, w&t.

Rep Rows 3 and 4 until 8 (10, 10, 10, 12, 12, 14) sts rem unwrapped in the middle, ending with a WS row.

Remove heel markers.

HEEL FLAP
Work the heel flap, reducing the gusset stitches as you go as foll.

ROW 1: (RS) Knit to first wrapped st, *knit the wrapped st tog with its wrap; rep until 1 wrapped st rem, ssk (final st tog with its wrap and the first gusset st), turn work.

ROW 2: (WS) Sl 1, purl to first wrapped st, *purl the wrapped st tog with its wrap; rep from * until 1 wrapped st rem, p2tog (final st tog with its wrap and the first gusset st), turn work.

ROW 3: Sl 1, k24 (22, 24, 30, 32, 36, 40), ssk, turn work.

ROW 4: Sl 1, p24 (22, 24, 30, 32, 36, 40), ssk, turn work.

Rep Rows 3 and 4 until only 1 gusset st rem on each side, ending with a WS row—58 (62, 66, 70, 74, 78, 82) sts rem.

Leg

Rejoin for working in rnds, working the final gusset decs in the first rnd as foll.

Note: Patt on back of leg begins on the same rnd as the instep sts.

First (third, fifth, seventh) sizes only

SET-UP RND: Sl 1, k24 (24, 32, 40), ssk, work instep sts in patt as set, k2tog, work patt rep starting at the second st to 2 sts before the instep—56 (64, 72, 80) sts rem.

Second size only

SET-UP RND: Sl 1, k22, p2tog through back loop (tbl), work instep sts in patt as set, p2tog, work patt rep starting at the first st to 3 sts before the instep—60 sts rem.

Fourth size only

SET-UP RND: Sl 1, [k10, M1] 2 times, k10, p2tog through back loop (tbl), work instep sts in patt as set, p2tog, work patt rep starting at first st to 3 sts before the instep—70 sts rem.

Sixth size only

SET-UP RND: Sl 1, [k7, M1] 4 times, k8, p2tog through back loop (tbl), work instep sts in patt as set, k2tog, work patt rep starting at second st to 2 sts before the instep—80 sts rem.

All sizes

This is the new start of rnd—56 (60, 64, 70, 72, 80, 80) sts. From here, you'll work the patt rep around all sts.

Work appropriate Leg chart (see pages 98 and 99) as set until leg measures 7 (7½, 8, 8, 8, 8½, 8½)" (18 [19, 20.5, 20.5, 20.5, 21.5, 21.5] cm) or desired length from top of heel, ending with Row 2 of patt.

Using the Russian lace method (see page 52), BO all sts, working [k2tog] 2 times across the 4 cable sts.

Finishing

Weave in loose ends. Block as desired (see page 18).

The **Secrets & Lies** Sock

FINISHED SIZE

Foot circumference, lightly stretched: 7½ (8, 8½, 9)" (19 [20.5, 21.5, 23] cm).

Ankle circumference, lightly stretched: 8 (8, 9, 9)" (20.5 [20.5, 23, 23] cm).

Leg length: 6 (6, 6¼, 6¼)" (15 [15, 16, 16] cm); adjustable to fit.

Foot length: Adjustable to fit; finished length should be about ½" (1.3 cm) shorter than actual foot length.

Sock shown measures 8" (20.5 cm) ankle/foot circumference.

YARN

#1, Super Fine.

Shown here: Zen Yarn Garden Serenity 20 (70% superwash merino, 20% cashmere, 10% nylon; 400 yd [366 m]/100 g): Jakey, 1 skein.

NEEDLES

Size U.S. 1.5 (2.5 mm): set of 4 double-pointed (dpn), two circular (cir) or one long cir, as you prefer (see page 20).

NOTIONS

Cable needle (cn); marker (m); tapestry needle.

GAUGE

32 sts and 46½ rnds = 4" (10 cm) in St st worked in rnds.

42½ sts and 46½ rnds = 4" (10 cm) in lace and cable patt worked in unstretched rnds.

I love the visual sophistication and complexity of this design. Being a mix of both lace and cables, it might be considered a little more challenging to knit, but there's nothing inherently difficult in what you need to do. Because lace patterning on the heel flap and toes can wear through very quickly, I've created riffs on the cabled areas of the pattern. I rather like the secret of a patterned heel and toe that's hidden from everyone but you. Notes are included for substituting a plain toe.

Notes

+ This pattern works for any sock yarn that specifies a gauge of 30 to 32 stitches in 4" (10 cm).

+ The instructions that follow are based on the Basic Pattern on page 40 worked at a gauge of 8 stitches per inch (2.5 cm) with finished sizes of 7½ (8, 8½, 9)" (19 [20.5, 21.5, 23] cm).

+ Choose a size based on foot circumference, allowing for the usual 10 percent negative ease; the leg pattern is very stretchy and accommodating.

THE SECRETS & LIES SOCK

Like The Wellesley Sock on page 94, the Secrets & Lies Sock is also sized by making adjustments to the stitch pattern. In this case, I've modified the basic repeat to allow for more stitch counts. The original stitch pattern repeated over 18 stitches, but I created a 16-stitch version by narrowing the purl columns. The cuff, toes, and sole are all worked on the number of stitches recommended in the tables in Chapter 3.

An additional challenge was that because the pattern looks best with an even number of repeats, there were few options when it came to the leg circumferences. I've provided only two leg sizes. But for each leg size, there are two different foot sizes, depending on the number of stitches in the sole. Although only two heel widths are included, two lengths are provided for each. In total, this allows for four overall sizes.

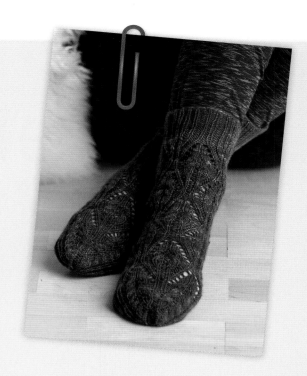

In the interest of aligning the pattern neatly at the toe, I modified the toe decrease rhythm slightly so that there are more alternations of decrease and even rounds.

STITCH GUIDE

2/2RC: Sl 2 sts onto cn and hold in back of work, k2, then k2 from cn.

2/2LC: Sl 2 sts onto cn and hold in front of work, k2, then k2 from cn.

Cuff

CO 56 (64, 64, 72) sts. Distribute sts across needles as you prefer and join for working in rnds, being careful not to twist sts.

Cont for your **size as** foll.

First size only

SET-UP RND: *K1, p2, [k1, p1] 4 times, p1, k1, p1; rep from *.

Second size only

SET-UP RND: *K1, p2, k2, [p1, k1] 2 times, p1, k2, p2, **k1, p1**; rep from *.

Third size only

SET-UP RND: *K1, p2, k1, p1, k1, p2, k1, p1, k1, p2, k1, p2; rep from *.

Fourth size only

SET-UP RND: *K1, p2, k2, p1, k1, p2, k1, p1, k2, p2, k1, p2; rep from *.

All sizes

Cont in ribbing as set until piece measures 1¾ (1¾, 2, 2)" (4.5 [4.5, 5, 5] cm) from CO.

Note: To lengthen the leg, work additional rnds of ribbing.

Inc on first and third sizes only as foll.

First size only

INC RND: *K1, p2, k1, M1R (see Glossary), [p1, k1] 2 times, p1, M1L (see Glossary), k1, p2, k1, p1; rep from *—64 sts.

Third size only

INC RND: *K1, p2, k1, M1R (see Glossary), p1, k1, p2, k1, p1, M1L (see Glossary), k1, p2, k1, p2; rep from *—72 sts.

All sizes

Proceed to Leg.

Leg

Work Rows 1–33 of Leg chart for your size once, then work Rows 2–17 again.

Heel
HEEL FLAP

The heel flap is worked back and forth in a cable patt on 33 (33, 36, 36) sts, beg and end with p1 as foll.

ROW 1: (RS) Work Row 1 of Heel Flap chart (see page 107) for your size across first 32 (32, 35, 35) sts, turn work.

ROW 2: (WS) Work Row 2 of chart across 33 (33, 36, 36) sts, turn work.

ROW 3: Work Row 3 of chart across 33 (33, 36, 36) sts.

ROW 4: Work Row 4 of chart across 33 (33, 36, 36) sts.

Cont in patt as set, rep Rows 2–5 of chart until a total of 24 (26, 28, 30) rows have been worked, ending with a WS row.

TURN HEEL

Work short-rows as foll.

ROW 1: (RS) K22 (22, 24, 24), ssk, turn work.

ROW 2: (WS) Sl 1, p11 (11, 12, 12), p2tog, turn work.

ROW 3: Sl 1, k11 (11, 12, 12), ssk (1 st each side of gap), turn work.

Leg chart, 1st and 2nd sizes

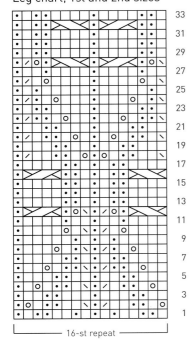

16-st repeat

Leg chart, 3rd and 4th sizes

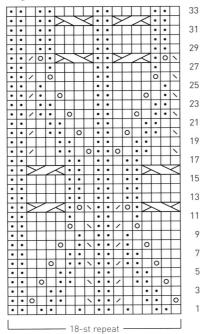

18-st repeat

□	k on RS; p on WS
•	p on RS; k on WS
○	yo
＼	ssk
／	k2tog
⟋	p2tog
⤬	2/2RC
⤬	2/2LC

ROW 4: Sl 1, p11 (11, 12, 12), p2tog (1 st each side of gap), turn work.

Rep Rows 3 and 4 until all sts have been worked, ending with a WS row—13 (13, 14, 14) sts rem.

Gusset

K13 (13, 14, 14) heel sts, then with the same needle, pick up and knit 14 (15, 16, 17) sts along selvedge edge at side of heel, using slipped sts as a guide (see page 36). With a new needle, work 31 (31, 36, 36) instep sts in patt as set. With another new needle, pick up and knit 14 (15, 16, 17) sts along selvedge edge at other side of heel, using slipped sts as a guide, then work the first 7 (7, 7, 7) sts from the first needle again—72 (74, 82, 84) sts total; 20 (21, 23, 24) sts between the start of the rnd and the start of the instep, 21 (22, 23, 24) sts between the end of the instep and the end of the rnd, 31 (31, 36, 36) instep sts.

Rnd begins at center of heel. If you're working on two cir needles or the magic-loop method, place a marker in this position.

From here on, the 31 (31, 36, 36) instep sts will be worked in patt as set. For the first and second sizes, the patt will begin with the first st of the rep and end with the 15th; for the third and fourth sizes, the patt will begin with the 18th st of the chart and end with the 17th. The top st of the gusset on each side will be worked as p1; the rest of the gusset and sole sts will be worked in St st.

SET-UP RND: K6 (6, 7, 7), k13 (14, 15, 16) through back loop (tbl), p1, work instep sts in patt as set, p1, k13 (14, 15, 16) tbl, knit to end of rnd.

DEC RND: Knit to 3 sts before instep, k2tog, p1, work instep sts in patt as set, p1, ssk, knit to end of rnd— 2 sts dec'd.

Work 1 rnd even, maintaining patt on instep.

Rep the last 2 rnds 5 (4, 6, 5) more times—60 (64, 68, 72) sts rem.

Foot

SET-UP RND: Knit to 1 st before instep, p1, work instep sts in patt as set, p1, knit to end of rnd.

Cont even in patt as set until a total of 3 reps have been worked from the cuff.

Note: To work a plain toe, change to St st for the remainder of the foot and toe.

Rep Rows 30–33 as necessary until foot measures about 1¾ (1¾, 2, 2)" (4.5 [4.5, 5, 5] cm) less than desired finished sock foot length, ending with Row 33 of patt.

Toe

Note: These instructions are for a patterned toe. For a plain toe, distribute the stitches evenly so that the sole and instep have the same number of stitches. Work the toe as for the Basic Sock pattern on page 40, following the numbers that correlate to your full stitch count.

Legend

☐	k on RS; p on WS
•	p on RS; k on WS
V	sl 1 wyb on RS; sl 1 wyf on WS
o	yo
\	ssk
/	k2tog
⩟	p2tog
⧓	2/2RC
⧓	2/2LC
▨	no stitch
☐	pattern repeat

DEC RND: Knit to 3 sts before instep, k2tog, p1, work Row 1 of Toe chart for your size across instep sts, p1, ssk, knit to end of rnd—4 sts dec'd.

NEXT RND: Knit to instep, work Row 2 of Toe chart across instep sts, p1, knit to end of rnd.

Rep the last 2 rnds 7 more times— 28 (32, 36, 40) sts rem.

Rep dec rnd every rnd 5 (6, 7, 7) times, ending with Row 21 (22, 23, 23) of chart—8 (8, 9, 13) sts rem.

Fourth size only

NEXT RND: Knit to 2 sts before instep, k2tog, [p1, k1] 2 times, p1, ssk, knit to end of rnd—11 sts rem.

All sizes

Cut yarn, leaving an 8" (20.5 cm) tail. Thread tail on a tapestry needle, draw through rem sts, and pull tight to close hole.

Finishing

Weave in loose ends. Block as desired (see page 18).

Heel Flap chart, 1st and 2nd sizes

Heel Flap chart, 3rd and 4th sizes

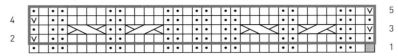

Toe chart, 1st and 2nd sizes

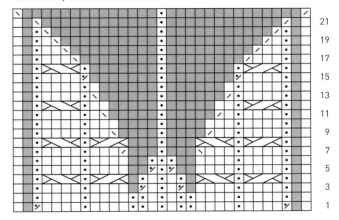

Toe chart, 3rd and 4th sizes

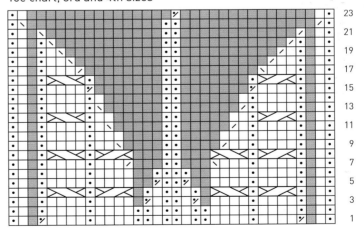

The JƏRVIS Sock

FINISHED SIZE

Foot circumference: 7 (7¼, 8, 8½)" (18 [18.5, 20.5, 21.5] cm).

Ankle circumference: 6¾ (6¾, 7½, 7½)" (17 [17 19, 19] cm).

Leg length: Adjustable to fit.

Foot length: Adjustable to fit; finished length should be about ½" (1.3 cm) shorter than actual foot length.

Sock shown measures 7¼" (18.5 cm) foot circumference.

YARN

CYCA #1, Super Fine.

Shown here: Madelinetosh Tosh Sock (100% superwash merino wool; 395 yd [361 m]/100 g): Briar, 1 (1, 1, 2) skein(s).

NEEDLES

All sizes: Size U.S. 1.5 (2.5 mm): set of 4 double-pointed (dpn), two circular (cir), or one long cir, as you prefer (see page 20).

Largest two sizes only: Size U.S. 2 (2.75 mm): set of 4 dpn, two cir, or one long cir, as you prefer.

NOTIONS

Marker (m); tapestry needle.

GAUGE

32 sts and 45 rnds = 4" (10 cm) in St st worked in rnds on smaller needle(s).

28 sts and 45 rnds = 4" (10 cm) in lace patt worked in rnds on smaller needle(s), slightly stretched after blocking.

26 sts and 42 rnds = 4" (10 cm) in lace patt worked in rnds on larger needle(s), slightly stretched after blocking.

This lace sock is worked from the toe up for the simple reason that I prefer how the pattern looks when aligned that way. I named these socks after a street in Toronto, where I live. Jarvis is a long road that takes some unusual paths—it's hilly and twisty, runs under one roadway and over another, and includes a rather unique shifting center lane. Knitting this sock is a bit like driving on Jarvis—you have to pay attention, but it's a lot of fun.

Notes

+ This pattern works for any sock yarn that specifies a gauge of 30 to 32 stitches in 4" (10 cm).

+ The following instructions are based on the Basic Pattern on page 54 worked at a gauge of 8 stitches per inch (2.5 cm), with finished sizes of 7 (7½, 8, 8½)" (18 [19, 20.5, 21.5] cm).

+ Choose a size based on foot circumference, allowing for the usual 10 percent negative ease—the leg pattern is very stretchy and very accommodating.

THE JARVIS SOCK

Using a pattern that repeats over 16 stitches with a "half-drop" repeat (the second half of the pattern repeat is shifted laterally by half a repeat), posed yet a different challenge for the Jarvis Sock. Not only is there only one option for the number of stitches in the leg (three pattern repeats for 48 stitches each), there isn't an easy way to adjust the basic pattern repeat—adding stitches in the ribbing portion would destroy the integrity of the central element of the offset motifs.

This pattern simply isn't adjustable without affecting the integrity and the look of the fabric that results. But even so, I was able to produce two leg circumferences and multiple foot and ankle circumferences.

To produce the larger leg circumference, I changed the gauge of the lace pattern by using needles one size larger for the leg. This loosens up the stitches in the lace pattern and results in a larger circumference on the same number of stitches—but the heel, foot, and toe are worked on needles of the appropriate size to maintain the integrity of the fabric where it matters. Because the lace pattern includes a ribbed component, the fabric compresses and stretches to fit a range of

sizes. The cuff is fully graded (that is, there's a different number of stitches for each size) to ensure a good, snug fit even if the lace portion doesn't extend to fully stretch around the leg.

As with some of the other patterns, some sizes have fewer heel stitches than specified on the tables in Chapter 3, but the overall construction is the same. For all sizes, the number of stitches in the gusset and in the center segment of the heel turn are based the numbers in the table on pages 56–58.

On Changing Needle Sizes: Don't Do It.

In general, I don't recommend a wholesale change in needle size as a means to create additional sock sizes. From a fit and construction perspective, you can run into trouble by adjusting the gauge. While working with larger needles will increase the circumference of the sock, it will also change the length of other parts. The length of the heel flap is important in a top-down sock, and the length of the gusset and heel turn is important in a toe-up sock. If you change the needle size to affect the gauge, be sure to check the row/round gauge as well to make sure you won't have to adjust the heels as a result.

A larger concern is about the fabric itself. I choose to work a particular yarn at a particular gauge because

I feel the combination makes a good fabric for a sock—dense enough to be comfortable underfoot and to withstand abrasion. If larger needles are used to loosen the fabric for a larger circumference, the fabric won't wear as well or feel as good. If smaller needles are used to tighten the fabric for a smaller circumference, the fabric may lose its elasticity and be more difficult to knit.

I've chosen to change the needle size only on the leg of the Jarvis Sock so that the heel is unaffected and so that the fabric in the foot remains dense, comfortable, and hardwearing.

Toe

Using Judy's magic method (see page 49), CO 20 (20, 20, 20) sts—10 (10, 10, 10) sts each on two needles.

RND 1: Work as foll, depending on the type of needle(s) used.

FOR DPN: K5 (5, 5, 5) with one needle, k5 (5, 5, 5) with a second needle, k10 (10, 10, 10) sts with a third needle.

FOR TWO CIR OR MAGIC LOOP: K10 (10, 10, 10) with one needle, k10 (10, 10, 10) with a second needle.

Place a safety pin or marker in the toe to indicate beg of rnd and a second one to indicate the center of the rnd.

INC RND: K1, M1R (see Glossary), knit to 1 st before center of rnd, M1L (see Glossary), k2, M1R, knit to 1 st before end of rnd, M1L, k1— 4 sts inc'd.

Knit 1 rnd even.

Rep the last 2 rnds 8 (9, 9, 10) more times, ending with an inc rnd—56 (60, 60, 64) sts total.

Cont for your size as foll.

First size only
NEXT RND: K4, [k2tog, k7] 3 times, knit to 1 st before end of rnd— 53 sts rem.

Second size only
NEXT RND: K2, [k2tog, k4] 5 times, knit to 1 st before end of rnd— 55 sts rem.

Third size only
NEXT RND: K14, k2tog, knit to 1 st before end of rnd—59 sts rem.

Fourth size only
NEXT RND: K15, k2tog, knit to end of rnd—63 sts rem.

All sizes
This position is the start of rnd. The first 27 (27, 31, 31) sts form the instep; the rem 26 (28, 28, 32) sts form the sole. Rearrange your sts or place markers as you require.

Foot

SET-UP RND: Work Instep chart (see page 112) for your size across 27 (27, 31, 31) sts, knit to end of rnd.

Cont even in patt as set until foot measures 3½ (3¾, 4, 4½)" (9 [9.5, 10, 11.5] cm) less than desired finished sock foot length.

Leg chart

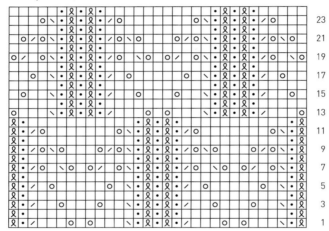

Instep chart, 1st and 2nd sizes

Instep chart, 3rd and 4th sizes

	knit
•	purl
ℚ	k tbl
○	yo
＼	ssk
／	k2tog

Gusset

Rearrange sts if necessary so that the sole sts are on one needle. Work the gusset incs at each end of the needle holding the sole sts as foll.

RND 1: Work instep sts in patt as set, M1R, place marker (pm) for beg of heel, knit to end of rnd, pm for end of heel, M1L—2 sts inc'd.

RND 2: Work instep sts in patt as set, knit to end of rnd.

RND 3: Work instep sts in patt as set, M1R, knit to end of rnd, M1L— 2 sts inc'd.

RND 4: Work instep sts in patt as set, knit to end of rnd.

Rep the last 2 rnds 9 (10, 11, 12) more times—75 (79, 85, 91) sts total.

Heel
TURN HEEL

Work short-rows (see Glossary) as foll.

ROW 1: (RS) Work instep in patt as set, knit to 1 st before second heel m, wrap next st and turn work (w&t).

ROW 2: (WS) Purl to 1 st before m, w&t.

Working only on the heel sts, cont as foll.

1 wrapped st rem, p2tog (final st tog with its wrap and the first gusset st), turn work.

ROW 3: (RS) Sl 1, k24 (26, 26, 30), ssk, turn work.

ROW 4: (WS) Sl 1, p24 (26, 26, 30), p2tog, turn work.

Rep Rows 3 and 4 until all but 1 gusset st rem on each side, ending with a WS row—55 (57, 61, 65) sts rem.

Leg

Rejoin for working in rnds, working the final gusset decs in the first rnd as foll.

SET-UP RND: Sl 1, k24 (26, 26, 30), ssk, work instep sts in patt as set, k2tog, knit to start of instep (new start of rnd)—53 (55, 59, 63) sts.

Note: You'll work the back of the leg in stockinette until you're in position to start a new pattern "tier," at which point you'll work decreases on the back of the leg to get to the appropriate stitch count. Then, you'll work the pattern all the way around the leg.

Change to larger needles for third and fourth sizes only.

ROW 3: (RS) Knit to st before last wrapped st, w&t.

ROW 4: (WS) Purl to st before last wrapped st, w&t.

Rep Rows 3 and 4 until 8 (10, 10,10) sts rem unwrapped in the middle, ending with a WS row.

Remove heel markers.

HEEL FLAP

Work the heel flap and dec gusset sts as foll.

ROW 1: (RS) Knit to first wrapped st, *knit the wrapped st tog with its wrap; rep from * until 1 wrapped st rem, ssk (final st tog with its wrap and the first gusset st), turn work.

ROW 2: (WS) Sl 1, purl to first wrapped st, *purl the wrapped st tog with its wrap; rep from * until

RND 1: Work in patt across instep sts, knit across back of leg.

Cont in patt as established through Row 10 or 22 of Instep chart, whichever comes first.

Cont for you size as foll.

First size only
DEC RND: Work next patt row (11 or 23) on instep, k1, [k2tog, k3]

5 times—48 sts rem; 27 instep sts, 21 back-of-leg sts.

Second size only
DEC RND: Work next patt row (11 or 23) on instep, [k2, k2tog] 7 times—48 sts rem; 27 instep sts, 21 back-of-leg sts.

Third size only
DEC RND: Work next patt row (11 or 23) on instep, [k2tog, k1, k2tog] 5 times, k1, k2tog—48 sts rem; 31 instep sts, 17 back-of-leg sts.

Fourth size only
DEC RND: Work next patt row (11 or 23) on instep, k1, [k2tog] 15 times, k1—48 sts rem; 31 instep sts, 17 back-of-leg sts.

Cont for your size as foll.

First and second sizes only
IF YOU'VE JUST COMPLETED ROW 11 OF PATT: Work Row 12 across instep, p1, k1tbl, p1—this will be the new start of rnd; you'll start the Leg chart on Rnd 13.

IF YOU'VE JUST COMPLETED ROW 23 OF PATT: Work Row 24 across instep, k3—this will be the new start of rnd; you'll start the Leg chart on Rnd 1.

Third and fourth sizes only
IF YOU'VE JUST COMPLETED ROW 11 OF PATT: Work Row 12 across instep, p1—this will be the new start of rnd; you'll start the Leg chart on Rnd 13.

IF YOU'VE JUST COMPLETED ROW 23 OF PATT: Work Row 24 across instep, k1—this will be the new start of rnd; you'll start the Leg chart on Rnd 1.

All sizes
NEXT RND: Work Leg chart Row 1 or 13 as specified for your size across all sts.

Cont through Row 24, then rep Rows 1–24 until leg measures about 5" (12.5 cm), or 2" (5 cm) less than desired total length, ending with Row 12 or 23 of patt.

If you've just finished Row 12, skip to Inc rnd; if you've just finished Row 23, work Row 24 to the last 8 sts—this will be the new start of rnd.

Inc for your size as foll.

First size only
INC RND: [K1 through back loop (tbl), p1, k4, M1, k3, M1, k4, p1, k1tbl, p1] 3 times—54 sts.

Second and third sizes only
INC RND: [K1 through back loop (tbl), p1, [k2, M1] 2 times, k3, [M1, k2] 2 times, p1, k1tbl, p1] 3 times—60 sts.

Fourth size only
INC RND: [K1 through back loop (tbl), p1, [k1, M1] 2 times, [k2, M1] 4 times, k1, p1, k1tbl, p1] 3 times—66 sts.

Cuff
SET-UP RND: *K1tbl, p1; rep from *.

Cont in twisted ribbing as set for 2" (5 cm).

Use the Russian Lace method (see page 52) to BO all sts.

Finishing
Weave in loose ends. Block as desired (see page 18).

The CƏRPITƏ Sock

Worked top down, this sock features a startlingly easy allover colorwork design. The very regular pattern is quickly memorized. Because a color is never worked for more than three consecutive stitches, it's relatively easy to maintain even tension, which makes this a good choice for first-time colorwork. The simplicity of the patterning makes it easy to adjust to different foot and leg lengths, too.

FINISHED SIZE

Ankle/foot circumference: 7¾ (8¼, 8¾, 9, 9½)" (19.5 [21, 22, 23, 24] cm).

Leg length: Adjustable to fit.

Foot length: Adjustable to fit; finished length should be about ½" (1.3 cm) shorter than the actual foot length.

Sock shown measures 8¼" (21 cm) ankle/foot circumference.

YARN

CYCA #1, Super Fine.

Shown here: Opal Sock Yarn (75% superwash wool, 25% nylon; 465 yd [425 m]/100 g): #3072 Violet (MC) and #3081 Natural (CC), 1 ball each.

NEEDLES

Size U.S. 2 (2.75 mm): set of 4 double-pointed (dpn), two circular (cir) or one long cir, as you prefer (see page 20).

NOTIONS

Tapestry needle.

GAUGE

40 sts and 40 rnds = 4" (10 cm) in colorwork patt worked in rnds.

Notes

+ Choose a size based on actual foot circumference, with zero, or even a little positive, ease.

+ This pattern works for any sock yarn that specifies a gauge of 30 to 32 stitches in 4" (10 cm).

+ The sock is calculated at the colorwork gauge, with zero ease.

+ You may need to use a larger needle than usual to achieve gauge.

+ When working corrugated ribbing, both yarns must sit at the back. When purling the CC stitches, bring the yarn to the front, purl the stitch, and then immediately take the yarn to the back again.

THE CARPITA SOCK

The Carpita Sock is an example of a straightforward stranded-colorwork sock worked from the top down.

For this sock, I used the formulas above for calculating the stitch count for the foot and leg, basing both on the actual ankle circumference without adjusting for negative ease. In other words, my ease adjustment for this sock is 1.

**Sock Stitches = Ankle Circumference ×
Stockinette Gauge in Stitches per Inch**

The number of rows in the heel flap is the same as a sock knitted in single-color stockinette stitch. My gauge with this yarn in single-color stockinette is 8 stitches per inch (2.5 cm). To determine the number of rows to work in the heel flap, I just looked up the number from the table on pages 42–45 for the appropriate finished sock circumference at that gauge. The heel turn numbers HT1 and HT2, however, had to be based on the actual stitch count in the heel flap—either by using the formulas or by using the numbers in the table that correspond to the same number of stitches in the heel.

To tighten the edge stitches and prevent gaps in the fabric, I held both yarns together when working the first and last stitch of the heel flap and heel turn rows. When working the heel flap, this is the stitch that was slipped at the beginning of every row and only worked at the end of the row. For the heel turn, this is the decrease stitch. The double-stranded stitches in the heel flap aren't visible in the finished sock—they get buried beneath the picked-up stitches. The double-stranded stitches at the edge of the heel turn end up on the bottom of your foot, so they're not visible either.

Tips for Working Stranded Colorwork

Whether you carry both yarns in the same hand or one in each hand, be sure to keep the positions of the two yarns the same throughout the sock. No matter how good and even and tidy a knitter you are, the two yarns travel in slightly different paths, which result in slightly different tensions. One will be slightly looser, which will create larger and more prominent stitches (this is considered the "dominant" color). The difference may be imperceptible as you work, but will be surprisingly noticeable in the finished piece, even after blocking. Make note of how you hold the two yarns at the beginning and be consistent throughout both socks.

Ladders of loose stitches (see page 24) at needle boundaries can cause an interesting problem in this type of colorwork design. Loose stitches will affect the appearance of the colorwork pattern and potentially change the color dominance. To minimize this effect, I used two circular needles and arranged the stitches so that a two-stitch "seam" was positioned at the start of each needle. If one of these stitches is a bit looser, it won't be noticeable in the solid stripe.

Cuff

Using the two-color alternating method (see page 120), CO in two colors as foll: *[1 CC, 1 MC] 18 (19, 20, 21, 22) times, 1 CC, 2 MC; rep from * once—78 (82, 86, 90, 94) sts total.

Distribute sts across needles as you prefer and join for working in rnds, being careful not to twist sts.

Keeping both yarns in back, work corrugated ribbing by knitting the MC sts and purling the CC sts, bringing the yarn to front to purl, then bringing the yarn to back again before the next st.

Cont in rib as set until piece measures 2" (5 cm) from CO.

Leg

NEXT RND: *Beg at right side of chart (see pages 121 and 122) for your size, work Row 1 of Leg chart to left side of chart; rep from * once more.

Work as set until leg is desired length, repeating Rows 2–13 (1–12, 2–13, 2–13, 1–12) and ending with Row 13 (1, 13, 13, 1).

Heel
HEEL FLAP

The heel flap is worked back and forth on the first 37 (39, 41, 43, 45) sts; rem 41 (43, 45, 47, 49) sts will be worked later for instep.

In the heel flap and heel turn, work the last st of each row with MC and CC held tog (noted as "MC&CC") to make the edges of the flap and heel turn tighter and tidier.

ROW 1: (RS) [K1CC, k1MC] 18 (19, 20, 21, 22) times, k1MC&CC.

ROW 2: (WS) Sl 1, [p1MC, p1CC] 17 (18, 19, 20, 21) times, p1MC, p1MC&CC.

ROW 3: Sl 1, [k1MC, k1CC] 17 (18, 19, 20, 21) times, k1MC, k1MC&CC.

ROW 4: Sl 1, [p1MC, p1CC] 17 (18, 19, 20, 21) times, p1MC, p1MC&CC.

Rep Rows 3 and 4 until a total of 26 (26, 28, 30, 32) rows have been worked, ending with a WS row.

TURN HEEL

Cont the vertical stripe patt in colors as set, work short-rows as foll.

ROW 1: (RS) Work 25 (26, 27, 29, 30) sts in patt as set, ssk with MC&CC, turn work.

ROW 2: (WS) Sl 1, work 13 (13, 13, 15, 15) sts in patt as set, p2tog with MC&CC, turn work.

ROW 3: Sl 1, work 13 (13, 13, 15, 15) sts in patt as set, ssk (1 st each side of gap) with MC&CC, turn work.

ROW 4: Sl 1, work 13 (13, 13, 15, 15) sts in patt as set, p2tog (1 st each side of gap) with MC&CC, turn work.

Rep the last 2 rows 9 (10, 11, 11, 12) more times until all sts have been worked, ending with a WS row—15 (15, 15, 17, 17) sts rem.

Cut yarn.

Gusset

Rejoin both yarns at end of instep/top of gusset.

Beg with MC and alternating yarns, pick up and knit 19 (19, 20, 21, 22) sts along selvedge edge at side of heel, using slipped sts as a guide (see page 36). Because you'll pick up more than the usual number of sts, you'll have to pick up 2 sts in some of the slipped sts. Knit the heel sts, alternating colors as you go (note that the colors may or may not align with the colors in the heel sts; it doesn't matter). Cont alternating colors, pick up and knit 19 (19, 20, 21, 22) sts along other selvedge edge of heel flap, using slipped sts as a guide and picking up 2 sts in some slipped sts as before—94 (96, 100, 106, 110) sts total; 53 (53, 55, 59, 61) sole sts, 41 (43, 45, 47, 49) instep sts.

Rnd begs at beg of instep sts.

From here on, the instep will cont in the charted patt as set with a 2-st MC

Two-Color Alternating Cast-On

This cast-on is based on the long-tail method (see page 34), but creates a clever two-color edge that flows nicely into the corrugated ribbing.

Holding MC (light) and CC (dark) together, make a slipknot and place on needle. The slipknot does not count as a stitch; drop it off the needle on the first row/round.

Set up as for the long-tail method, wrapping MC around your thumb and CC around your index finger. *Cast on 1 st with CC as for the long-tail method (Figure 1). Bring the needle over to pick up the far strand on your finger, coming around and under it, then back toward you and under the nearest strand on your thumb, picking it up from under, and then back through the loop on your finger (Figure 2). Remove your finger from the loop, then tension the yarn to cast on 1 st with MC (Figure 3).

Repeat from * for the desired number of stitches.

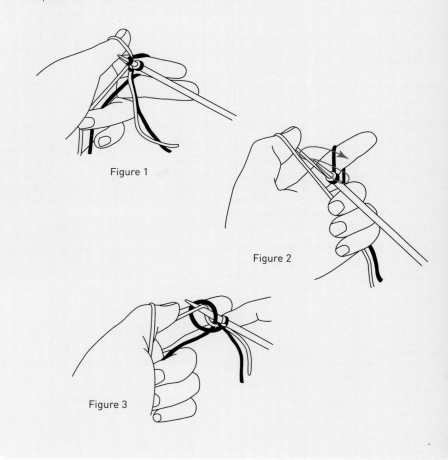

Figure 1

Figure 2

Figure 3

"seam" on each side; the sole will be worked in a simple salt-and-pepper patt of alternating colors.

SET-UP RND: Work instep sts in patt as set but work them through their back loops (tbl), [k1tblCC, ktblMC] 9 (9, 10, 10, 10, 11) times, k1tblCC 1 (1, 0, 1, 0) time, knit heel sts as established, k1tbl CC 1 (1, 0, 1, 0) time, [k1tblMC, k1tblCC] 9 (9, 10, 10, 10, 11) times.

RND 1: Work instep sts in patt as set, ssk with CC, *k1MC, k1CC; rep from * to 3 sts before end of sole, k1MC, k2tog with CC—2 sts dec'd.

RND 2: Work instep sts in patt as set, *k1MC, k1CC; rep from * to last sole st, k1MC.

RND 3: Work instep sts in patt as set, ssk with MC, *k1CC, k1MC; rep from * to 3 sts before end of sole, k1CC, k2tog with MC—2 sts dec'd.

RND 4: Work instep sts in patt as set, *k1CC, k1MC; rep from * to last sole st, k1CC.

Rep these 4 rnds 3 (2, 2, 3, 3) more times, then rep Rnds 1 and 2 only 0 (1, 1, 0, 0) more time—78 (82, 86, 90, 94) sts rem; 37 (39, 41, 43, 45) sole sts.

Leg chart, 1st size

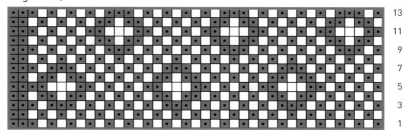

39 sts

Leg chart, 2nd size

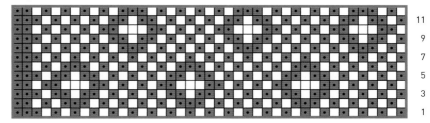

41 sts

Leg chart, 3rd size

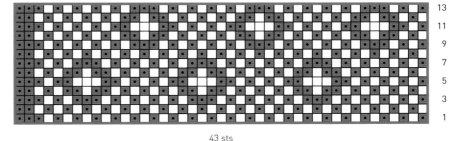

43 sts

☐ MC   ▣ CC   ☐ pattern repeat

Foot

Work even in patt as set until foot measures 2 (2, 2, 2½, 2½)" (5 [5, 5, 6.5 6.5] cm) less than desired finished sock foot length, ending with Rnd 7 or 13 (6 or 12, 7 or 13, 7 or 13, 6 or 12) of instep patt.

NEXT RND: Alternate 1 st of each color, reversing the colors of the previous rnd.

Toe

To set up for the toe, k1MC—this is the new beg of rnd. Slip the last instep st to the start of the sole, so that the instep and sole both beg and end with k1MC.

Note: It doesn't matter how the colors are lined up in the transition between foot and toe; you're going to change the pattern to create vertical stripes, and on the first toe round they might

line up with the last foot round, which means that your striping is established immediately; if they don't, your striping will be set one round later.

RND 1: K1MC, sskCC, *k1CC, k1MC; rep from * to 4 sts before end of instep, k1CC, k2togCC, k1MC; k1MC, sskCC, **k1CC, k1MC; rep from ** to 4 sts before end of sole, k1CC, k2togCC, k1MC—4 sts dec'd.

Leg chart, 4th size

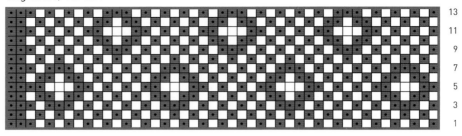

45 sts

Leg chart, 5th size

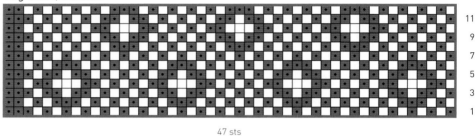

47 sts

☐ MC   ▪ CC   ☐ pattern repeat

RND 2: K1MC, k2CC, *k1MC, k1CC; rep from * to last 2 sts of instep, k1CC, k1MC; k1MC, k2CC, **k1MC, k1CC; rep from * to last 2 sts of rnd, k1CC, k1MC.

RND 3: K1MC, sskCC, *k1MC, k1CC; rep from * to 4 sts before end of instep, k1MC, k2togCC, k1MC; k1MC, sskCC, **k1 MC, k1 CC; rep from * to 4 sts before end of rnd, k1MC, k2togCC, k1MC—4 sts dec'd.

RND 4: *K1MC, k1CC; rep from * to last st of instep, k1MC; **k1MC, k1CC; rep from ** to last st of sole, k1MC.

Rep these 4 rnds 2 (2, 2, 3, 3) more times, then work Rnds 1 and 2 once more—50 (54, 58, 54, 58) sts rem.

RND 5: K1MC, sskCC, *k1MC, k1CC; rep from * to 4 sts before end of instep, k1MC, k2togCC, k1MC; k1MC, sskCC, **k1MC, k1CC; rep from ** to 4 sts before end of rnd, k1MC, k2togCC, k1MC—4 sts dec'd.

RND 6: K1MC, sskCC, *k1CC, k1MC; rep from * to 4 sts before end of instep, k1CC, k2togCC, k1MC; k1MC, sskCC, **k1MC, k1CC; rep from ** to 4 sts before end of sole, k1CC, k2togMC, k1MC—4 sts dec'd.

Rep the last 2 rnds 2 more times, then work Rnd 5 only 0 (1, 1, 0, 1) more time—26 (26, 30, 30, 30) sts rem.

Cut CC. Adjust sts if necessary so that 13 (13, 15, 15, 15) sts are on each of two needles.

Finishing

Cut MC, leaving a 20" (51 cm) tail. Thread tail on a tapestry needle and use the Kitchener st (see Glossary) to graft rem sts tog.

Weave in loose ends. Block as desired (see page 18).

The Carpita Sock   123

The LINDISFARNE Sock

|||||||||||||||||||||||||||||||||||||||||||||||||||||||||||||||||||||||||||||||

FINISHED SIZE

Ankle circumference: 8 (8, 9, 9, 9¾)" (20.5 [20.5, 23, 23, 25] cm).

Foot circumference: 7½ (8, 8½, 9, 9¼)" (19 [20.5, 21.5, 23, 23.5] cm).

Leg length: Adjustable to fit.

Foot length: Adjustable to fit; finished length should be about ½" (1.3 cm) shorter than actual foot length.

Sock shown measures 8" (20.5 cm) foot circumference.

YARN

CYCA #1, Super Fine.

Shown here: Austermann Step Classic (75% superwash wool, 25% nylon; 459 yd [420 m]/100 g): #1002 Chocolate Brown (MC), #1015 Orange (CC), 1 ball each.

NEEDLES

Size U.S. 2 (2.75 mm): set of 4 double-pointed (dpn), two circular (cir) or one long cir, as you prefer (see page 20).

NOTIONS

Markers (m); tapestry needle.

GAUGE

40½ sts and 44 rnds = 4" (10 cm) in colorwork patt worked in rnds, after blocking.

These socks feature colorwork patterns reminiscent of ancient runes and the symbols on the *Lindisfarne Gospels manuscript* in colors that the 1970s band Lindisfarne might have approved of. Worked from the toe up, this is the more challenging of the colorwork socks in this book. The patterning is a little more complex, and a little bit of thinking is required when working the gusset increases into the pattern to ensure that the pattern on the heel flap aligns with that in the leg.

Notes

+ This pattern works for any sock yarn that specifies a gauge of 30 to 32 stitches in 4" (10 cm).

+ The sock is calculated at the colorwork gauge, with zero ease, for circumferences of 7½ (8, 8½, 9, 9½)" (19 [20.5, 21.5, 23, 24] cm).

+ Choose a size based on actual foot circumference—the sock should be worn with zero, or even a little positive, ease.

+ You may need to use a larger needle than usual to achieve the correct gauge.

+ See page 118 for tips on working stranded colorwork.

+ When working the heel flap, be sure to catch both wraps when working the wrapped stitches tog with their wraps.

+ To create a tidier edge on the heel flap, the decreases are worked with both strands held together.

THE LINDISFARNE SOCK

The Lindisfarne Sock is an example of a toe-up sock worked in stranded colorwork.

The complexity and the size of the pattern repeat in the Lindisfarne Sock forced me into some creative adjustments when it came to providing multiple sizes. There are five foot sizes, but only three leg sizes. Two of the leg sizes use the instep patterning divided by a seam element to add more stitches while preserving the integrity of the pattern; the other leg size uses the basic 18-stitch repeat all the way around.

There are also two versions of the instep pattern—a smaller pattern for smallest two sizes and a larger pattern for the three larger sizes. To compensate for the different numbers of instep stitches, the number of sole stitches isn't the same as the number of instep stitches. This posed a bit of a problem from the very beginning. Judy's magic cast-on requires the same number of stitches on each of two needles. To get the "uneven" numbers of stitches, I had to work some extra increases on half of the cast-on stitches.

The gusset and heel are worked on the modified number of sole stitches (rather than 50 percent of the sock stitches). For the second and third sizes, there's a pretty big difference between the number of sole stitches and 50 percent of the sock stitches, which meant that the sole stitch count doesn't scale with the overall foot size. I based the gusset number based on 50 percent of the sock stitches and, instead of just dividing the sole stitches in thirds to set the heel turn, I played a little with the ratio of heel stitches to heel base stitches. My objective was to keep the number of *wraps* proportionate to the size. (This means that the number of unwrapped stitches remaining in the middle might seem out of line for these two sizes.)

I chose to continue the leg pattern along the heel flap, which required two "tricky" maneuvers—I had to figure out where to start the pattern on the heel flap so that it would align with the established foot pattern at the top

Heels and Toes

One of my earliest colorwork socks was knitted in a gray-and-white hound's-tooth pattern. I had trouble fitting the heel, so I decided to dodge the issue entirely by working the heel and the toe in a solid color.

Of all the socks I've made, these were fastest to wear out. I'd used larger needles for the colorwork portion, and I hadn't thought to change back to smaller needles for the plain heels and toes. Although the fabric was reinforced on the leg and the foot, there was just a single thickness, worked too loosely, on the areas that are most likely to wear out. And wear out they did.

Since then, I always continue a colorwork pattern on the heels and toes. In fact, I once designed a sock that had colorwork patterning *only* on the heels and toes. It doesn't have to be complicated patterning—the simple vertical stripes in The Carpita Sock on page 116 are quite attractive.

If you really do want a solid heel and toe for a particular look, then reinforce those sections with yarn designed for this purpose or work the heel and toes with a double strand of the main yarn (see page 29).

of the heel. For the four sizes for which the sole and instep stitch counts differ, I had to adjust the number of stitches in the first row of the heel flap.

This was one of the more challenging socks in the book to design (certainly the most challenging to write up), and it does require some attention and planning to knit. But I think it's absolutely worth it.

Toe

Using CC and Judy's magic method (see page 49), CO 28 (28, 34, 34, 34) sts—14 (14, 17, 17, 17) sts each on two needles.

Following the chart for your size, work Instep Toe chart across first half of rnd and work Sole Toe chart (see pages 129 and 130) across second half of rnd (note that there are different numbers of instep and sole sts for sizes small, medium, and large)—77 (81, 86, 90, 94) sts when charts are complete; 38 (38, 47, 47, 47) instep sts and 39 (43, 39, 43, 47) sole sts.

Foot

Following the charts for your size, work Instep chart (see pages 130 and 131) across first 38 (38, 47, 47, 47) sts and work Sole chart (see page 131) across rem sts until foot measures 5 (5¼, 5½, 5¾, 6¼)" (12.5 [13.5, 14, 14.5, 16] cm) less than desired finished sock length.

Gusset

Rearrange sts if necessary so that the sole sts are on one needle. Work the gusset incs at each end of the needle holding the sole sts.

Note: The gusset increases are worked into the sole pattern. The color with which you should work the increase depends on where you are in the pattern. If the next sole pattern row is to start (and end) with 2 CC stitches, work the increases in MC. If the next sole pattern row is to start (and end) with 2 MC stitches, work the increases in CC. If the next sole pattern row is to start (and end) with 1 CC stitch, work the increases in CC; if the next sole pattern row is to start (and end) with 1 MC stitch, work the increases in MC.

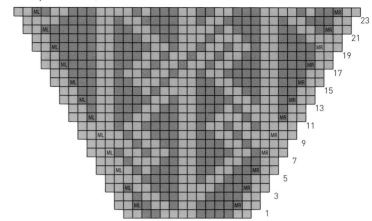

Instep Toe chart, 1st and 2nd sizes

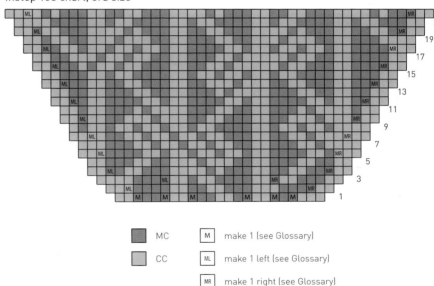

Instep Toe chart, 3rd size

	MC		M	make 1 (see Glossary)
	CC		ML	make 1 left (see Glossary)
			MR	make 1 right (see Glossary)

RND 1: Work instep sts in patt as set, M1R (see Glossary), place marker (pm) for beg of heel, knit to end of rnd, pm for end of heel, M1L (see Glossary)—2 sts inc'd.

RND 2: Work instep sts in patt as set, knit to end of rnd.

RND 3: Work instep sts in patt as set, M1R, knit to end of rnd, M1L—2 sts inc'd.

RND 4: Work instep sts in patt as set, knit to end of rnd.

Rep the last 2 rnds 13 (14, 15, 16, 17) more times—15 (16, 17, 18, 19) gusset sts per side; 107 (113, 120, 126, 132) sts total.

Heel

Note: After Row 1 is complete, make a note of the last instep pattern row worked. Use both yarns for the wrap in the wrap & turn.

TURN HEEL

Work short-rows (see Glossary) as foll.

Instep Toe chart, 4th size

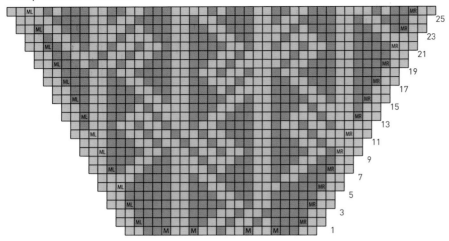

Instep Toe chart, 5th size

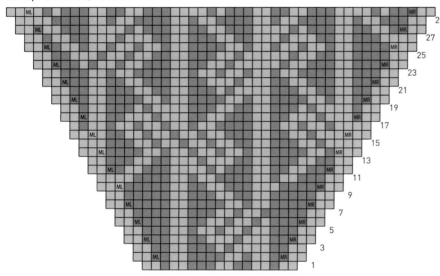

ROW 1: (RS) Work instep in patt as set, knit to 1 st before second heel m, wrap next st and turn work (w&t).

ROW 2: (WS) Purl to 1 st before m, w&t.

Working only on the heel sts, cont as foll.

ROW 3: (RS) Knit to st before last wrapped st, w&t.

ROW 4: (WS) Purl to st before last wrapped st, w&t.

Rep Rows 3 and 4 until 13 (17, 13, 15, 17) sts rem unwrapped in the middle, ending with a WS row—13 (13, 13, 14, 15) wraps on each side.

Remove heel markers.

HEEL FLAP

Notes: Please read the following before you proceed.

1. At this point, the pattern begins on the back of the leg—to figure out where to start, count back from the end of the instep pattern. There are 26 (26, 26, 28, 30) rows in the heel flap; the last row should be the same as the last instep row. Count back that many rows in the Instep chart from the last row worked. For example, if you ended the instep pattern on Row 12, and you're working 28 heel flap rows, count back 18 rows (to Row 13) and then another 10 rows (to Row 3); you'll begin the heel flap on Row 3.

2. For all but the fourth size, you'll have to adjust the stitch count when working the first row of the heel flap. See the individual pattern rows for details. Because I can't predict what row you'll be on, there's no way for me to tell you how to place the increases/decreases. Work across the stitches of the chart indicated, working increases or decreases in the color pattern to bring you to the required stitch count. The backward-loop method (see Glossary) is the easiest increase to work in this case.

3. For the first, second, and fifth sizes, the leg patterning is as follows: [k2 MC, Instep chart as set] 2 times. The heel flap is worked as follows: first stitch with both yarns, 1 MC, Instep chart, 1 MC, last stitch with both yarns.

4. For the third and fourth sizes, the Leg chart is worked 5 times around. The rows line up with the Instep pattern, but you'll change over to using the Leg chart in the place of the Instep chart. The heel flap is worked as follows: first stitch with both yarns, stitches 2–18 of leg pattern, stitches 1–18 of leg pattern, stitches 1–8 of leg pattern, last st with both yarns.

Work the heel flap and dec gusset sts for your size as foll.

First size only

ROW 1: (RS) Starting with the 12th st of next patt row (see notes above), work 13 unwrapped heel sts and *at the same time* inc 3 sts; cont in patt, knit the next 11 wrapped sts tog with their wraps, with MC knit 1 wrapped st tog with its wrap, then use both yarns to work sssk (see Glossary) on this final st tog with its wraps and the first 2 gusset sts—42 heel flap sts; 2 gusset sts on one side dec'd.

Second size only

ROW 1: (RS) Starting with the 12th st of next patt row (see Notes above), work 17 unwrapped heel sts and *at the same time* work k2tog in the center of these sts; cont in patt, knit the next 11 wrapped sts tog with their wraps, with MC knit 1 wrapped st tog with its wrap, then use both yarns to work sssk (see Glossary) on this final st tog with its wraps and the first 2 gusset sts—42 heel flap sts; 2 gusset sts on one side dec'd.

Third size only

ROW 1: (RS): Starting with the 14th st of next patt row (see Notes above), work 13 unwrapped heel sts and *at the same time* inc 4 sts; cont in patt, knit the next 12 wrapped sts tog with their wraps, then use both yarns to work sssk (see Glossary) on this final st tog with its wraps and the first 2 gusset sts—43 heel flap sts; 2 gusset sts on one side dec'd.

Fourth size only

ROW 1: (RS) Starting with the 15th st of next patt row (see Notes above), work 15 unwrapped heel sts; cont in patt, knit the next 13 wrapped sts tog with their wraps, then use both yarns to work sssk (see Glossary) on

Sole Toe chart, 1st size

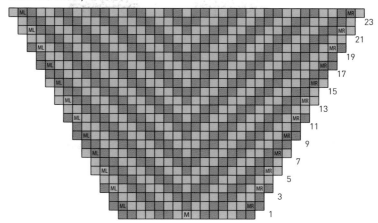

Sole Toe chart, 2nd size

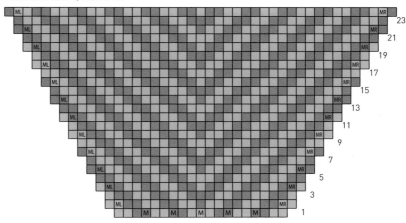

Sole Toe chart, 3rd size

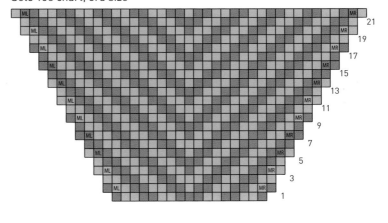

	MC		M	make 1 (see Glossary)
	CC		ML	make 1 left (see Glossary)
			MR	make 1 right (see Glossary)

Sole Toe chart, 4th size

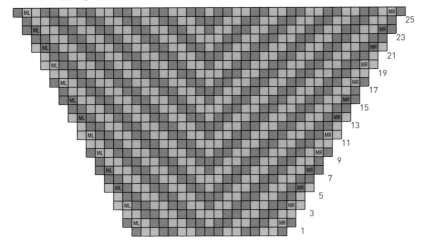

Sole Toe chart, 5th size

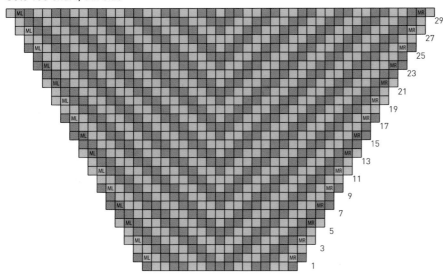

Instep chart, 1st and 2nd sizes

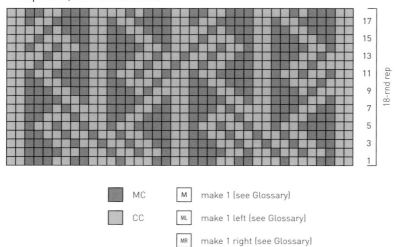

18-rnd rep

	MC		M	make 1 (see Glossary)
	CC		ML	make 1 left (see Glossary)
			MR	make 1 right (see Glossary)

this final st tog with its wraps and the first 2 gusset sts—43 heel flap sts; 2 gusset sts on one side dec'd.

Fifth size only

ROW 1: (RS) Starting with the 14th st of next patt row (see notes above), work 17 unwrapped heel sts and *at the same time* inc 4 sts; cont in patt, knit the next 13 wrapped sts tog with their wraps, with MC knit 1 wrapped st tog with its wraps, then use both yarns to work sssk (see Glossary) on this final st tog with its wraps and the first 2 gusset sts—51 heel flap sts; 2 gusset sts on one side dec'd.

All sizes

Cont as foll.

ROW 2: (WS) Sl 1, purl in color pattern, working 12 (12, 12, 13, 14) wrapped sts tog with their two wraps, and with both yarns, work p3tog on this final st tog with its wrap and the first two of the gusset sts—2 gusset sts dec'd on one side. Turn work.

ROWS 3 AND 5: (RS) Sl 1, work 40 (40, 41, 41, 49) sts in color patt as set, sssk—2 gusset sts dec'd.

ROWS 4 AND 6: (WS) Sl 1, work 40 (40, 41, 41, 49) sts in color patt as set, p3tog—2 gusset sts dec'd.

ROW 7: Sl 1, work 40 (40, 41, 41, 49) sts in color patt as set, ssk—1 gusset st dec'd.

ROW 8: Sl 1, work 40 (40, 41, 41, 49) sts in color patt as set, p2tog—1 gusset st dec'd.

Rep Rows 7 and 8 until 1 gusset st rem on each side, ending with a WS row—82 (82, 92, 92, 100) sts rem.

Instep chart, 3rd, 4th, and 5th sizes

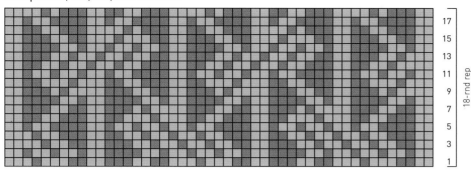

18-rnd rep

17 15 13 11 9 7 5 3 1

Leg chart, 3rd and 4th sizes

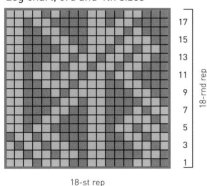

18-rnd rep

17 15 13 11 9 7 5 3 1

18-st rep

Sole chart, 1st, 3rd, and 5th sizes

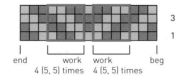

3 1

end · · · work 4 (5, 5) times · · · work 4 (5, 5) times · · · beg

Sole chart, 2nd and 4th sizes

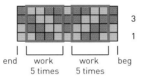

3 1

end · · · work 5 times · · · work 5 times · · · beg

Leg

Rejoin for working in rnds, working the final gusset decs in the first rnd as foll.

SET-UP RND 1: Sl 1, work 40 (40, 41, 41, 49) sts in color patt as set, ssk in color as set by chart patt, work across instep in patt as set. This is the new start of rnd.

SET-UP RND 2: K2tog in color set by chart, work to end of rnd in color patt as set—80 (80, 90, 90, 98) sts rem.

Cont for your size as foll.

First, second, and fifth sizes only
RND 1: [Work Instep patt as set, k2MC] 2 times.

Third and fourth sizes only
RND 1: Work Leg chartt 5 times around.

All sizes
Cont even in patt as set until leg measures 1" (2.5 cm) less than desired total length.

Cuff

Set up the ribbing for your size as foll.

First and second sizes only
SET-UP RND: *[K2CC, (k1MC, k1CC) 3 times, k1MC] 4 times, k2CC, k2MC; rep from * once more.

RND 1: *[K2CC, (p1MC, k1CC) 3 times, p1MC] 4 times, k2CC, p2MC; rep from * once more.

Third and fourth sizes only
SET-UP RND: *[K1MC, k1CC] 3 times, k1MC, k2CC; rep from *.

RND 1: *[P1MC, k1CC] 3 times, p1MC, k2CC; rep from *.

Fifth size only
SET-UP RND: *[K2CC, (k1MC, k1CC) 3 times, k1MC] 5 times, k2CC, k2MC; rep from * once more.

RND 1: [K2CC, (p1MC, k1CC) 3 times, p1MC] 5 times, k2CC, p2MC; rep from * once more.

All sizes
Cont in ribbing as set for 1" (2.5 cm).

Cut CC.

With MC, knit 2 rnds.

BO all sts knitwise. This creates a small rolled top that harmonizes nicely with the patt. It also eliminates the need for a special stretchy BO because the yarn worked singly has a much looser gauge than the color-work patt.

Finishing

Weave in loose ends. Block as desired (see page 18).

The HARCOURT Sock

FINISHED SIZE

Leg circumference: 6½ (7¼, 8¼, 8¼)" (16.5 [18.5, 21, 21] cm).

Foot circumference: 6½ (7¼, 8, 8½)" (16.5 [18.5, 20.5, 21.5] cm).

Leg length: Adjustable to fit.

Foot length: Adjustable to fit; finished length should be about ½" (1.3 cm) shorter than actual foot length.

Sock shown measures 7¼" (18.5 cm) foot circumference.

YARN

CYCA #1, Super Fine.

Shown here: Skeinny Dipping Cannonball (80% superwash merino, 20% nylon; 390 yd [357 m]/100 g): Persimmon, 1 skein.

NEEDLES

Size U.S. 1.5 (2.5 mm): set of 4 double-pointed (dpn), two circular (cir) or one long cir, as you prefer (see page 20).

NOTIONS

Markers (m); tapestry needle.

GAUGE

32 sts and 48 rnds = 4" (10 cm) in St st worked in rnds.

29½ sts and 48 rnds = 4" (10 cm) in lace patt worked in rnds, after blocking.

These socks follow an impactful, but easy-to-work, lace pattern that looks particularly nice in not-entirely solid hand-dyed yarns. The instructions here are for working the sock both from the cuff down and the toe up. The direction will affect the appearance of the lace pattern, but you have to look closely to see the difference.

Notes

+ This pattern works for any sock yarn that specifies a gauge of 30 to 32 stitches in 4" (10 cm).

+ Choose a size based on foot circumference, allowing for the usual 10 percent negative ease; the leg pattern is very stretchy and accommodating.

+ Choose pattern size based on foot circumference.

+ The lace pattern is very straightforward except for one small tricky step: the decrease worked at the start of Round 15 of the pattern is worked over the last stitch of the previous round and the first stitch of the next round; for the leg of both socks and the foot of the toe-up sock, this is straightforward. For the foot of the top-down sock, it requires a bit of a cheat: the first decrease is worked over the last sole stitch and the first instep stitch; the resulting stitch remains part of the sole, and the final instep stitch is worked as a plain knit stitch.

THE HARCOURT SOCK

For the Harcourt Sock, I chose a lace pattern with a 6-stitch repeat, which limited the number of stitches in the leg to multiples of 6. I created additional sizes by adjusting the number of stitches in the foot.

Although the number of cuff stitches might seem smaller than normal for the first three sizes (the stockinette gauge suggests 56, 60, and 64 stitches, respectively, but I'm using 48, 54, and 60 stitches), I took advantage of the stretchy properties of the ribbing to keep things simple. For the largest size, the cuff has a slightly irregular ribbing, followed by a decrease round to achieve the proper stitch count for the lace pattern in the leg.

The various heel sizes involve changes in both the length and width of the heel flap. To ensure full 6-stitch pattern repeats on the instep, the heel is worked on the same number of stitches for the two smallest sizes.

In the top-down version, the number of heel rows (and, therefore, the number of picked-up gusset stitches) is not set by the number of heel flap stitches, but rather by what you'd work for a sock of the same circumfer-

ence in in plain stockinette stitch. For the two smaller sizes, the heel turn itself is adjusted so that the center strap is the same width as it would be for stranded stockinette stitch. For these two sizes, the center heel strap is proportionately wider than the typical one-third and therefore the sides are a little narrower, there are fewer gusset decreases, and the heel flap is shorter. As a consequence, the gusset decreases end a little earlier in the foot. If the socks feel tight across the gusset area, you can adjust the gusset length (and therefore, make a wider foot in this area) by working an extra round even between the gusset decrease rounds (i.e., work two even rounds instead of just one between decrease rounds).

In the toe-up version, the number of gusset stitches is also determined by the number you'd need for a plain stockinette-stitch sock of the same circumference, which also determines the number of rows in the heel flap. The number of stitches in the center portion of the heel base is proportionate to the number of stitches that would be in the equivalent stockinette sock.

The same lace chart is worked for both the top-down and toe-up versions. Upon close examination, the patterns are slightly different—the diagonal decrease lines are to the left of the eyelets in the toe-up version (on the left in the photo), while they're to the right of the eyelets in the top-down version (on the right in the photo). However, the overall zigzag pattern looks the same.

top down   *toe up*

TOP-DOWN VERSION

Cuff

CO 48 (54, 60, 66) sts. Distribute sts across needles as you prefer and join for working in rnds, being careful not to twist sts.

Cont for your size as foll.

First, second, and third sizes only
SET-UP RND: *K1, p1; rep from *.

Fourth size only
SET-UP RND: *[K1, p1] 4 times, k1, p2; rep from *.

All sizes
Cont in ribbing as set until piece measures 1" (2.5 cm) from CO.

Leg

First, second, and third sizes only
SET-UP: K1—this becomes the new start of rnd.

Fourth size only
SET-UP: *[K1, p1] 4 times, k1, p2tog; rep from * to end of rnd, then k1 (first st of next rnd)—60 sts; this becomes the new start of rnd.

All sizes
Work Rows 1–16 of Zigzag Lace chart until leg measures about 7" (18 cm) from CO or desired length to top of heel, ending with an even-numbered rnd.

Heel
HEEL FLAP
The heel flap is worked back and forth on half of the leg sts.

Cont for your size as foll.

First size only
ROW 1: (RS) K24, turn work—24 heel sts.

Second size only
ROW 1: (RS) [K8, M1] 2 times, k8, turn work—26 heel sts.

Third and fourth sizes only
ROW 1: (RS) K30, turn work—30 heel sts.

All sizes
Place rem 24 (28, 30, 30) sts onto spare needle or holder to work later for instep.

Beg with a WS row, work 24 (26, 30, 30) heel sts back and forth in rows as foll.

ROW 2: (WS) Sl 1, p23 (25, 29, 29).

ROW 3: (RS) Sl 1, k23 (25, 29, 29).

ROW 4: Sl 1, Sl 1, p23 (25, 29, 29).

Rep Rows 3 and 4 until a total of 22 (24, 26, 28) rows have been worked, ending with a WS row.

TURN HEEL
Work short-rows as foll.

ROW 1: (RS) K16 (18, 20, 20), ssk, turn work.

ROW 2: (WS) Sl 1, p8 (10, 10, 10), p2tog, turn work.

ROW 3: Sl 1, k8 (10, 10, 10), ssk (1 st each side of gap), turn work.

ROW 4: Sl 1, p8 (10, 10, 10), p2tog (1 st each side of gap), turn work.

Rep Rows 3 and 4 until all sts have been worked, ending with a WS row—10 (12, 12, 12) sts rem.

Zigzag Lace chart

✓					o	15
				o	✓	13
			o	✓		11
		o	✓			9
✗	o					7
✗	o					5
	✗	o				3
	✗	o				1

- ☐ knit
- ⊙ yo
- ✗ ssk
- ✓ k2tog
- ☐ pattern repeat

Gusset

K10 (12, 12, 12) heel sts, then, with the same needle, pick up and knit 13 (14, 15, 16) sts along selvedge edge at side of heel, using slipped sts as a guide (see page 36). With a new needle, work lace patt as set across 24 (28, 30, 30) instep sts. With another new needle, pick up and knit 13 (14, 15, 16) sts along selvedge edge at other side of heel, using slipped sts as a guide, then work the first 5 (6, 6, 6) sts from the first needle again—60 (68, 72, 74) sts total; 24 (28, 30, 30) instep sts, 18 (20, 21, 22) sts between end of rnd and each side of instep.

Rnd begins at center of heel. If you're working on two cir needles or using the magic-loop method, place a marker in this position.

SET-UP RND: K5 (6, 6, 6), k13 (14, 15, 16) through back loop (tbl), work instep sts in patt as set, k13 (14, 15, 16) tbl, knit to end of rnd.

DEC RND: Knit to 3 sts before instep, k2tog, k1, work instep sts in patt, k1, ssk, knit to end of rnd—2 sts dec'd.

NEXT RND: Knit to instep, work instep sts in patt as set, knit to end of rnd.

Rep the last 2 rnds 4 (5, 5, 4) more times—50 (56, 60, 64) sts rem.

Foot

Work even in patt as set until foot measures 1¼ (1½, 1¾, 1¾) (3.2 [3.8, 4.5, 4.5] cm) less than desired finished sock foot length.

Toe

Rearrange sts if necessary so that there are 25 (28, 30, 32) sts each for the sole and instep. Cont in St st as foll.

DEC RND: Knit to 3 sts before start of instep, k2tog, k2, ssk, knit to 3 sts before end of instep, k2tog, k2, ssk, knit to end of rnd—4 sts dec'd.

Work 1 rnd even.

Rep the last 2 rnds 4 (5, 6, 6) more times—30 (32, 32, 36) sts rem.

Rep dec rnd every rnd 5 (6, 6, 7) times—10 (8, 8, 8) sts rem.

Cut yarn, leaving an 8" (20.5 cm) tail. Thread tail on a tapestry needle, draw through rem sts, pull tight to close hole, and secure on WS.

Finishing

Weave in loose ends. Block as desired (see page 18).

TOE-UP VERSION

Toe

Using Judy's magic method (see page 49), CO 18 (20, 20, 24) sts— 9 (10, 10, 12) sts each on two needles.

Place a safety pin or marker in the toe to indicate beg of rnd and a second one to indicate the center of the rnd.

INC RND: K1, M1R (see Glossary), knit to 1 st before center of rnd, M1L (see Glossary), k2, M1R, knit to 1 st before end of rnd, M1L, k1— 4 sts inc'd.

Knit 1 rnd even.

Rep the last 2 rnds 7 (8, 9, 9) more times—50 (56, 60, 64) sts total.

Foot

Cont for your size as foll.

First and Fourth sizes only
SET-UP: K1—this becomes the new start of rnd.

Second size only
SET-UP: Knit to 1 st before end of rnd—this becomes the new start of rnd.

All sizes
Rnd starts at start of instep sts.

NEXT RND: Work Row 1 of Zigzag Lace chart across 24 (24, 30, 30) sts for instep, knit to end of rnd for sole.

Rearrange sts on needles or place markers as desired.

Cont even in patt as set until foot measures 3¼ (4, 3¾, 4¼)" (8.5 [10, 9.5, 11] cm) less than desired finished sock foot length.

Gusset

Rearrange sts if necessary so that the sole sts are on one needle. Work the gusset incs at each end of the needle holding the sole sts.

RND 1: Work instep sts in patt as set, M1R, place marker (pm) for beg of heel, knit to end of rnd, pm for end of heel, M1L—2 sts inc'd.

RND 2: Work instep sts in patt as set, knit to end of rnd.

RND 3: Work instep sts in patt as set, M1R, knit to end of rnd, M1L—2 sts inc'd.

RND 4: Work instep sts in patt as set, knit to end of rnd.

Rep the last 2 rnds 9 (10, 11, 12) more times—72 (80, 86, 92) sts total.

Heel
TURN HEEL
Work short-rows (see Glossary) as foll.

ROW 1: (RS) Work instep in patt as set, knit to 1 st before second heel m, wrap next st and turn work (w&t).

ROW 2: (WS) Purl to 1 st before m, w&t.

Working only on the heel sts, cont as foll.

ROW 3: (RS) Knit to st before last wrapped st, w&t.

ROW 4: (WS) Purl to st before last wrapped st, w&t.

Rep Rows 3 and 4 until 8 (8, 10,12) sts rem unwrapped in the middle, ending with a WS row.

Remove heel markers.

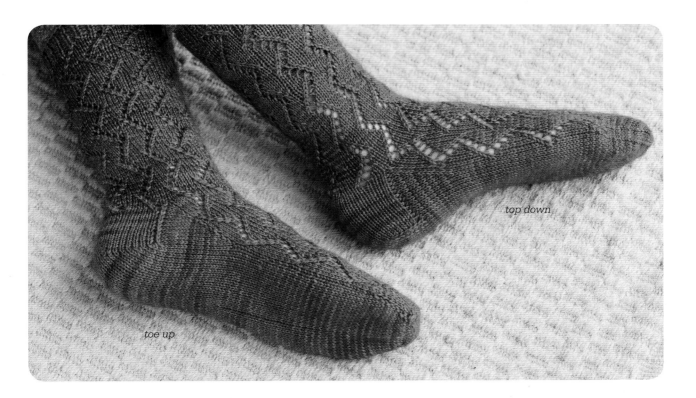

toe up

top down

HEEL FLAP

Work the heel flap and dec gusset sts as foll.

ROW 1: (RS) Knit to first wrapped st, *knit the wrapped st tog with its wrap; rep from * until 1 wrapped st rem, ssk (final st tog with its wrap and the first gusset st), turn work.

ROW 2: (WS) Sl 1, purl to first wrapped st, *purl the wrapped st tog with its wrap; rep from * until 1 wrapped st rem, p2tog (final st tog with its wrap and the first gusset st), turn work.

ROW 3: Sl 1, k24 (30, 28, 32), ssk, turn work.

ROW 4: Sl 1, p24 (30, 28, 32), p2tog, turn work.

Rep Rows 3 and 4 until only 1 gusset st rem on each side, ending with a WS row—52 (58, 62, 66) sts rem.

Leg

Note: The first round of the leg adjusts the stitch count on the heel to make an even multiple of 6 stitches; the final gusset stitches are decreased in this round.

Cont for your size as foll.

First (second) sizes only

RND 1: Sl 1, k7 (9), k2tog, k6 (8), k2tog, k7 (9), ssk, work instep sts in patt as set—49 (55) sts rem.

Third size only

RND 1: Sl 1, k28, ssk, work instep sts in patt as set—61 sts rem.

Fourth size only

RND 1: Sl 1, [k5, k2tog] 2 times, k4, [k2tog, k5] 2 times, ssk, work instep sts in patt as set—61 sts rem.

All sizes

RND 2: K2tog, k23 (29, 29, 29)—48 (54, 60, 60) sts; this is the new start of the rnd.

Cont in patt as set until Rnd 8 or 16 of patt is completed.

NEXT RND: Work patt across all sts.

Cont in patt as set until leg measures 6" (15 cm), or 1" (2.5 cm) less than desired total length.

Note: The pattern looks best if it ends on Rnd 8 or 16, but it's not critical.

Cuff

Work in k1, p1 ribbing for 1" (2.5 cm).

Using a stretchy method (see page 52), BO all sts.

Finishing

Weave in loose ends. Block as desired (see page 18).

The WELLINGTON ROAD Sock

|||||||||||||||| | | | — | — | — | — | — | — | — | — | — |||| | | | — | — | — |||| | | | — | — | — ||||| |||

FINISHED SIZE
Ankle/foot circumference, lightly stretched: 7 (7½, 8, 8½, 9, 9½)" (18 [19, 20.5, 21.5, 23, 24] cm).

Leg length: 7¾" (19.5 cm) with an option for 4" (10 cm) alternative.

Foot length: Adjustable to fit; finished length should be about ½" (1.3 cm) shorter than actual foot length.

Sock shown measures 7½" (19 cm) ankle/foot circumference.

YARN
CYCA #1, Super Fine.

Shown here: Miss Babs Cosmic Hand-Painted Sock Yarn (80% superwash merino, 20% nylon; 400 yd [366 m]/100 g): Roasted Pumpkin, 1 (1, 2, 2, 2, 2) skein(s).

NEEDLES
Size U.S. 1.5 (2.5 mm): set of 4 double-pointed (dpn), two circular (cir) or one long cir, as you prefer (see page 20).

NOTIONS
Cable needle (cn); markers (m); tapestry needle.

GAUGE
32 sts and 45 rnds = 4" (10 cm) in St st worked in rnds.

This top-down sock features a striking asymmetrical cable that contrasts nicely against the mostly stockinette-stitch background. It also makes the knitting a littler easier and faster than an allover cabled sock. There are left and right versions of the cables, depending on the direction of the central cable. It's a minor detail that has a nice effect—it adds a bit of fun in the knitting and helps combat second-sock syndrome.

Notes
+ This pattern works for any sock yarn that specifies a gauge of 30 to 32 stitches in 4" (10 cm).

+ The instructions that follow are based on the Basic Pattern on page 40 worked at a gauge of 8 stitches per inch (2.5 cm) with finished sizes of 7 (7½, 8, 8½, 9, 9½)" (18 [19, 20.5, 21.5, 23, 24] cm).

+ Choose a size based on foot circumference, allowing for the usual 10 percent negative ease.

+ The cable element splits at the start of the instep to create two smaller cable repeats for the heel and foot.

THE WELLINGTON ROAD SOCK

The Wellington Road Sock is a nice example of how a bit of detail can be added without significantly increasing the complexity of the knitting.

For partially patterned socks, you need to knit two gauge swatches—one for the stockinette-stitch portion and the other for the pattern panel. For the Wellington Road Sock, I've placed a medium-sized cable panel at the side of the foot, but worked the rest of the sock in plain stockinette stitch. With this yarn, my stockinette gauge is 8 stitches per inch (2.5 cm), and the 28-stitch cable panel measures 2.6 inches (6.6 cm) wide.

To maintain the proper circumference while adding the cable pattern, 2.6 inches (6.6 cm) worth of stockinette gauge has to be replaced with the cable gauge. The first step is to determine how many stockinette stitches are represented by this 2.6 inches (6.6 cm).

8 stitches per inch × 2.6" = 20.8 stitches

To simplify the math, I rounded this number up to 22 so I'd be working with an even number of stitches. This means that the 28 cable stitches will replace 22 plain stitches, so 6 extra stitches are needed.

28 cable stitches – 22 stockinette stitches = 6 stitches

Therefore, to add this 28-stitch cable element on a sock that normally would have 60 stitches, I had to increase 6 stitches to 66 stitches—28 stitches are worked in the cable pattern; 38 stitches are worked in stockinette.

Because the cable panel extends into the cuff, the entire leg is worked on 66 stitches. If the cuff were worked in a simple rib pattern instead, the cuff would be worked on 60 stitches, then increases would be worked to get the necessary 66 stitches for the leg. If you plan to do this, the increases will look best if they're added in the 28-stitch section where the cable pattern will be worked.

Consider the placement of the cable when determining the division of the heel and instep. It's simple if the cable element sits entirely on the instep—the heel is worked on 50 percent of the stockinette stitch count. If, on the other hand, even a portion of the cable panel is worked on the heel flap, you'll have to pay close attention to the division. For the top-down Wellington Road Sock, half of the cable panel continues into the heel. Because there are 66 stitches in the leg, 33 stitches each are worked for the heel and instep.

As with any other patterned sock, work the sole on 50 percent of the unaltered stitch count, which is 30 stitches in this example. For simplicity, I decreased 3 stitches when changing to stockinette for the heel turn so I'd have the necessary 30 stitches for this portion. This works better than the adjusted heel turn that I used for The Man of Aran Sock on page 146 because the cable element is off-center. Otherwise, the heel turn would be unbalanced without some clever math, which adds unnecessary complexity.

I also chose to include the pattern on the toe. This meant that I could continue the different stitch counts on the instep and sole to almost the end of the toe. In this case, the initial decreases are worked in the plain section of the instep, then decreases are included in the cable pattern in the final rounds. At that point, there are so few stitches that the gauge difference doesn't matter.

RIGHT SOCK

Cuff

CO 62 (66, 70, 74, 78, 82) sts. Distribute sts across needles as you prefer and join for working in rnds, being careful not to twist sts.

SET-UP RND: K2, work Row 1 of Right Leg chart (see page 143) across 28 sts, *k2, p2; rep from *.

Cont in patt as set until piece measures 2" (5 cm) from CO.

Leg

SET-UP RND: K2, work the next row of Right Leg chart across 28 sts, knit to end of rnd.

Cont in patt as set through Row 60 of chart, then work Rows 17–45 once more.

Note: For a shorter leg, just work Rows 1–45 of the chart once.

Heel
HEEL FLAP

The heel flap is worked back and forth in rows on half of the leg sts so that a single cable element runs along the far side of the flap.

ROW 1: (RS) K2, work Row 1 of Right Heel chart over next 13 sts, turn work.

ROW 2: (WS) Work Row 2 of chart over next 13 sts, p18 (20, 22, 24, 26, 28), turn work.

ROW 3: Sl 1, k17 (19, 21, 23, 25, 27), work Row 3 of chart over next 13 sts.

ROW 4: Work Row 4 of chart over next 13 sts, p18 (20, 22, 24, 26, 28).

Cont in patt as set until a total of 23 (25, 27, 29, 31, 33) rows have been worked, ending with a RS row.

NEXT ROW: (WS) Sl 1, k2, [p2tog] 3 times, k4, p18 (20, 22, 24, 26, 28)—28 (30, 32, 34, 36, 38) sts rem.

TURN HEEL

Work short-rows as foll.

ROW 1: (RS) K19 (20, 21, 23, 24, 25), ssk, turn work.

ROW 2: (WS) Sl 1, p10 (10, 10, 12, 12, 12), p2tog, turn work.

ROW 3: Sl 1, k10 (10, 10, 12, 12, 12), ssk (1 st each side of gap), turn work.

ROW 4: Sl 1, p10 (10, 10, 12, 12, 12), p2tog (1 st each side of gap), turn work.

Rep Rows 3 and 4 until all sts have been worked, ending with a WS row—12 (12, 12, 14, 14, 14) sts rem.

Gusset

K12 (12, 12, 14, 14, 14) heel sts, then use the same needle to pick up and knit 15 (16, 17, 18, 19, 20) sts along selvedge edge at side of heel flap, using slipped sts as a guide (see page 36). With a new needle, work 31 (33, 35, 37, 39, 41) instep sts as foll: starting with st 2, work Right Foot chart across next 15 sts, knit to end of instep. With another new needle, pick up and knit 15 (16, 17, 18, 19, 20) sts along selvedge edge at other side of heel flap, using slipped sts as a guide, then work the first 6 (6, 6, 7, 7, 7) sts from the first needle again—73 (77, 81, 87, 91, 95) sts total.

Rnd begins at base of foot.

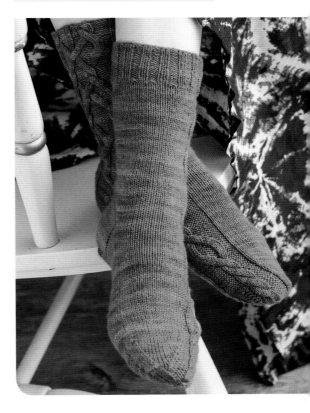

RND 1: K6 (6, 6, 7, 7, 7), k14 (15, 16, 17, 18, 19) through back loops (tbl), work Right Foot chart across next 16 sts, knit to end of instep, k15 (16, 17, 18, 19, 20) tbl, knit to end of rnd.

Note: The last of the first set of gusset sts becomes part of the instep; rearrange the sts on your needles if desired.

RND 2: Knit to 2 sts before instep, k2tog, work instep sts patt as set, k1, ssk, knit to end of rnd—2 sts dec'd.

RND 3: Knit to instep, work instep sts in patt as set, knit to end of rnd.

Rep the last 2 rnds 6 (6, 6, 7, 7, 7) more times—59 (63, 67, 71, 75, 79) sts rem.

Foot

SET-UP RND: Knit to instep, work instep sts in patt as set, knit to end of rnd.

Cont even in patt as set until foot measures 1¾ (1¾, 2, 2, 2, 2¼)" (4.5 [4.5, 5, 5, 5, 5.5] cm) less than desired finished sock foot length, ending between Rows 1–8 or 22–30 of chart if possible.

Note: If you're at that point of the chart, continue the 6-round 6-stitch basic cable repeat rounds only; if you're not at that point of the chart, continue working the chart pattern as you work the toe, until you reach Row 22 or 44. At that point, just start working the 6-round 6-stitch basic cable repeat (Rnds 1–6 of Right Foot chart).

If you're working the first size, and you're at rounds 9, 10, 31, or 32, work 2 more even rounds before you begin the toe to make sure the patterns line up neatly. These two extra rounds are required to make the patterning close up neatly, and they won't make a significant difference in the fit of the sock.

Toe

DEC RND: Knit to 2 sts before instep, k2tog, work chart as set, ssk, knit to 3 sts before end of instep, k2tog, k2, ssk, knit to end of rnd—4 sts dec'd.

NEXT RND: Knit to instep, work instep sts as set, knit to end of rnd.

Rep these 2 rnds 5 (6, 7, 8, 9, 10) more times—35 sts rem; 20 instep sts and 15 sole sts.

At this point, no matter where you ended the instep, you'll be working the 6-rnd 6-st basic cable rep on the toe. As you work the later decs, you'll be removing sts from the charted area and maintain the cable patt as long as possible.

From here, you'll be working the first instep decrease in the patterned area.

NEXT RND: Knit to 2 sts before instep, k2tog, p1, p2tog, work rest of chart to last 4 sts of instep, k1, k2tog, k2, ssk, knit to end of rnd—31 sts rem; 18 sts on instep and 13 sts on sole.

NEXT RND: Knit to 2 sts before instep, k2tog, p1, p2tog, work rest of chart to last 3 sts of instep, k2tog, k2, ssk, knit to end of rnd—27 sts rem; 16 sts on instep and 11 sts on sole.

The final decs depend on how the cable is aligned.

If there are 2 purl sts before the cable

NEXT RND: Knit to 2 sts before instep, k2tog, p2, work cable as set, p2tog, purl to last 3 sts of instep, k2tog, k2, ssk, knit to end of rnd—23 sts rem; 14 sts on the instep and 9 sts on the sole.

Rep the last rnd once more—19 sts rem; 12 sts on the instep, and 7 sts on the sole.

NEXT RND: Knit to 2 sts before the instep, k2tog, p2tog, [k2tog] 3 times, p1, k2tog, k2, ssk, knit to end of rnd—12 sts rem; 7 sts on instep and 5 sts on sole.

FINAL RND: Knit to the instep, p1, ssk, k1, k2tog, knit to end of rnd—10 sts rem; 5 sts each on sole and instep.

If there are 4 purl sts before the cable

NEXT RND: Knit to 2 sts before the instep, k2tog, p1, p2tog, work chart to last 3 sts of instep, k2tog, k2, ssk, knit to end of rnd—23 sts rem; 14 sts on instep, and 9 sts on sole.

Rep the last rnd once more—19 sts rem; 12 sts on the instep, and 7 sts on sole.

NEXT RND: Knit to 2 sts before instep, k2tog, p2tog, [k2tog] 3 times, purl to last 3 sts of instep, k2tog, k2, ssk, knit to end of rnd—12 sts rem; 7 sts on instep, and 5 sts on sole.

Right Leg chart

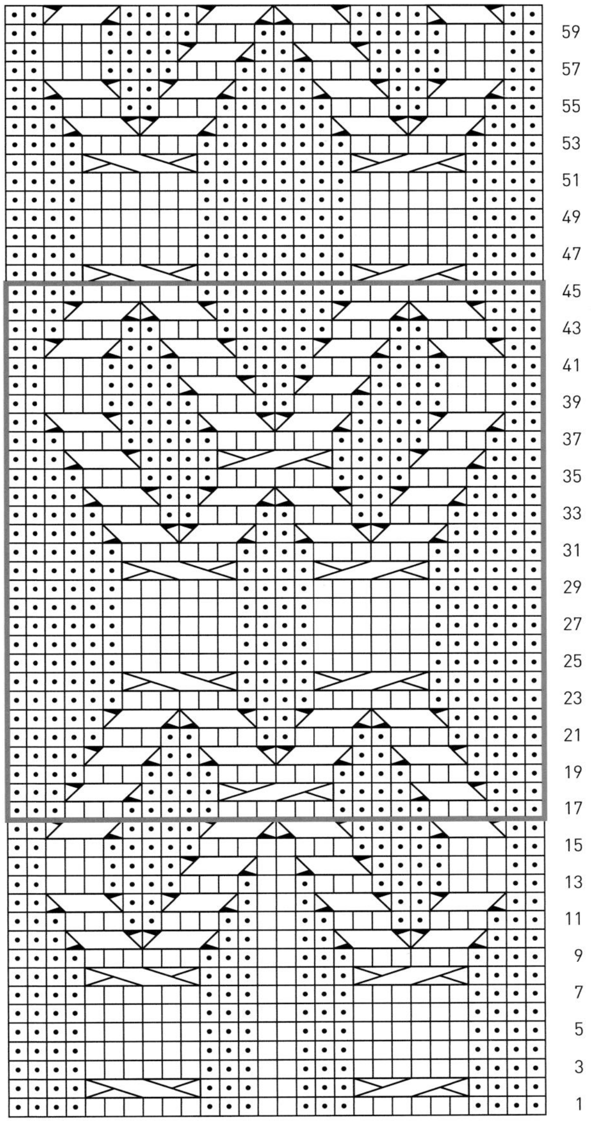

Right Heel chart

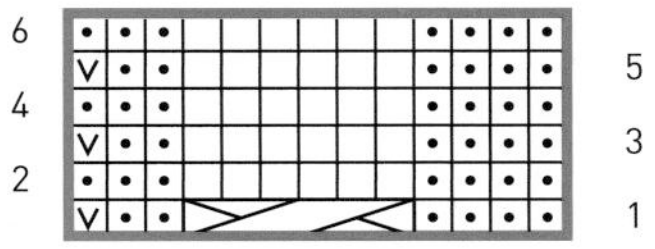

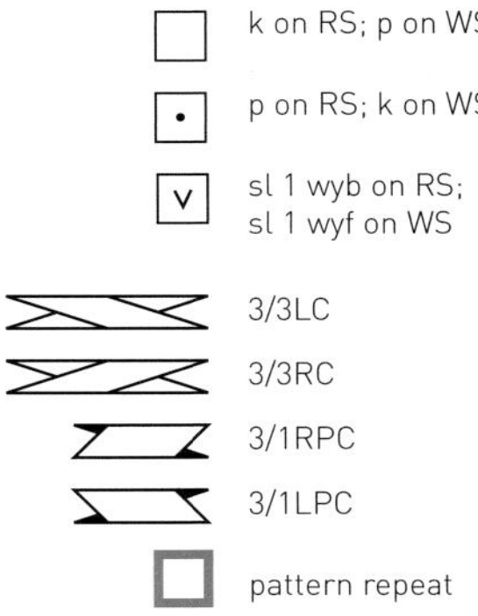
k on RS; p on WS
p on RS; k on WS
sl 1 wyb on RS; sl 1 wyf on WS
3/3LC
3/3RC
3/1RPC
3/1LPC
pattern repeat

Right Foot chart

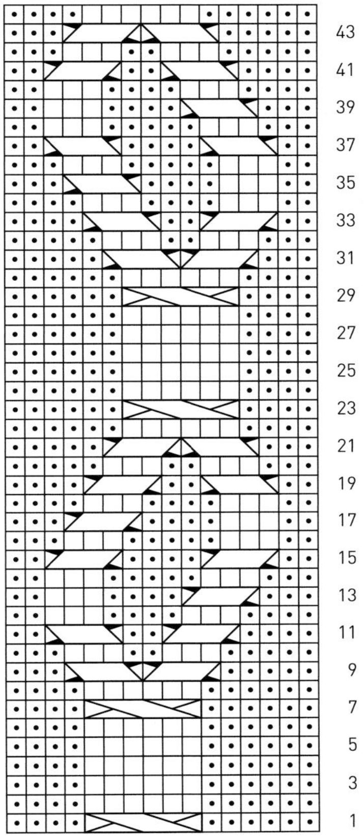

FINAL RND: Knit to instep, p2tog, k2tog, knit to end of rnd—10 sts rem; 5 sts each on sole and instep.

All versions

Cut yarn, leaving an 8" (20.5 cm) tail. Thread the tail on a tapestry needle, draw through rem sts, and pull tight to close the hole.

LEFT SOCK

Cuff

CO 62 (66, 70, 74, 78, 82) sts. Distribute sts across needles as you prefer and join for working in rnds, being careful not to twist sts.

SET-UP RND: K2, work Row 1 of Left Leg chart (see page 144) across 28 sts, *k2, p2; rep from *.

Cont in patt as set until piece measures 2" (5 cm) from CO.

Leg

SET-UP RND: K2, work Row 1 of Left Leg chart across 28 sts, knit to end of rnd.

Cont in patt as set through Row 60 of chart, then work Rows 17–44 once more.

Note: For a shorter leg, just work Rows 1–44 of the chart once.

Heel

HEEL FLAP

The heel flap is worked back and forth in rows on half of the leg sts so that a single cable element runs along the far side of the flap.

ROW 1: (RS) K2, work Row 45 of Left Leg chart as set, k18 (20, 22, 24, 26, 28), turn work.

ROW 2: (WS) Sl 1, p17 (19, 21, 23, 25, 27), work Row 2 of Left Heel chart over next 13 sts, turn work.

ROW 3: Work Left Heel chart over next 13 sts, k18 (20, 22, 24, 26, 28).

ROW 4: Sl 1, p17 (19, 21, 23, 25, 27), work Left Heel chart Row 4 over next 13 sts.

Cont in patt as set until a total of 23 (25, 27, 29, 31, 33) rows have been worked, ending with a RS row.

NEXT ROW: (WS) Sl 1, p17 (19, 21, 23, 25, 27), k4, [p2tog] 3 times, k3— 28 (30, 32, 34, 36, 38) sts rem.

TURN HEEL

Work as for right sock.

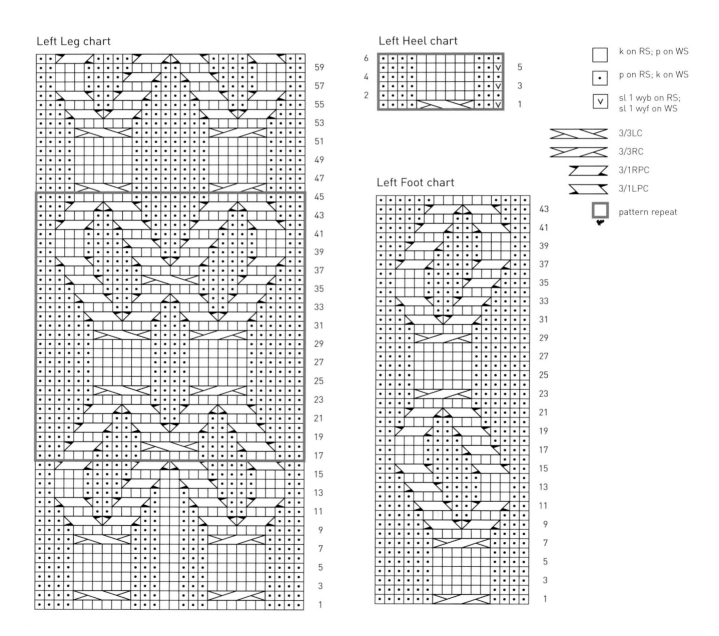

Left Leg chart

Left Heel chart

Left Foot chart

k on RS; p on WS

p on RS; k on WS

sl 1 wyb on RS; sl 1 wyf on WS

3/3LC

3/3RC

3/1RPC

3/1LPC

pattern repeat

Gusset

K12 (12, 12, 14, 14, 14) heel sts, then use the same needle to pick up and knit 15 (16, 17, 18, 19, 20) sts along selvedge edge at side of the heel flap, using slipped sts as a guide (see page 36). With a new needle, work 31 (33, 35, 37, 39, 41) instep sts as foll: k16 (18, 20, 22, 24, 26), work Left Foot chart across next 15 sts (skipping st 16) to end of instep. With another new needle, pick up and knit 15 (16, 17, 18, 19, 20) sts along selvedge edge at other side of heel flap, using slipped sts as a guide, then work the first 6 (6, 6, 7, 7, 7) sts from the first needle again—73 (77, 81, 87, 91, 95) sts total.

Rnd begins at base of foot.

RND 1: K6 (6, 6, 7, 7, 7), k15 (16, 17, 18, 19, 20) tbl, k16 (18, 20, 22, 24, 26), work Left Foot chart across next 16 sts, (this takes you 1 st into gusset), k14 (15, 16, 17, 18, 19) tbl, knit to end of rnd.

Note: The first of the second set of gusset stitches becomes part of the instep; rearrange the sts on your needles if desired.

RND 2: Knit to 3 sts before instep, k2tog, k1, work instep sts in patt as set, ssk, knit to end of rnd—2 sts dec'd.

RND 3: Knit to instep, work instep sts in patt as set, knit to end of rnd.

Rep the last 2 rnds 6 (6, 6, 7, 7, 7) more times—59 (63, 67, 71, 75, 79) sts rem.

Foot

Work as for Right Sock.

Toe

DEC RND: Knit to 3 sts before instep, k2tog, k2, ssk, knit to 2 sts before chart, k2tog, work chart as set across instep, ssk, knit to end of rnd—4 sts dec'd.

NEXT RND: Knit to instep, work instep sts as set knit to end of rnd.

Rep these 2 rnds 5 (6, 7, 8, 9, 10) more times—35 sts rem; 20 sts on instep and 15 sts on sole.

At this point, no matter where you ended the instep, you'll be working the 6-rnd, 6-st basic cable rep (Rnds 1–6 of Left Foot chart) on the toe. As you work the later decs, you'll be removing sts from the charted area and maintain the cable patt as long as possible.

From here on, you'll be working the second instep decrease in the patterned area.

NEXT RND: Knit to 3 sts before instep, k2tog, k2, ssk, k1, work chart to 3 sts before end of instep, p2tog, p1, k1, ssk, knit to end of rnd—31 sts rem; 18 sts on instep and 13 sts on sole.

NEXT RND: Knit to 3 sts before instep, k2tog, k2, ssk, work chart to 3 sts before end of instep, p2tog, p1, k1, ssk, knit to end of rnd—27 sts rem; 16 sts on instep and 11 sts on sole.

The final decs depend on how the cable is aligned.

If there are 4 purl sts before the cable

NEXT RND: Knit to 3 sts before instep, k2tog, k2, ssk, purl to cable, work cable as set, purl to 3 sts before end of instep, p2tog, p1, ssk, knit to end of rnd—23 sts rem; 14 sts on instep and 9 sts on sole.

Rep the last rnd once more—19 sts rem; 12 sts on instep and 7 sts on sole.

NEXT RND: Knit to 3 sts before instep, k2tog, k1, ssk, p1, [k2tog] 3 times, p2tog, k1, ssk, knit to end of rnd—12 sts rem; 7 sts on instep and 5 sts on sole.

FINAL RND: Knit to instep, k1, ssk, p1, k1, k2tog, p1, knit to end of rnd—10 sts rem; 5 sts each on sole and instep.

If there are 6 purl sts before the cable

NEXT RND: Knit to 3 sts before instep, k2tog, k2, ssk, purl to 2 sts before cable, p2tog, work cable as set, p2, k1, ssk, knit to end of rnd—23 sts rem; 14 sts on instep and 9 sts on sole.

Rep the last rnd once more—19 sts rem; 12 sts on instep and 7 sts on sole.

NEXT RND: Knit to 3 sts before instep, k2tog, k2, ssk, p1, [k2tog] 3 times, p2tog, ssk, knit to end of rnd—12 sts rem; 7 sts on instep and 5 sts on sole.

FINAL RND: Knit to instep, k1, ssk, k1, k2tog, p1, knit to end of rnd—10 sts rem; 5 sts each on sole and instep.

All versions

Cut yarn, leaving an 8" (20.5 cm) tail. Thread tail on a tapestry needle, draw through rem sts, pull tight to close hole, and secure on WS.

Finishing

Weave in loose ends. Block as desired (see page 18).

The MƏN OF ƏRƏN Sock

FINISHED SIZE
Ankle/foot circumference, lightly stretched: 7 (7¾, 8¼, 9, 10)" (18 [19.5, 21, 23, 25.5] cm).

Leg length: Adjustable to fit.

Foot length: Adjustable to fit; finished length should be about ½" (1.3 cm) shorter than actual foot length.

Sock shown measures 8¼" (21 cm) ankle/foot circumference.

YARN
CYCA #1 Super Fine.

Shown here: Paton Kroy Socks 4-Ply (75% superwash merino, 25% nylon; 166 yd [152 m]/50 g): #1208 Muslin, 3 (3, 3, 3, 4) balls.

NEEDLES
Size U.S. 2 (2.75 mm): set of 4 double-pointed (dpn), two circular (cir) or one long cir, as you prefer (see page 20).

NOTIONS
Markers (m); cable needle (cn); tapestry needle.

GAUGE
29 sts and 42 rnds = 4" (10 cm) in St st worked in rnds.

About 48 sts and 47 rnds = 4" (10 cm) in honeycomb cable patt worked in rnds.

Presented as a documentary, the 1934 film, *Man of Aran* includes a significant degree of artifice in the staging. The concept of Aran sweaters is also somewhat artificial. Heavily cabled, off-white sweaters would have been impractical for fishermen of old—cables require more yarn and time in the making and off-white would get filthy very quickly. Just like the film, the "Aran sweater" as we know it was, effectively, invented to be sold to tourists—representative, but staged.

Notes
+ This pattern works for any sock yarn that specifies a gauge of 28 stitches in 4" (10 cm).

+ The following instructions are based on the Basic Patterns on pages 40 and 54 worked at a gauge of 7 stitches per inch (2.5 cm), with finished sizes of 7 (7¾, 8¼, 9, 10)" (18 [19.5, 21, 23, 25.5] cm).

+ Choose a size based on foot circumference, allowing for the usual 10 percent negative ease.

+ There is a lot going on in this pattern—you should be comfortable working seed stitch and cable patterns on varying numbers of stitches in both in rows and rounds. There's also some interesting cabled increases and decreases.

+ Two versions are provided—the toe-up version is a bit more challenging than the top-down version, as it requires a bit of calculation to make the patterning align along the back of the leg.

THE MAN OF ARAN SOCK

Inspired by a variety of patterns used in classic Aran sweaters, the Man of Aran Sock has patterns throughout the leg, heel flap, and instep. The various sizes are achieved through varying the numbers of stitches in the different patterns—seed stitch in the side panels, purl stitches between the cables, and the main honeycomb cable pattern.

There's a large difference between the stockinette gauge for the gussets, sole, and toe, and the cable gauge used elsewhere. Because the patterned heel flap compresses laterally, it's worked on many more stitches than in a standard stockinette sock—but the length of the heel flap remains proportionate to the stockinette gauge.

The heel turn is worked on the full stitch count of the flap, but instead of dividing the stitches into the usual thirds for the turn, I've based the number of stitches in the center third on the number of stitches in the cuff. This requires more decreases than normal for the heel turn, which, in turn, produces a longer heel cup. But this extra length compensates nicely for the lack of stretch and the lateral compression in the heel flap— and it also ensures a proportionate sole and gusset.

For the toe-up version, I've worked the heel as usual for a stockinette sock, but I added a set of increases in the heel flap to get the required number of stitches. The increases are cleverly hidden within the first cable-turning row as described in the sidebar at right. If this is a bit too "tricky," you can simply work the increases in the last round of stockinette stitch.

Hidden Cable Increases and Decreases

When adjusting stitch counts to accommodate the different gauges between stockinette and cables, this pattern hides the increases or decreases within the cable turns.

INCREASE 3 STITCHES INTO 4: Slip 1 stitch onto a cable needle and hold in back of work, k2, then k1f&b (see Glossary) from the cable needle—3 stitches increased to 4.

DECREASE 4 STITCHES INTO 3: Slip 2 stitches onto a cable needle and hold in back of work, k2, then k2tog from the cable needle—4 stitches decreased to 3.

TOP-DOWN VERSION

Cuff

CO 52 (56, 64, 68, 68) sts. Distribute sts across needles as you prefer and join for working in rnds, being careful not to twist sts.

RND 1: [P1 (1, 2, 2, 1), k2, p1 (1, 2, 2, 1), [k4, p2] 2 (2, 2, 2, 3) times, k4, p1 (1, 2, 2, 1), k2, p1 (1, 2, 2, 1), k2 (4, 4, 6, 4)] 2 times.

RND 2: [P1 (1, 2, 2, 1), RT (see Stitch Guide), p1 (1, 2, 2, 1), (k4, p2) 2 (2, 2, 2, 3) times, k4, p1 (1, 2, 2, 1), LT (see Stitch Guide), p1 (1, 2, 2, 1), k2 (4, 4, 6, 4)] 2 times.

Rep Rnds 1 and 2 until piece measures 1½" (3.8 cm) from CO, ending with Rnd 1.

Leg

INC RND: *P1 (1, 2, 2, 1), RT, M1P (see Stitch Guide), p0 (0, 1, 1, 0), [2/1RCInc (see Stitch Guide), 2/1LCInc (see Stitch Guide)] 3 (3, 3, 3, 4) times, p0 (0, 1, 1, 0), M1P, LT, p1 (1, 2, 2, 1), work seed st (see Stitch Guide) across next 2 (4, 4, 6, 4) sts; rep from * once more—68 (72, 80, 84, 88) sts.

RND 1: [P1 (1, 2, 2, 1), k2, p1 (1, 2, 2, 1), work Row 1 of Honeycomb Cable chart (see page 151) 3 (3, 3, 3, 4) times, p1 (1, 2, 2, 1), k2, p1 (1, 2, 2, 1), work seed st across next 2 (4, 4, 6, 4) sts] 2 times.

RND 2: [P1 (1, 2, 2, 1), RT, p1 (1, 2, 2, 1), work Row 2 of Honeycomb Cable chart 3 (3, 3, 3, 4) times, p1 (1, 2, 2, 1), LT, p1 (1, 2, 2, 1), work seed st across next 2 (4, 4, 6, 4) sts] 2 times.

Work even in patts as set until sock measures 6¼" (16 cm) or desired length to top of heel, ending with an odd-numbered rnd of chart.

Heel

HEEL FLAP

The heel flap is worked back and forth on half of the leg sts.

ROW 1: (RS) Work 33 (34, 38, 39, 42) sts in patts as set.

The heel flap is worked on 34 (36, 40, 42, 44) sts, beg and ending midway through the seed st column and slipping the first st of every row.

ROW 2: (WS) Sl 1, work 33 (35, 39, 41, 43) sts in patt as set.

ROW 3: Sl 1, work 33 (35, 39, 41, 43) sts in patt as set.

ROW 4: Sl 1, work 33 (35, 39, 41, 43) sts in patt as set.

Cont in patt as set until a total of 24 (26, 26, 28, 30) rows have been worked.

TURN HEEL

Work short-rows as foll.

ROW 1: (RS) K22 (23, 26, 27, 28), ssk, turn work.

ROW 2: (WS) Sl 1, p10 (10, 12, 12, 12), p2tog, turn work.

ROW 3: Sl 1, k10 (10, 12, 12, 12), ssk (1 st each side of gap), turn work.

ROW 4: Sl 1, p10 (10, 12, 12, 12), p2tog (1 st each side of gap), turn work.

Rep the last 2 rows 9 (10, 11, 12, 13) more times, ending with WS Row 4—all sts have been worked; 12 (12, 14, 14, 14) sts rem.

STITCH GUIDE

RT: Skip first st and knit into second st on left needle, knit first st, then slip both sts off the needle.

LT: Skip first st and knit into the back of the second st on the left needle, knit first st, then slip both sts off the needle.

2/2RC: Slip 2 sts onto cn and hold in back of work, k2, then k2 from cn.

2/2LC: Slip 2 sts onto cn and hold in front of work, k2, then k2 from cn.

2/1RCInc: Slip 2 sts onto cn and hold in back of work, k2, then k1f&b (see Glossary) from cn— 3 sts inc'd to 4 sts.

2/1LCInc: Slip 2 sts onto cn and hold in front of work, k1f&b (see Glossary), then k2 from cn—3 sts inc'd to 4 sts.

2/2RCDec: Slip 2 sts onto cn and hold in back of work, k2, then k2tog from cn—4 sts dec'd to 3 sts.

2/2LCDec: Slip 2 sts onto cn and hold in front of work, k2tog, then k2 from cn—4 sts dec'd to 3 sts.

M1P: Insert tip of left needle from back to front under the horizontal bar between the last st on the right needle and the first st on the left needle, then purl this strand through the front loop to twist it— 1 st inc'd.

SEED STITCH (EVEN NUMBER OF STS WORKED IN RNDS)

Rnd 1: *K1, p1; rep from *.

Rnd 2: *P1, k1; rep from *.

Rep Rnds 1 and 2 for patt.

Gusset

K12 (12, 14, 14, 14) heel sts, then, with the same needle, pick up and knit 14 (15, 15, 16, 17) sts along selvedge edge at side of heel flap, using slipped sts as a guide (see page 36). With a new needle, work in patts as set across 34 (36, 40, 42, 44) instep sts. With another new needle, pick up and knit 14 (15, 15, 16, 17) sts along selvedge edge at other side of heel flap, using slipped sts as a guide, then work the first 6 (6, 7, 7, 7) sts from the first needle again—74 (78, 84, 88, 92) sts total; 20 (21, 22, 23, 24) sts between the start of the rnd and the start of the instep, 34 (36, 40, 42, 44) instep sts, and 20 (21, 22, 23, 24) sts between the end of the instep and the end of the rnd.

Rnd begins at center of heel. If you're working on two cir needles or the magic-loop method, place a marker in this position.

From here on, the 34 (36, 40, 42, 44) instep sts will be worked in patts as set; the gusset and sole sts will be worked in St st (knit every rnd).

SET-UP RND: K6 (6, 7, 7, 7), k14 (15, 15, 15, 16, 17) through back loop (tbl), work instep sts in patt as set, k14 (15, 15, 16, 17) tbl, knit to end of rnd.

DEC RND: Knit to 2 sts before instep, k2tog, work instep sts in patt, ssk, knit to end of rnd—2 sts dec'd.

Work 1 rnd even, maintaining patt on instep.

Rep the last 2 rnds 6 more times—26 (28, 30, 32, 34) sole sts rem; 60 (64, 70, 74, 78) sts total.

Foot

Work even in patt as set until foot measures 1¾ (1¾, 2, 2, 2¼)" (4.5

[4.5, 5, 5, 5.5] cm) less than desired finished sock foot length, ending with Rnd 3 or 7 of patt.

DEC RND: In this rnd, you'll work decs on the central cable element— the way that the decs are worked depends on which cable rnd you ended on.

IF YOU ENDED ON HONEYCOMB CABLE RND 3: Knit to instep, work seed st as set over next 1 (2, 2, 3, 2) st(s), p1 (1, 2, 2, 1), k2tog, p1 (1, 0, 0, 1), [p2tog] 0 (0, 1, 1, 0) time, [2/2LCDec (see Stitch Guide), 2/2RCDec (see Stitch Guide)] 3 (3, 3, 3, 4) times, [p2tog] 0 (0, 1, 1, 0) time, p1 (1, 0, 0, 1), k2tog, p1 (1, 2, 2, 1), work seed st as set over next 1 (2, 2, 3, 2) st(s), knit to end of rnd—52 (56, 60, 64, 68) sts rem.

IF YOU ENDED ON HONEYCOMB CABLE RND 7: Knit to instep, work seed st as set over next 1 (2, 2, 3, 2) sts, p1 (1, 2, 2, 1), k2tog, p1 (1, 0, 0, 1), [p2tog] 0 (0, 1, 1, 0) time, [2/2RCDec, 2/2LCDec] 3 (3, 3, 3, 4) times, [p2tog] 0 (0, 1, 1, 0) time, p1 (1, 0, 0, 1), k2tog, p1 (1, 2, 2, 1), work seed st as set over next 1 (2, 2, 3, 2) st(s), knit to end of rnd—52 (56, 60, 64, 68) sts rem.

Toe

Rearrange sts if necessary so that there are 26 (28, 30, 32, 34) sts each for the sole and the instep. Cont in St st as foll.

DEC RND: Knit to 3 sts before start of instep, k2tog, k2, ssk; knit to 3 sts before end of instep, k2tog, k2, ssk, knit to end of rnd—4 sts dec'd.

Knit 1 rnd even.

toe up

top down

Honeycomb Cable chart

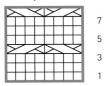

7
5
3
1

- ☐ k on RS; p on WS
- ⟋⟍ 2/2RC
- ⟍⟋ 2/2LC
- ☐ pattern repeat

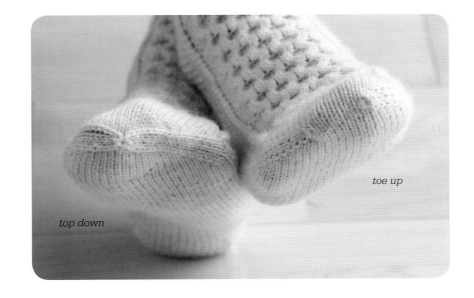

top down

toe up

Rep the last 2 rnds 5 (5, 6, 6, 7) more times—28 (32, 32, 36, 36) sts rem.

Rep dec rnd every rnd 5 (6, 6, 7, 7) times—8 sts rem.

Cut yarn, leaving an 8" (20.5 cm) tail. Thread tail on a tapestry needle, draw through rem sts, pull tight to close hole, and secure on WS.

Finishing

Weave in loose ends. Block as desired (see page 18).

||||||||||||||||||||||||||||||||||||||

TOE-UP VERSION

Toe

Using Judy's magic method (see page 49), CO 16 (20, 20, 24, 24) sts—8 (10, 10, 10, 12) sts each on two needles.

RND 1: Work as foll, depending on the type of needle(s) used.

FOR DPN: K4 (5, 5, 5, 6) with one needle, k4 (5, 5, 5, 6) with a second

needle, k8 (10, 10, 10, 12) with a third needle.

FOR TWO CIR OR MAGIC-LOOP METHOD: K8 (10, 10, 10, 12) with one needle, k8 (10, 10, 10, 12) with a second needle.

Place a safety pin or marker in the toe to indicate beg of rnd and a second one to indicate the center of the rnd.

INC RND: K1, M1R (see Glossary), knit to 1 st before center of rnd, M1L (see Glossary), k2, M1R, knit to 1 st before end of rnd, M1L, k1—4 sts inc'd.

Knit 1 rnd even.

Rep the last 2 rnds 8 (8, 9, 9, 10) more times—52 (56, 60, 64, 68) sts total.

Foot

INC RND: Work seed st across 1 (2, 2, 3, 2) st(s), p1 (1, 2, 2, 1), k1f&b (see Glossary), [M1P (see Stitch Guide)] 0 (0, 1, 1, 0) time, p1, [2/1RCInc (see Stitch Guide), 2/1LCInc (see Stitch Guide)] 3 (3, 3, 3, 4) times, p1, [M1P] 0 (0, 1, 1, 0) time, k1f&b, p1 (1, 2, 2,

1), work seed st across next 1 (2, 2, 3, 2) st(s), knit to end of rnd—60 (64, 70, 74, 78) sts; 34 (36, 40, 42, 44) instep sts; 26 (28, 30, 32, 34) sole sts.

RND 1: Work seed st as set over next 1 (2, 2, 3, 2) st(s), p1 (1, 2, 2, 1), RT (see Stitch Guide), p1 (1, 2, 2, 1), work Rnd 1 of Honeycomb Cable chart 3 (3, 3, 3, 4) times, p1 (1, 2, 2, 1), LT (see Stitch Guide), p1 (1, 2, 2, 1), work seed st as set over next 1 (2, 2, 3, 2) st(s), knit to end of rnd.

RND 2: Work seed st as set over next 1 (2, 2, 3, 2) st(s), p1 (1, 2, 2, 1), k2, p1 (1, 2, 2, 1), work Rnd 2 of Honeycomb Cable chart 3 (3, 3, 3, 4) times, p1 (1, 2, 2, 1), k2, p1 (1, 2, 2, 1), work seed st as set over next 1 (2, 2, 3, 2) st(s), knit to end of rnd.

Work even in patts as set until foot measures 3¼ (3¼, 3¾, 4, 4½)" (8.5 [8.5, 9.5, 10, 11.5] cm) less than desired finished sock foot length, ending with an odd-numbered rnd of chart. Make note of the last rnd worked so you'll be able to align the patt on the back of the leg.

Gusset

Rearrange sts if necessary so that the sole sts are on one needle. Work the gusset incs at each end of the needle holding the sole sts.

RND 1: Work instep in patt as set, M1R, place marker (pm) for beg of heel, knit to end of rnd, pm for end of heel, M1L—2 sts inc'd.

RND 2: Work instep sts in patt as set, knit to end of rnd.

RND 3: Work instep sts in patt as set, M1R, knit to end of rnd, M1L—2 sts inc'd.

RND 4: Work instep sts in patt as set, knit to end of rnd.

Rep the last 2 rnds 8 (9, 10, 10, 11) more times—80 (86, 94, 98, 104) sts total.

Heel
TURN HEEL

Work short-rows (see Glossary) as foll.

ROW 1: (RS) Work instep in patt as set, knit to 1 st before second heel m, wrap next st and turn work (w&t).

ROW 2: (WS) Purl to 1 st before m, w&t.

Working only on the heel sts, cont as foll.

ROW 3: (RS) Knit to st before last wrapped st, w&t.

ROW 4: (WS) Purl to st before last wrapped st, w&t.

Rep Rows 3 and 4 until 8 (8, 10, 10, 12) sts rem unwrapped in the middle, ending with a WS row.

Remove heel markers.

HEEL FLAP

Work the heel flap and dec gusset sts as foll.

ROW 1: (RS) Knit to first wrapped st, *knit the wrapped st tog with its wrap; rep from * until 1 wrapped st rem, ssk (final st tog with its wrap and the first gusset st), turn work.

ROW 2: (WS) Sl 1, purl to first wrapped st, *purl the wrapped st tog with its wrap; rep from * until 1 wrapped st rem, p2tog (final st tog with its wrap and the first gusset st), turn work.

Beg working the heel sts in patt as foll.

IF YOU FINISHED THE FOOT ON RND 3 OF CHART: Beg with Rnd 4 of patt. Count back 16 (18, 20, 20, 22) rows in patt from that next row. In this example, if you need to be ready to work Rnd 2, you'll need to start the heel flap with Rnd 2 (8, 6, 6, 4). You'll also need to pick up seed st on the sides of the heel and work them in patt on the next row of the heel flap.

IF YOU'RE STARTING THE HEEL FLAP PATT ON RND 2 OR 6 OF CHART: Work the cable incs as [K3, M1R, M1L, k3] 3 (3, 3, 3, 4) times—24 (24, 24, 24, 32) sts inc'd from 18 (18, 18, 18, 24) sts.

IF YOU'RE STARTING THE HEEL FLAP PATT ON RND 4 OF CHART: Work the cable incs as [2/1LCInc, 2/1RCInc] 3 (3, 3, 3, 4) times—24 (24, 24, 24, 32) sts inc'd from 18 (18, 18, 18, 24) sts.

IF YOU'RE STARTING THE HEEL FLAP PATT ON RND 8 OF CHART: Work the cable incs as [2/1RCInc, 2/1LCInc] 3 (3, 3, 3, 4) times—24 (24, 24, 24, 32) sts inc'd from 18 (18, 18, 18, 24) sts.

All versions

ROW 3: (RS) Sl 1, work seed st across next 0 (1, 1, 2, 1) st(s), p1 (1, 2, 2, 1), k1f&b, p1 (1, 2, 2, 1), work cable incs as outlined above, p1 (1, 2, 2, 1), k1f&b, p1 (1, 2, 2, 1), work seed st across next 0 (1, 1, 2, 1) st(s), ssk, turn work.

ROW 4: (WS) Sl 1, work seed st across next 0 (1, 1, 2, 1) st(s), k1 (1, 2, 2, 1), p2, k1 (1, 2, 2, 1), work honeycomb patt across next 24 (24, 24, 24, 32) sts, k1 (1, 2, 2, 1), p2, k1 (1, 2, 2, 1), work seed st across next 0 (1, 1, 2, 1) st(s), p2tog, turn work.

ROW 5: (RS) Sl 1, work seed st across next 0 (1, 1, 2, 1) st(s), p1 (1, 2, 2, 1), RT, p1 (1, 2, 2, 1), work honeycomb patt across next 24 (24, 24, 24, 32) sts, p1 (1, 2, 2, 1), LT, p1 (1, 2, 2, 1), work seed st across next 0 (1, 1, 2, 1) st(s), ssk, turn work.

ROW 6: (WS) Sl 1, work seed st across next 0 (1, 1, 2, 1) st(s), k1 (1, 2, 2, 1), p2, k1 (1, 2, 2, 1), work honeycomb patt across next 24 (24, 24, 24, 32) sts, k1 (1, 2, 2, 1), p2, k1 (1, 2, 2, 1), work seed st across next 0 (1, 1, 2, 1) st(s), p2tog, turn work.

Rep Rows 5 and 6 until 2 gusset sts rem on each side, ending with a WS row—70 (74, 82, 86, 90) sts rem.

Leg

Rejoin for working in rnds, working in patt across all sts and working the final gusset decs in the first rnd as foll.

RND 1: Sl 1, work heel sts in patt as set, ssk, work instep sts in patt as set—69 (73, 81, 85, 89) sts rem.

RND 2: K2tog, work in patt as set to end of rnd—68 (72, 80, 84, 88) sts rem.

At this point, the rnd starts in the middle of the first seed st column. Beg and ending rnds in the center of seed st will throw off the patt so that the sts won't line up. We need to shift the start of the round, and "cheat" a little to ensure the seed st aligns. (If by some quirk, your seed st is okay at this point, then don't slip those sts but work them to shift the beg of the rnd. If it's okay at the start of the round, you might find that it's off in the second seed st column at the center of the rnd. If so, slip the sts as required in the first half of the column on the next round.)

SET-UP: Sl 1 (2, 2, 3, 2) st(s)—this is the new start of rnd.

RND 1: [P1 (1, 2, 2, 1), RT, p1 (1, 2, 2, 1), work next row of chart 3 (3, 3, 3, 4) times, p1 (1, 2, 2, 1), LT, p1 (1, 2, 2, 1), work seed st across next 2 (4, 4, 6, 4) sts] 2 times.

RND 2: [P1 (1, 2, 2, 1), k2, p1 (1, 2, 2, 1), work next row of chart 3 (3, 3, 3, 4) times, p1 (1, 2, 2, 1), k2, p1 (1, 2, 2, 1), work seed st across next 2 (4, 4, 6, 4) sts] 2 times.

Work even in patt as set until leg measures 2" (5 cm) less than desired total length, ending with Rnd 3 of chart.

Cuff

SET-UP RND 1: *P1 (1, 2, 2, 1), RT, p1 (1, 0, 0, 1), [p2tog] 0 (0, 1, 1, 0) time, [2/2LCDec, 2/2RCDec] 3 (3, 3, 3, 4) times, [p2tog] 0 (0, 1, 1, 0) time, p1 (1, 0, 0, 1), LT, p1 (1, 2, 2, 1), work seed st across next 2 (4, 4, 6, 4) sts; rep from * once—56 (60, 64, 68, 72) sts rem.

SET-UP RND 2: *P1 (1, 2, 2, 1), k2, p0 (0, 2, 2, 0), [p2tog] 1 (1, 0, 0, 1) time, [k4, p2] 2 (2, 2, 2, 3) times, k4, [p2tog] 1 (1, 0, 0, 1) time, p0 (0, 2, 2, 0), k2, p1 (1, 2, 2, 1), work seed st across next 2 (4, 4, 6, 4) sts; rep from * once—52 (56, 64, 68, 68) sts rem.

RND 1: *P1 (1, 2, 2, 1), RT, p1 (1, 2, 2, 1), [k4, p2] 2 (2, 2, 2, 3) times, k4, p1 (1, 2, 2, 1), LT, p1 (1, 2, 2, 1), k2 (4, 4, 6, 4); rep from * once.

RND 2: [P1 (1, 2, 2, 1), k2, p1 (1, 2, 2, 1), [k4, p2] 2 (2, 2, 2, 3) times, k4, p1 (1, 2, 2, 1), k2, p1 (1, 2, 2, 1), k2 (4, 4, 6, 4); rep from * once.

Rep Rnds 1 and 2 for 2" (5 cm), ending with Rnd 2.

Using a stretchy method (see page 52), BO all sts.

Finishing

Weave in loose ends. Block as desired (see page 18).

Chapter 5
On Adjustments for Non-Average Feet

All of the patterns in the previous chapter are designed to fit an "average-" shaped foot. Such a foot conforms to the following basic rules:

+ The foot circumference and ankle circumference are about the same.

+ The gusset circumference is about 10 to 15 percent larger than the foot circumference.

+ The low-calf circumference is no more than 30 percent larger than the ankle circumference.

+ The heel diagonal circumference is about 35 to 40 percent larger than the foot circumference.

+ Adult toes are about 1¾ inches to 2¼ inches (4.5 to 5.5 cm) long; children's toes are about 1 inch to 2 inches (2.5 to 5 cm) long.

If your foot—or the foot you're knitting for—doesn't conform to all of these rules, you'll do well to make at least one of the adjustments described in this chapter.

Two Rules That Are Easily Broken

Two key assumptions in standard sock design can be broken without adverse effects on the construction. The foot and ankle circumferences don't have to be the same, and the right and left socks don't have to be identical.

The Foot Circumference Doesn't Have to Match the Ankle Circumference

Standard sock patterns have the same number of stitches in the foot as the leg. When working a top-down sock, this means that the gusset stitches are decreased away so that the stitch count for the foot is the same as for the leg; for a toe-up sock the gusset stitches are decreased away so that the stitch count for the leg is the same as for the foot before the gusset increases began.

But there's nothing sacred about this convention. Although it reflects average foot proportions, it's not critical for sock construction. Indeed, many of the fit adjustments discussed in this chapter involve changing one of these circumferences. It's, therefore, a good idea to measure both your foot and ankle circumferences, then calculate the ankle and foot stitches separately (allowing for appropriate negative ease, of course).

Adjusting a pattern to reflect different ankle and foot circumferences can be very simple. If you're working from the top down, simply end the gusset decreases when you hit the necessary number of stitches, which may be more or fewer than expected for a standard sock. Once you achieve the required number of stitches, be sure to adjust them so that 50 percent are on the instep and 50 percent are on the sole before you begin the toe decreases. If you're working from the toe up, simply end the heel flap/gusset decreases when you hit the stitch count you need.

Be aware that this simple solution does have limitations. For a top-down sock, the heel is proportionate to the leg; for a toe-up sock, the heel is proportionate to the foot. See page 165 for ways to fine-tune the fit for a variety of heel sizes and shapes.

There are times when you'll want different stitch counts on the leg and foot to accommodate a pattern stitch or repeat. Indeed, many of the patterned socks in the book work this way—see the sidebar on page 70 for how and why this is done.

If you're working a plain stockinette heel in a top-down sock, the simplest solution is to base the number of stitches in the heel (and thereby the size of the heel and gusset) on the foot circumference, not the ankle circumference. Specifically, work increases or decreases at the bottom of the leg to adjust to the necessary foot stitches before you work the heel flap.

In a toe-up sock, the number of gusset stitches (and therefore the number of rows in the heel flap) is proportionate to the foot circumference and the gauge (if you're working a half-patterned foot, it's specifically the stockinette gauge). You'll work the gusset and heel as usual to match the number of stitches in the sole of the sock, then, in the first round of the leg, you'll work increases or decreases to adjust to the necessary number of stitches for the leg.

Ultimately, the fit of the foot is critical, but there's wiggle room in the leg. In general, it's best to err on the side of too many stitches for the leg rather than too few. The leg can afford to be a bit looser—you can tighten the cuff with ribbing, if necessary.

THE TWO SOCKS DON'T HAVE TO BE IDENTICAL

The two socks in a pair don't have to be exactly the same. If you're knitting for someone with mismatched feet—whether simply because one is larger than the other or due to an injury or other medical problem—you can knit mismatched socks.

It's actually a useful exercise to measure both of your feet in full detail. It's not that uncommon for the two feet to be such different sizes that they don't fit the same shoe size. Even among people who wear the same size of shoe on each foot, there can be surprising variance between the two. Statistically, it's highly unlikely that both feet share

Socks for Diabetics and Other Special Medical Needs

Diabetics who experience poor circulation and swelling in their feet rely on special socks to provide comfort and relief. Indeed, other medical conditions can cause similar symptoms, and therefore these "diabetic socks" are useful to many. There are three characteristics in such socks, all of which knitters can easily accommodate—they need to wick away moisture and breathe (to help combat impaired healing), they should be soft and protective (to cushion and protect extra-fragile feet), and they should not be constricting in any way (to help aid poor circulation).

Wool is an ideal fiber for such socks—its moisture-wicking and breathability characteristics are also very helpful for those who have issues regulating their temperature or have difficulty with their body's ability to sense temperature.

To ensure a soft yarn, consider a blend that contains some alpaca or angora and that has a lofty spin. But work the fabric tightly so that the socks will wear well and feel smooth on the foot. Also, consider working the sole so that the knit side of the fabric is against the foot (see page 62).

To ensure a comfortable, non-binding cuff use the twisted German cast-on (see page 35) for a top-down sock or Jeny's surprisingly stretchy bind-off (see page 52) for a toe-up sock. For legs prone to swelling, also add a few more stitches in the upper leg/cuff—for a top-down sock, cast on about a third more stitches and then work some gradual decreases to shape down the leg; for a toe-up sock, work some increases in the top third of the leg.

all the same measurements. But, as long as they're within about 5 percent of each other—for example, your right foot measures 8½ inches (20.5 cm) in circumference and your left foot measures 8¾ inches (22 cm)—then the same sock will fit each foot equally well. Knit fabrics stretch.

If you do make different socks for the left and right feet, be sure to indicate which sock is which. I like to make a very obvious mistake—purl a few stitches that should be knitted, for example—in the ribbing or toe of the left sock so I'll know that the "right" sock is the right sock, and the "wrong" sock is the left sock.

Do note, however, that foot-specific socks tend to wear out faster because each sock always experiences the same friction in the same area. If you knit such socks, I highly recommend choosing a hard-wearing yarn and working at a tight gauge (see Chapter 2).

Leg Circumference Adjustments

There are a variety of reasons why you might want to adjust the "standard" leg circumference. The key is in the relationship between the foot, ankle, and low-calf circumferences. A couple of quick calculations can tell you what sorts of adjustments you need to make.

First divide your foot circumference by your ankle circumference. The calculation for an "average" foot should be very close to 1.

foot circumference ÷ ankle circumference = 1

If your calculated number is greater than 1, your foot circumference is larger than that of your ankle. If your calculated number is less than 1, your ankle circumference is larger than that of your foot. If the different is minor (between 0.91 and 1.09), the difference isn't worth addressing. But if your number is greater than 1.1 or less than 0.9, you'll want to make some adjustments.

Before we continue, let's examine the way we expect the leg of a sock to fit. Although the fit is based on the smallest part of the ankle circumference (with negative ease), it relies on the stretchy properties of knitted fabrics so that the leg will fit the larger circumference of the low calf as well. In fact, a sock stays up because of that stretch at the top of the leg. A knitted fabric will happily stretch to accommodate a low-calf circumference that's 30 percent greater than the ankle circumference.

Next, divide your low-calf circumference by your ankle circumference. This calculation should be between 1 and 1.3 because we expect the ankle to be a little narrower than the low-calf circumference.

low-calf circumference ÷ ankle circumference = 1 to 1.3

If your calculated number is less than 1, your leg is skinnier than expected; if your number is greater than 1.3, your leg is shapelier than expected. In either case, you'll benefit from some special adjustments to your socks.

A common fit problem arises when the foot, heel, and ankle fit well, but the sock leg doesn't stay up (see sidebar below). There are a number of factors that cause this to happen, each with its own solution.

Let's examine some situations in which leg adjustments are necessary and how they should be made.

Why Sock Legs Fall Down

There are a number of reasons why sock legs fall down, and not all of them require recalculations.

If the leg (and foot) of a sock doesn't allow for about 10 percent negative ease, it won't hug the leg and will slouch down.

If the leg is sized for the wider circumference of the lower calf but it doesn't actually reach that wider circumference, it will be too baggy and will fall down. This often happens because the leg shortens when it's stretched to full circumference—be sure to allow for this when determining the final length of the sock leg.

If the cast-on edge for a top-down sock isn't flexible, it won't stretch to accommodate the slightly larger low-calf circumference. See pages 34 and 35 for suitable cast-ons.

If the bind-off edge of a toe-up sock isn't flexible, it also won't stretch to accommodate the slightly larger low-calf circumference. See page 52 for suitable bind-offs.

If the leg is sized for the narrowest part of the ankle but reaches well into the wider circumference of the calf, it might not be able to stretch to fit that circumference and will fall down. If you don't want to shorten the leg, you can simply fold over the cuff for an effectively shorter length.

SITUATION: SKINNY LEGS

Ankle Circumference ÷ Low-Calf Circumference ≤ 1

If the ankle, heel, and foot circumferences conform to the standard rules but the low-calf circumference is smaller than or very close to the ankle circumference, the sock leg may not stay up. The solution is reasonably straightforward for a calf-length sock, because skinny legs tend to be skinny all the way down to the ankle for a constant circumference throughout.

Solution: Make the sock shorter
Simply fold over the upper part of the leg to make a cuff or end the leg sooner to make ankle-length socks.

Solution: Make the leg tighter
Make the leg tighter by using smaller needles or by working a "tighter" stitch pattern—such as ribbing or cables—that compresses the stitches around the leg.

Solution: Make the leg narrower
To make a narrower leg while keeping the heel, foot, and toes the same, you'll want to allow for more-than-standard negative ease. Multiply the ankle circumference by 0.8 (instead of 0.9) to get the target leg circumference, then use that number in the tables or formulas to calculate the number of stitches to work in the leg of the sock. Use the standard amount of ease (0.9) for the foot.

For a top-down sock, work the leg on the recalculated number of stitches for the desired length to the heel. Then work an increase round to achieve the necessary number of stitches for the standard heel and foot.

For a toe-up sock, work the foot on the standard number of stitches to the end of the gusset decrease/heel flap section. Then work a decrease round to reduce the stitch count to the recalculated number for the leg.

There are limitations to this. If the difference between the foot and ankle circumferences is greater than 30 percent, you can end up with a "gathered" look at the ankle, which isn't attractive. This solution also doesn't work for a foot that has a narrow heel—see page 168 for that.

SITUATION: SHAPELY LEGS

Low-Calf Circumference ÷ Ankle Circumference = 1.3 or more

If the ankle, heel, and foot circumferences conform to the standard rules, but the low-calf circumference is more than 30 percent larger than the ankle circumference, the sock leg may not stretch enough to accommodate the larger low-calf circumference. The upper part of the sock leg will fall down to where the circumference requires less stretch. The solution lies in allowing for the additional curve in the leg.

Solution: Make the leg shorter
A simple solution is to adjust the length of the leg so that the upper edge (the cast-on edge if knitting from the top down; the bind-off edge if knitting from the toe up) falls within the narrow ankle circumference. In other words, the sock doesn't cover the curvy portion of the calf. You can get this effect by knitting a shorter leg or simply folding down the upper part of the sock leg to create a folded cuff.

Solution: Make the leg wider
For legs that are consistently wide from the ankle to the low-calf, make the leg of the sock larger than normal for the same foot and heel size. This solution works best for socks that are mid-calf or shorter and where the low-calf circumference is no more than 10 percent larger than the ankle circumference.

Low-Calf Circumference ÷ Ankle Circumference = 1.3 to 1.4

In this case, you'll want to base the number of stitches in the sock leg on the wider circumference at the low-calf, instead of the circumference at the ankle. Multiply the low-calf circumference by 0.9 to get the target leg circumference, then use that number in the tables or formulas to calculate the number of stitches to work in the leg of the sock. Use the standard amount of ease for the foot.

For a top-down sock, work the leg on the recalculated number of stitches for the desired length to the heel. Then work a decrease round to achieve the necessary number of stitches for the standard heel and foot.

For a toe-up sock, work the foot on the standard number of stitches to the end of the gusset decrease/heel flap section. Then work an increase round to achieve the recalculated number of stitches for the leg.

The risk with this solution is that the sock leg may be baggy around the narrowest part of the ankle. You can remedy this by adding ribbing in this area to condense the stitches, or you can tailor the sock to fit the actual curve of the leg. Read on.

Solution: Tailor the sock to the curve of the leg

If there is a lot of difference between the ankle and low-calf circumferences, you'll do best to tailor the sock leg to match these measurements.

To tailor the shape of the leg, you'll need to measure the leg in four places—the low-calf circumference (or where you want the top of the leg to end), the ankle circumference (measure the narrowest part), the circumference halfway between these two measurements, and the length between the ankle and low-calf circumferences.

For example, let's say we're designing a sock for a leg that has an ankle circumference of 8 inches (20.5 cm), mid-height circumference of 9½ inches (24 cm) and low-calf circumference of 11½ inches (29 cm). Let's also say that we want the leg of the sock to be 8 inches (20.5 cm) long, and we're working at a gauge of 7.5 stitches and 10 rounds per inch (2.5 cm).

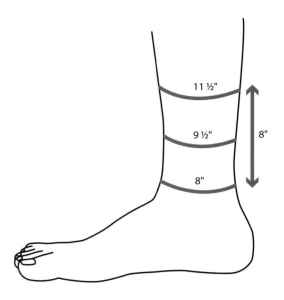

You'll want to slope the leg if there is a big difference between your low calf and ankle circumferences.

The first step is to convert the measurements into numbers of stitches and rows by multiplying them by the gauge (stitch gauge for horizontal measurements; row/round gauge for vertical measurements) and allow for the proper amount of negative ease to ensure a snug fit.

Low-Calf (Top Circumference) Stitches:

(Low-Calf Circumference × Gauge in Stitches per Inch) × 0.9

(11.5" × 7.5 stitches per inch) × 0.9

= 86.25 stitches × 0.9

= 77.62 stitches, which we'll round to nearest even number = 78 stitches

Mid-Leg Stitches:

(Mid-Leg Circumference × Gauge in Stitches per Inch) × 0.9

= (9.5" × 7.5 stitches per inch) × 0.9

= 71.25 stitches × 0.9

= 64.12 stitches, which we'll round to the nearest even number = 64 stitches

Ankle Stitches:

$$\textbf{(Ankle Circumference × Gauge in Stitches per Inch) × 0.9}$$

$$= (8" × 7.5\ \text{stitches per inch}) × 0.9$$

$$= 60\ \text{stitches} × 0.9$$

$$= 54\ \text{stitches}$$

Leg Rounds:

$$\textbf{Leg Length × Gauge in Rounds per Inch}$$

$$= 8" × 10\ \text{rounds per inch}$$

$$= 80\ \text{rounds}$$

To work from the top down, we'd cast on 78 stitches, decrease 14 stitches to 64 stitches over the first half of the leg (over 40 rounds), then decrease 10 stitches to 54 stitches over the second half of the leg (over the remaining 40 rounds).

To work from the toe up, we'd begin with 54 stitches at the ankle, increase 10 stitches to 64 stitches over the first half of the leg (40 rounds), then increase 14 stitches to 78 stitches over the second half of the leg (remaining 40 rounds).

In general, sock leg shaping is centered along the back of the leg with two mirrored decreases or increases worked in each shaping round (see sidebar above right). Therefore, there will be 7 shaping rounds in the upper half of the sock where there's a difference of 14 stitches between the low-calf and mid-sock circumferences. There will be 5 shaping rounds in the lower half of the sock where there's a difference of 10 stitches between the ankle and mid-sock circumferences.

The tricky part is determining how to space those decreases or increases. We have 80 rounds in the entire length of the leg, which allows 40 rounds for each of the two shaping sections.

Low Cuff to Mid-Point

In the 40 rounds between the top of the sock and the mid-point, we want 7 shaping rounds. To determine the placement of these rounds, divide the number of rounds by the number of shaping rounds plus 1 (see sidebar at right).

Shaping Rounds

Depending on whether you're knitting top down or toe up, you'll work 2 increases or 2 decreases in each shaping round. To center the shaping over the center back leg, place two markers in the middle of the back of the leg. If you've got an even number of stitches on the back of the leg, place a marker on each side of the center two stitches; if you've got an odd number of stitches, place a marker on each side of the center stitch.

Work mirrored increases or decreases as follows.

INCREASE ROUND: Knit to first marker, M1R (see Glossary), slip marker, knit to next marker, slip marker, M1L (see Glossary), knit to end of round—2 stitches increased.

DECREASE ROUND: Knit to 2 stitches before first marker, ssk (see Glossary), slip marker, knit to next marker, slip marker, k2tog (see Glossary), knit to end of round—2 stitches decreased.

Why Add 1?

We add "1" to the number of shaping rounds to ensure there will be an even number of rounds both before and after the shaping. If we simply divide the total number of rounds by the number of shaping rounds, we'd end up with a shaping round in either the first or last round of that section. The fit is best when the shaping rounds are spaced out evenly, with a few even rounds before the first and after the last shaping round in a section.

Number of Rounds ÷ (Number of Shaping Rounds + 1)

40 rounds ÷ (7 shaping rounds +1)

= 40 rounds ÷ 8 shaping rounds

= 5 rounds per shaping interval

This tells us that we'll work 5 rounds before the first shaping round, then we'll work the shaping every following 5th round. In other words, we'll work 5 rounds even, then we'll work a shaping round followed by 4 rounds even until a total of 40 rounds and 7 shaping rounds have been completed.

The instructions would read: Work 5 rounds even, [work a shaping round, work 4 rounds even] 7 times.

Mid-Point to Ankle

We have another 40 rounds in which to work the shaping between the mid-point of the leg and the ankle. We need to adjust the stitch count by 10 stitches in this interval, which means there will be 5 shaping rounds.

Number of Rounds ÷ (Number of Shaping Rounds + 1)

40 rounds ÷ (5 shaping rounds + 1)

= 40 rounds ÷ 6 shaping rounds

= 6.66 rounds per shaping interval

We obviously can't work with fractions when it comes to numbers of rounds to work, so we'll round to the nearest whole number, which, in this case, is 7.

This tells us that every 7th round will be a shaping round. In other words, we'll work 6 rounds even between the shaping rounds. But, because the calculation didn't produce a whole number, we can't assume that we'll work 7 rounds even before the first shaping round. To figure out the number of even rounds to begin with, subtract the number of shaping rounds from the total number of rounds in the shaping interval.

Number of Rounds − (Number of Rounds in Shaping Interval × Number of Shaping Intervals)

40 rounds − (7 rounds per shaping interval × 5 shaping intervals)

= 40 rounds − 35 rounds

= 5 rounds

This tells us that we'll work 5 rounds before the first shaping round. The instructions would read: Work 5 rounds even, [work a shaping round, work 6 rounds even] 5 times.

In summary, the top-down leg instructions would read:

Cast on 78 stitches. Work 5 rounds even. [Work decrease round, work 4 rounds even] 7 times—64 stitches remain. Work 5 rounds even. [Work decrease round, work 6 rounds even] 5 times—54 stitches remain.

The toe-up instructions would begin with 54 stitches at the end of the heel. The leg instructions would read:

Work 5 rounds even. [Work increase round, work 6 rounds even] 5 times—64 stitches. Work 5 rounds even. [Work increase round, work 4 rounds even] 7 times—78 stitches.

Bind off all stitches.

Of course, these types of calculations can be refined to best fit the shape of the leg you're dealing with. Instead of breaking the two calculations exactly at the mid-length of the sock leg, you can work one set of shaping over more rounds than the other. For example, for a muscular leg, you might want to work the calf expansion over a shorter distance. In this case, measure the circumference at the point at which the calf shape changes, then measure the distance from the ankle to that point and the distance from that point to the top of the sock and use those circumferences and lengths in your calculations.

Math Check

I always like to check my math when doing this sort of thing—add up the number of even rounds, then add up the number of shaping rounds, then add them all together to make sure you're working the desired total number of rounds.

For our example, for the Low Cuff to Midpoint shaping, we'll work 5 rounds even, [work a shaping round, work 6 rounds even] 5 times.

The first 5 rounds will be worked even, plus 6 rounds will be worked even 5 times. In other words, there will be 5 + (6 × 5) = 35 even rounds.

There will also be a total of 5 shaping rounds.

35 even rounds + 5 shaping rounds = 40 rounds.

A Bit of Fudge

Don't be afraid to include a little fudging in these types of calculations when the math doesn't work out perfectly. As long as you have the correct stitch counts in the correct places, you'll be fine. Don't worry if you need to work an extra increase or decrease round or if the lengths are a bit off. A few rounds aren't going to make a significant difference in the finished sock.

For example, let's look at what would happen if we wanted to work 5 shaping rounds over a total of 38 rounds.

Number of Rounds ÷ (Number of Shaping Rounds + 1)

$$38 \text{ rounds} \div (5 \text{ shaping rounds} + 1)$$

$$= 38 \text{ rounds} \div 6 \text{ shaping rounds}$$

$$= 6.33 \text{ rounds in shaping interval; which we'll}$$
$$\text{round to the nearest whole number} = 6$$

This tells us that the shaping will be worked every 6th round 5 times with some rounds left over to work even before the first shaping round. We'll determine the number of rounds to work even before the first shaping round as before.

Number of Rounds – (Number of Rounds in Shaping Interval × Number of Shaping Intervals)

$$38 \text{ rounds} - (6 \text{ rounds per shaping interval} \times$$
$$5 \text{ shaping intervals})$$

$$= 38 \text{ rounds} - 30 \text{ rounds}$$

$$= 8 \text{ rounds}$$

This tells us we'll work 8 rounds even before the first shaping round. The instructions would read: Work 8 rounds even, [work a shaping round, work 5 rounds even] 5 times.

This works fine, but the shaping rounds could be distributed a bit more evenly. We could take 3 of the even rounds from the beginning of the instructions and distribute them evenly within the shaping intervals by adding an extra round in three of the repeats.

The modified instructions would read: Work 5 rounds even, work a shaping round, work 6 rounds even, work a shaping round, work 5 rounds even, work a shaping round, work 6 rounds even, work a shaping round, work 5 rounds even, work a shaping round, work 6 rounds even.

SITUATION: KNEE SOCKS

Whether or not your foot conforms to standard sock fit, knee-length socks always require leg shaping. Keep in mind that the shaping on handknitted knee socks can appear extreme when the sock isn't being worn. Commercially manufactured knee socks are typically made out of much stretchier fabrics so that the same circumference sock fits the entire leg—it stretches more where it needs to. Handknitted socks are not quite as stretchy, which is why shaping is necessary.

In general, a knee sock should be shaped between the under-knee circumference and the fullest part of the calf and again from the fullest part of the calf to the ankle. In addition, the upper part of the leg should be worked with more negative ease than the rest of the leg—about 20 percent negative ease in the middle of the leg and 25 percent negative ease around the cuff—than the usual 10 percent. This extra negative ease helps the sock legs stay put, even if they begin to stretch over the day. The Fitzcarraldo Knee Sock on page 178 is an example of a knee-length sock worked from the toe up, which allows it to be tried on to check the fit as it's knitted.

To custom-fit a knee sock, you'll need five leg measurements—the circumferences of the narrowest part of the ankle, fullest part of the calf, and narrowest part under the knee (where you want the top of the sock to hit). You'll also need the distances between the ankle and the fullest part of the calf, the distance between the fullest part of the calf and the under-knee measurement, as well as your stitch and round gauge.

For example, let's say we're designing a knee sock for a leg that has an ankle circumference of 8 inches (20.5 cm), full-calf circumference of 15½ inches (39.5 cm), and top-of-calf circumference of 14 inches (35.5 cm). Let's also say that we want the leg to measure 10 inches (25.5 cm) from the ankle to fullest part of calf 4 inches (10 cm) from the fullest part of calf to the top of the calf and that we're working at a gauge of 7.5 stitches and 10 rounds per inch (2.5 cm).

Again, the first step is to convert the measurements into numbers of stitches and rows by multiplying them by the gauge (stitch gauge for horizontal measurements; row/round gauge for vertical measurements) and allow for the proper amount of negative ease to ensure a snug fit—25 percent negative ease in the cuff, 20 percent negative ease in the full calf, and 10 percent negative ease in the ankle.

Cuff Stitches:

(Top Circumference × Gauge in Stitches per Inch) × 0.75

(14" × 7.5 stitches per inch) × 0.75

= 105 stitches × 0.75

= 78.75 stitches, which we'll round to the nearest even number = 78 stitches

Full-Calf Stitches:

(Full-Calf Circumference × Gauge in Stitches per Inch) × 0.8

= (15.5" × 7.5 stitches per inch) × 0.8

= 116.25 stitches × 0.8

= 93 stitches, which well round to 94 stitches (we could just have easily rounded to 92)

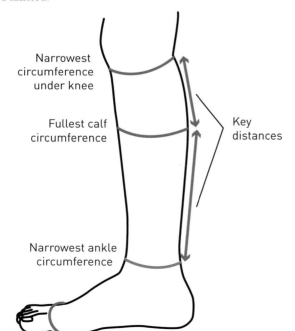

Narrowest circumference under knee

Fullest calf circumference

Key distances

Narrowest ankle circumference

Ankle and foot circumference

Ankle Stitches:

$$\textbf{(Ankle Circumference × Gauge in Stitches per Inch) × 0.9}$$

$$(8" × 7.5 \text{ stitches per inch}) × 0.9$$

$$= 60 \text{ stitches} × 0.9$$

$$= 54 \text{ stitches}$$

Upper Leg Rounds:

$$\textbf{(Length between Full Calf and Cuff) × Gauge in Rounds per Inch}$$

$$4" × 10 \text{ rounds per inch}$$

$$= 40 \text{ rounds}$$

Lower Leg Rounds:

$$\textbf{(Length between Ankle and Full Calf) × Gauge in Rounds per Inch}$$

$$10" × 10 \text{ rounds per inch}$$

$$= 100 \text{ rounds}$$

To work from the top down, we'd cast on 78 stitches, increase 16 stitches to 94 stitches over the first 40 rounds, then decrease 40 stitches to 54 stitches over the next 100 rounds.

To work from the toe up, we'd begin with 54 stitches at the ankle, increase 40 stitches to 94 stitches over the first 100 rounds, then decrease 16 stitches to 78 stitches over the next 40 rounds.

Again, the shaping will be centered along the center back of the leg with two mirrored decreases or increases worked in each shaping round (see sidebar on page 159). Therefore, there will be 8 shaping rounds in the upper 40 rounds where there's a difference of 16 stitches between the cuff and full-calf circumferences; there will be 20 shaping rounds in the lower 100 rounds where there's a difference of 40 stitches between the ankle and full-calf circumferences.

We'll use the same formulas we used for a calf-length sock (see page 158) to calculate the spacings of the shaping rounds.

On Ribbing for Knee-Sock Cuffs

Because the ribbing in a knee sock must stretch to a larger degree than the rest of the sock, it will have to be worked longer than you might expect. This is because the stitches shrink in length when they're stretched horizontally. Therefore, be sure to stretch the stitches widthwise when measuring the length of the cuff.

In most cases, handknitted knee socks fall down because they're too loose at the upper leg and cuff, which is why I've specified more negative ease in the upper sections of the leg. But if your socks still fall down, there are a number of solutions.

Work the cuff on smaller needles, or work a twisted ribbing (see page 64).

Add a hem by working an additional 2 inches to 3 inches (5 to 7.5 cm) of ribbing, fold the ribbing in half to the inside of the sock, insert a length of 1 inch (2.5 cm) elastic, and sew the cast-on edge to the last row of ribbing to secure the elastic in place.

Work the hem as above, but make two small buttonholes about 1 inch (2.5 cm) down from the top at the center back. Turn the hem down to the outside, thread a length of ribbon through the folded edge, beginning and ending at each buttonhole, then tie it into a snug bow.

Shaping Between Cuff and Full Calf

Between the top of the sock and the full calf, we have 40 rounds in which to work 8 shaping rounds. Of the 4 inches (10 cm) in this section, we want 2 inches (5 cm) to be ribbing, which leaves us with 20 rounds over which to work the 8 rounds of shaping.

$$\textbf{Number of Rounds ÷ (Number of Shaping Rounds + 1)}$$

$$20 \text{ rounds} ÷ (8 \text{ shaping rounds} + 1)$$

$$= 20 \text{ rounds} ÷ 9 \text{ shaping rounds}$$

$$= 2.22 \text{ rounds, which we'll round to the nearest whole number} = 2 \text{ rounds}$$

This tells us that we'll work 2 rounds before the first shaping round, then we'll work the shaping round every 2nd round 8 times. Let's check the number of rounds this will take.

$$2 \text{ rounds} + [\text{shaping round}, 1 \text{ round even}] \text{ 8 times}$$

$$= 2 \text{ rounds} + 16 \text{ rounds}$$

$$= 18 \text{ rounds}$$

We need to work 2 more rounds to get to the target 20 rounds, so we can add those extra rounds in the middle of the sequence as follows.

Work 2 rounds even, [(work shaping round, work 1 even) 3 times, (work shaping round, work 2 rounds even)] twice for a total of 20 rounds and 8 shaping rounds.

Shaping Between Full Calf and Ankle

Between the full calf and the ankle, we have 100 rounds in which to work 20 shaping rounds.

Number of Rounds ÷ (Number of Shaping Rounds + 1)

$$100 \text{ rounds} \div (20 \text{ shaping rounds} + 1)$$

$$= 100 \text{ rounds} \div 21 \text{ rounds}$$

$$= 4.76 \text{ rounds, which we'll round to the nearest whole number} = 5 \text{ rounds}$$

This tells us that we'll work 5 rounds before the first shaping round, then we'll work the shaping round every 5th round 20 times. Let's check the number of rounds this will take.

$$5 \text{ rounds} + [\text{shaping round}, 4 \text{ rounds even}] \text{ 20 times}$$

$$= 5 \text{ rounds} + [5 \text{ rounds}] \text{ 20 times}$$

$$= 5 \text{ rounds} + 100 \text{ rounds}$$

$$= 105 \text{ rounds}$$

We're 5 rounds over the target number of 100 rounds, so we'll have to remove those excess rounds in the middle of the sequence as follows.

Work 5 even rounds, [work shaping round, work 4 rounds even] 15 times, [work shaping round, work 3 rounds even] 5 times for a total of 100 rounds and 20 shaping rounds.

To distribute the shaping rounds a little more evenly, we can alternate the 5- and 4-round intervals as follows.

Work 5 even rounds, [(work shaping round, work 4 rounds even) 3 times, (work shaping round, work 3 rounds even)] 5 times.

In summary, the top-down instructions would read:

Cast on 78 sts.

Work ribbing for 2" (5 cm).

Work 2 rounds even, [(work increase round, work 1 even) 3 times, (work increase round, work 2 rounds even)] 2 times—94 stitches.

Work 5 even rounds, [(work decrease round, work 4 rounds even) 3 times, (work decrease round, work 3 rounds even)] 5 times—54 stitches remain.

The toe-up instructions would begin with 54 stitches at the end of the heel. The leg instructions would read:

Work 5 even rounds, [(work increase round, work 4 rounds even) 3 times, (work increase round, work 3 rounds even)] 5 times—94 stitches.

Work 2 rounds even, [(work decrease round, work 1 round even) 3 times, (work decrease round, work 2 rounds even)] 2 times—78 stitches remain.

Work ribbing for 2" (5 cm).

Bind off all stitches.

Of course, these calculations can be further refined to best fit the shape of the leg you're dealing with. For a particularly shapely leg, you might want to include another circumference—mid-way between the full-calf and ankle, for example—and calculate three shaping intervals instead of just the two we calculated here. See The Fitzcarraldo Knee Sock on page 178 for a case study.

Foot Circumference Adjustments

If the ankle and foot circumferences aren't proportionate, you'll first want to determine whether it's the ankle (or indeed, the leg) or the foot that's "out of line." In other words, is the problem a disproportionate ankle or leg on a well-proportioned foot or is the problem a disproportionate foot on a well-proportioned ankle and leg? For example, tall skinny men often have very skinny legs compared to their feet, and short women with larger feet often have even larger ankles and calves. On the other hand, I know a woman who has a larger-than-usual forefoot with big bunions and swollen toes resulting from years of wearing high heels while working as a model.

A number of formulas that involve the Diagonal Heel Circumference will help determine where the problem lies.

If the heel is proportionate to the foot

**Diagonal Heel Circumference ÷
Foot Circumference = 1.3 to 1.4**

If the heel is proportionate to the leg

**Diagonal Heel Circumference ÷
Ankle Circumference = 1.3 to 1.4**

If the leg and foot are about the same, then these two formulas will give the same (or close to the same) number. If there's a discrepancy of more than 20 percent between the two, then there are number of possibilities. Let's examine them.

As Goes the Foot, So Goes the Toe

Keep in mind that if you adjust the number of stitches in the foot of a sock, the number of stitches in the toe may change accordingly. This isn't an issue when working a sock from the top down because you'll simply work the decreases until 8 or 10 stitches remain. But the number of stitches cast on for a toe-up sock depends on the number of stitches that will be in the foot.

Given that 4 stitches are increased in each increase round, you'll want to make sure to cast on a number of stitches that's a multiple of 4 stitches less than the desired number of stitches in the foot.

For example, if you want 60 stitches in the foot, which is a multiple of 4 stitches, you can cast on a multiple of 4 stitches—8, 12, 16, 20, 24, etc.

But if the number of stitches needed in the foot isn't a multiple of 4 stitches, you'll need to begin by determining how many stitches that number deviates from a multiple of 4.

For example, 62 foot stitches is a multiple of 4 stitches + 2 stitches. In this case, you'd need to cast on a multiple of 4 + 2 stitches—10, 14, 18, 22, 26, etc.

Because an even number of stitches has to be cast on for a toe-up sock, you'll have to make another adjustment if the foot requires an odd number of stitches. In these cases, increase in groups of 4 stitches until you get to the closest even number, then work a single final increase or decrease to get to the necessary odd number of stitches.

SITUATION:
ANKLE IS LARGER THAN FOOT; HEEL IS PROPORTIONATE TO FOOT

Ankle Circumference Is Larger than Foot Circumference

and

Diagonal Heel Circumference ÷ Foot Circumference = 1.3 to 1.4

In this situation, the leg is proportionately larger than the foot, but the foot is proportionate to the heel.

Solution: Work the leg on more stitches than the foot and heel

Determine the stitch count for the leg by the ankle circumference and the stitch count for the foot by the smaller foot circumference, allowing for 10 percent negative ease.

Leg Stitches = (Ankle Circumference × Gauge in Stitches per Inch) × 0.9

Foot Stitches = (Foot Circumference × Gauge in Stitches per Inch) × 0.9

Work increases or decreases at the boundary between the heel and leg to adjust between the two stitch counts so that the heel is worked on 50 percent of the foot stitches.

For a top-down sock, work the leg on the calculated number of leg stitches (adding leg shaping if desired). On the final round of the leg, decrease as necessary to achieve the calculated number of stitches for the foot and work the heel on 50 percent of the foot stitches.

For a toe-up sock, work the toe, foot, gusset, and heel on the calculated number of foot stitches. Once the heel is complete, work an increase round to achieve the calculated number of stitches for the leg.

SITUATION:
ANKLE IS LARGER THAN FOOT; HEEL IS PROPORTIONATE TO ANKLE

Ankle Circumference Is Larger than Foot Circumference

and

Diagonal Heel Circumference ÷ Ankle Circumference = 1.3 to 1.4

In this situation, the ankle and the heel are proportionate to each other, but they're both larger than the foot.

Solution: Work the foot on fewer stitches than the leg and heel

Determine the stitch count for the leg by the ankle circumference and the stitch count for the foot by the smaller foot circumference, allowing for 10 percent negative ease.

Leg Stitches = (Ankle Circumference × Gauge in Stitches per Inch) × 0.9

Foot Stitches = (Foot Circumference × Gauge in Stitches per Inch) × 0.9

For a top-down sock, work the leg on the calculated number of stitches (adding leg shaping if desired), then work the heel on 50 percent of these stitches. Work more gusset decreases than usual to achieve the calculated number of stitches for the foot. Before beginning the toe decreases, rearrange the stitches as necessary so that there is the same number of stitches on the instep as on the sole.

For a toe-up sock, work the toe and foot on the calculated number of foot stitches. Work additional gusset increases to make up the difference between the foot and the leg stitch counts. If you need 6 more stitches for the leg, for example, work 3 additional gusset stitches each side. Work the heel on 50 percent of the leg stitches and decrease the heel flap to the proper stitch count for the leg. Because more stitches will be increased in the gusset, the gusset shaping will have to begin earlier than usual—use the formulas on page 61 to calculate when to begin the gusset increases.

SITUATION:
ANKLE IS LARGER THAN HEEL; HEEL IS LARGER THAN FOOT

Ankle Circumference Is Greater than Foot Circumference

and

Diagonal Heel Circumference ÷ Foot Circumference Is Greater than 1.4

and

Diagonal Heel Circumference ÷ Ankle Circumference Is Less than 1.4

In this situation, the ankle is proportionately larger than the heel, which, in turn, is proportionately larger than the foot.

Solution: There are two factors at play here, and you'll need two solutions

In short, the heel needs to be larger than the foot, and the leg needs to be larger than the heel.

To enlarge the heel, you'll need to enlarge the gusset as described below.

Leg Stitches = (Ankle Circumference × Gauge in Stitches per Inch) × 0.9

Foot Stitches = (Foot Circumference × Gauge in Stitches per Inch) × 0.9

For a top-down sock, work the leg on the calculated number of stitches (adding leg shaping if desired), work the heel rows (as determined by the gusset adjustment), then work additional gusset decreases to achieve the calculated number of stitches for the foot.

For a toe-up sock, work the toe and foot on the calculated number of foot stitches and work additional gusset increases. Again, because more stitches will be increased in the gusset, the gusset shaping will have to begin earlier than usual. Once the heel is complete, work an additional increase round to achieve the calculated number of stitches for the leg.

SITUATION:
ANKLE IS SMALLER THAN HEEL; HEEL IS SMALLER THAN FOOT

Ankle Circumference Is Smaller than Foot Circumference

and

Diagonal Heel Circumference ÷ Ankle Circumference Is Less than 1.3

and

Diagonal Heel Circumference ÷ Foot Circumference Is Greater than 1.3

In this situation, the ankle is proportionately smaller than the heel, which, in turn, is proportionately smaller than the foot.

Solution: Work the heel on fewer stitches than the foot; work the leg on fewer stitches than the heel

There are two factors at play here, so you'll need two solutions. In short, the heel needs to be smaller than the foot, and the leg needs to be smaller than the heel.

Determine the stitch count for the leg by the ankle circumference, the size of the heel by the gusset circumference using either the short-cut gusset formula on page 169 or the full gusset adjustment as outlined on page 170), and the stitch count for the foot by the smaller foot circumference.

Leg Stitches = (Ankle Circumference × Gauge in Stitches per Inch) × 0.9

Foot Stitches = (Foot Circumference × Gauge in Stitches per Inch) × 0.9

For a top-down sock, work the leg on the calculated number of leg stitches (adding leg shaping if desired).

Work the heel on 50 percent of the leg stitches, but work more heel rows as determined by the gusset adjustment calculation, then work fewer gusset decreases to achieve the calculated number of stitches for the foot. To compensate for the fewer gusset decreases and ensure a suitable gusset length, work 2 rounds even (instead of just 1) between the decrease rounds. Rearrange the stitches if necessary so that there is the same number of instep as sole stitches when you begin the toe shaping.

For a toe-up sock, work the toe and foot on the calculated number of foot stitches. Work the gusset increases as per the gusset adjustment and then once the heel is complete, work the decreases in the first round of the leg to get to the specified number of leg stitches.

SITUATION:
FOOT AND ANKLE ARE PROPORTIONATE, BUT HEEL IS LARGER

Ankle Circumference = Foot Circumference

and

**Diagonal Heel Circumference ÷
Ankle Circumference is Greater than 1.4**

See Fine-Tuning the Gusset Circumference on page 170.

SITUATION:
FOOT AND ANKLE ARE PROPORTIONATE, BUT HEEL IS SMALLER

Ankle Circumference = Foot Circumference

and

**Diagonal Heel Circumference ÷
Ankle Circumference is Less than 1.3**

See Fine-tuning the Gusset Circumference on page 170.

Gusset Circumference Adjustments

The basic formulas assume that your gusset circumference is about 10 percent greater than the foot circumference.

Gusset Circumference = Foot Circumference × 1.1

If the foot you're knitting for has a high or low arch that doesn't fit that assumption, you can make some simple tweaks (without a lot of math) to improve the fit. If the tweaks aren't enough, you can fine-tune the fit by calculating the correct number of stitches for the gusset, then including that number in the overall calculations.

SITUATION: HIGH ARCH

Gusset Circumference ÷ Foot Circumference Is Greater than 1.1

If you have a high arch (i.e., a larger gusset circumference), chances are that your socks fit well in the foot and leg, but are tight and pull around the heel diagonal.

Solution: Increase the number of gusset stitches and lengthen the heel flap

For a Top-Down Sock
Adjust the number of rows in the heel flap as follows.

High-Arch Heel Flap Rows = Heel Rows (from table) × 1.25

or

High-Arch Heel Flap Rows = Number of Heel Stitches (from formula)

Use one of the two formulas above to determine the number of rows to work in the heel flap, rounding up to an even number if necessary. For each additional pair of heel flap rows, pick up 1 more gusset stitch at each side. Decrease the gusset stitches as usual to the desired number of foot stitches.

For a Toe-Up Sock
Adjust the gusset stitches calculation as follows.

Gusset Stitches Per Side = Sock Stitches × 0.25 or 0.3

You'll need to recalculate the number of gusset stitches according to the formula above. The basic toe-up sock pattern (see page 54) adds 20 percent more stitches to each side of the foot—for a high instep, you'll want to increase that to 25 to 30 percent more stitches, according to the formula above. The heel flap works on the revised number of gusset stitches.

SITUATION: LOW ARCH

Gusset Circumference ÷ Foot Circumference Is Less than 1.1

If you have a lower arch (i.e., a smaller gusset circumference), your socks might wrinkle around the heel diagonal but fit well around the foot and leg.

Solution: Reduce the number of gusset stitches and shorten the heel flap

For a Top-Down Sock
Adjust the number of rows in the heel flap as follows.

Low-Arch Heel Flap Rows = Heel Rows (from table) × 0.8

or

Low-Arch Heel Flap Rows = Number of Heel Stitches (from formula) × 0.65

Use one of the formulas above to determine the number of rows to work in the heel flap, rounding to an even number if necessary. Pick up 1 gusset stitch for every 2 rows in the heel flap, plus 2 extra stitches at the top of the gusset as described on page 36. Decrease the gusset stitches as usual to the desired number of foot stitches.

For a Toe-Up Sock
Adjust the gusset stitches calculation as follows.

Gusset Stitches Per Side = Sock Stitches × 0.15

You'll need to recalculate the number of gusset stitches according to the formula above. The basic toe-up sock pattern (see page 55) adds 20 percent more stitches to each side of the foot—for a low arch, you'll want to decrease that to about 15 percent more stitches, according to the formula above, then the heel flap works on that revised number of gusset stitches.

FINE-TUNING THE GUSSET CIRCUMFERENCE

If you find that the high-instep and low-arch adjustments don't produce a good fit, or if you're comfortable working out a few more calculations, you can fine-tune the gusset circumference and heel flap length for a precise fit. Some of the calculations will be the same whether you plan to work from the top down or from the toe up; others will depend on the direction you plan to knit.

To begin, you'll want to know how many stitches there should be in the gusset at its fullest circumference, allowing for 10 percent negative ease (you can, of course, adjust the amount of negative ease as required to accommodate a stitch pattern).

The Gusset Total for a Top-Down Sock = (Gusset Circumference × Gauge in Stitches per Inch) × 0.9

If working from the top down, this is the stitch count you'll want after the gusset pick-up is complete; if working from the toe up, this is the stitch count you'll want after the gusset increases are complete.

The circumference around the gusset is directly related to the length of the heel flap. For a sock worked from the top down, the circumference of the sock at this point is a function of the number of stitches in the instep, the number of stitches that remain after the heel turn, and the number of stitches in each gusset.

Instep Stitches + Stitches Remaining after the Heel Turn + (2 × Gusset Stitches)

The number of gusset stitches is determined by the number of rows in the heel flap.

Gusset Stitches = (Heel Flap Rows ÷ 2) + 2

For a sock that's worked from the toe up, the full gusset circumference stitch count involves simple addition.

Full Gusset Circumference for Toe-Up Socks = Sock Stitches + (2 × Gusset Stitches per Side)

The numbers of rows in the heel flap is determined by the number of stitches increased—2 heel flap rows are worked for every 2 gusset stitches increased.

If the number of stitches changes in the gusset, the number of rows will change in the heel flap. But that's appropriate—the length of the heel flap determines where the sock divides for the instep and heel, which should coincide with the top of the instep.

Top-Down Socks

If you're working top down, first determine the number of rows you'll need to work in the heel flap so that you'll end up with the correct number of stitches after picking up stitches for the gussets.

Total Number of Gusset Stitches to Pick Up = Full Gusset Total – Heel Stitches – (HT2 +2)

In other words, the number of gusset stitches to be picked up (both sides added together) is equal to the number of stitches for the desired gusset circumference, less the instep stitches (which is the same as the Heel Stitches) and less the number of stitches that remain when the heel turn is complete (which is HT2 + 2).

Because the gusset stitches are evenly divided between the two sides of the foot, the number of gusset stitches on each side will be half of the total number of gusset stitches.

Gusset Stitches per Side = Total Number of Gusset Stitches to Pick Up ÷ 2

Because 1 gusset stitch is picked up at each side every other row, 2 rows will be worked in the heel flap for every gusset stitch to be picked up along one side of the heel flap. But, we also have to account for the 2 gusset stitches that are picked up in the leg (see page 36) in addition to the stitches picked up along the chain edge heel flap stitches. Therefore, the number of rows to work in the heel flap is twice the number of gusset stitches on each side, less 4 stitches.

Heel Flap Rows = (2 × Gusset Stitches per Side) − 4

This calculation is independent of others in the sock, making it nice and simple: If we need to pick up 20 gusset stitches on each side, then there will be 36 heel flap rows.

$$(2 \times 20) - 4 = 36$$

Toe-Up Socks

If you're working toe up, first determine the number of gusset stitches to be increased at each side, which is based on the difference between the total gusset stitches and the foot stitches.

Number of Gusset Stitches to Increase Each Side = (Full Gusset Total − Foot Stitches) ÷ 2

For example, if you're knitting a sock for a foot that a 9½ inches (24 cm) circumference and 12 inches (30.5 cm) full gusset circumference at a gauge is 8 stitches per inch (2.5 cm), the calculations would be as follows.

$$Sock\ Stitches = 9\frac{1}{2}" \times 0.9 \times 8$$

$$= 68.4\ stitches;\ which\ rounds\ to\ 68\ stitches$$

$$Full\ Gusset\ Total = 12 \times 0.9 \times 8$$

$$= 86.4\ stitches;\ which\ rounds\ to\ 86\ stitches$$

This tells you that you'll need a total of 18 gusset stitches, or 9 gusset stitches on each side.

$$86 - 68 = 18$$

$$18 \div 2 = 9$$

Next, determine when to begin the increases based on the formulas on page 61.

Length of Heel and Gusset = [(Gusset Stitches × 2) + (Heel Stitches − Heel Base Stitches)] ÷ Rounds per Inch

Therefore, you'd work the foot to the prescribed length, then increase 1 gusset each side of the foot every other round until the recalculated total number of stitches is achieved. Work the heel on 50 percent of the original number of Sock Stitches, decreasing the gussets and working the heel flap according to the revised number of heel stitches. Work the leg as usual (adding shaping if desired).

Foot Length Adjustments

The basic patterns in this book assume that the foot length corresponds to those in the tables on pages 12–14. If you find that your sock feet are too long or too short—even when you take precise measurements—there are a number of solutions. But before you start recalculating any numbers, make sure you're knitting the correct size.

A sock that's too narrow (and therefore stretches a lot to fit the circumference) won't have as much lengthwise stretch, and the foot will feel too short. Equally, a sock that's too wide (and therefore doesn't stretch at all to fit the circumference) will have too much lengthwise stretch, and the foot will feel too long.

SITUATION:
NEGATIVE EASE ISN'T INCLUDED

Keep in mind that the elasticity of wool is bound to cause a sock to stretch out. If, when you put the sock on in the morning, it's exactly the same length as your foot (or even a bit longer), the foot of the sock will simply be too long after you've worn it a few hours.

Solution: Allow for About 5 Percent Negative Ease

A finished sock should be about ½ inch (1.3 cm) shorter than the actual foot length for an adult or about ¼ inch (6 mm) shorter than the actual foot length for a child.

Proper Sock Foot Length

Be cautious when following a sock pattern that specifies working the foot to a particular length. If that length isn't right for your foot, the finished sock won't fit well. You'll do better to work a few calculations and adjust the length according to the length you really need.

Top-Down Socks

To determine where to start the toe shaping on a top-down sock, subtract the negative ease (¼ inch to ½ inch, as above) and the toe cup length from the actual foot length.

Foot Length before Toe Shaping = Actual Foot Length – Negative Ease – Toe Cup Length

The toe cup length is determined by the number of rounds in the toe shaping.

Toe Cup Length = Number of Rounds in Toe ÷ Gauge in Rounds per Inch

Toe-Up Socks

To determine where to start the gusset shaping on a toe-up sock, calculate the length of the gusset and heel, then add a bit of negative ease. You'll need to look at the construction of the heel and gusset in the pattern to figure this out.

For example, if the gusset increases are worked every other round as part of the foot, then the gusset length is a function of the number of stitches increased each side and the round gauge.

Gusset Length = (2 × Gusset Stitches per Side) ÷ Gauge in Rounds per Inch (2.5 cm)

The heel length is a function of the number of rows/rounds in the sole portion of the heel turn and the round gauge.

Heel Length = Heel Rows/Rounds ÷ Gauge in Rounds per Inch (2.5 cm)

For the patterns in this book, the number of rounds in the base of the heel is the difference between the total number of heel stitches and the number of stitches in the heel base.

Heel Base Rounds = Total Heel Stitches – Heel Base Stitches

To allow for negative ease, add ½ inch (1.3 cm) for adult socks; add ¼ inch (6 mm) for children's socks as follows.

For an adult, begin the gusset increases when the foot measures:

Foot length – Gusset Length – Heel Length – ½" (1.3 cm)

For a child, begin the gusset increases when the foot measures:

Foot length – Gusset Length – Heel Length – ¼" (6 mm)

SITUATION: TOES DON'T MATCH THE STANDARD LENGTH

If you're knitting for an adult and the longest toe is less than 1¾ inches (4.5 cm) or longer than 2¼ inches (5.5 cm), the toe cup will be too short or too long for a comfortable fit. For children's feet, in general, the toe cup length doesn't have as much effect on the fit so adjustments aren't needed.

Solution: Adjust the Toe Length
See Toe Shaping on page 176.

Toe Length Adjustments

The toe construction for the socks in this book assumes that the longest toe is between 1¾ inches and 2¼ inches (4.5 and 5.5 cm) long and that there's a gentle slope from the smallest toe to the big toe. It doesn't matter if the first or second toe is the longest. What is important is the length of the longest toe and the difference in length between the longest and shortest toes. A large difference between those two lengths requires more curve in the toe shaping; a small difference requires a flatter top.

The table below gives the standard length of the sock toes for the basic top-down and toe-up sock patterns in this book, based on the foot circumference. In general, a larger foot circumference corresponds to a longer foot, which, in turn, corresponds to longer toes. Therefore, it's safe to assume that the larger the foot, the more rounds will be necessary in the toe shaping. Note that in general, the toe shaping for toe-up socks is a bit longer than that for top-down socks because the shaping I've used for the toe-up toes has a few more rounds.

If your longest toe is significantly shorter or longer than these figures, you'll need to adjust the rate of toe shaping to adjust the length of your longest toe.

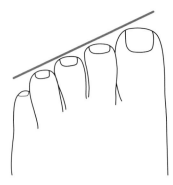

A flat shape requires less curve in the toe shaping.

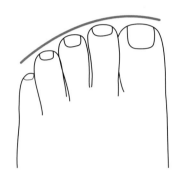

A curvier shape requires more curve in the toe shaping.

TOE LENGTH IN THE BASIC SOCK PATTERNS AS A FUNCTION OF FOOT CIRCUMFERENCE

FOOT CIRCUM IN INCHES	TOP-DOWN TOE SHAPING (THE HALF & HALF) LENGTH		TOE-UP TOE SHAPING (THE SIMPLE TOE) LENGTH	
	inches	cm	inches	cm
5	1	2.5	1.2	3
5½	1.2	3	1.3	3.25
6	1.3	3.25	1.4	3.5
6½	1.4	3.5	1.6	4
7	1.6	4	1.75	4.5
7½	1.75	4.5	1.75	4.5
8	1.9	4.75	2	5
8½	2	5	2.1	5.25
9	2.2	5.5	2.2	5.5
9½	2.3	5.75	2.3	5.75
10	2.4	6	2.5	6.25
10½	2.5	6.25	2.5	6.25

SITUATION:
THE SOCK TOE IS TOO SHORT

If the sock is for a foot with longer-than-expected toes, the standard toe shaping will result in a toe that's too short.

Solution: Work more rounds in the toe

The solution is to lengthen the toe by spreading the shaping over more rounds.

Top-Down Sock

For a top-down sock with fewer than 88 stitches, use the Barn Toe (see page 177), which adds more rounds to the toe cap for a nice curve and a no-graft tip. For a top-down sock with more than 88 stitches, work the adjusted shape that produces a slightly longer toe cup.

No matter how you adjust the toe, prevent a pointy no-graft tip by working the decreases more slowly at first (more "plain" rounds between decrease rounds), then more rapidly as you approach the tip of the toe (fewer "plain" rounds between the decrease rounds).

Toe-Up Sock

When it comes to working from the toe up, you have two choices. If the tip of the toe is the appropriate width, cast on the same number of stitches but work a "slower" increase by introducing some extra "even" rounds between the increases—a variation of the top-down Half & Half Toe shaping (see page 176). Work the first half of the increases in a 2-round pattern that alternates a "plain" round with an increase round, then work the remaining increases in a 3-round pattern that alternates 2 "plain" rounds with an increase round.

For example, let's say we cast-on 24 stitches and we want to increase 48 stitches to a total of 72 stitches. Because 4 stitches are increased on each increase round, we'll need to work a total of 12 increase rounds. We'll work half (6) of these increase rounds in the first shaping section and the other half (6) in the second shaping section.

The instructions would read: [Work 1 round even, work increase round] 6 times, then [work 2 rounds even, work increase round] 6 times.

If the tip of the toe is too wide, then start with fewer stitches as described on page 175.

SITUATION:
THE SOCK TOE IS TOO LONG

If the sock is for a foot with shorter-than-expected toes, the standard toe shaping will result in a toe that's too long.

Solution: Work fewer rounds in the toe

Top-Down Sock

For a top-down sock, work a Half & Half Toe (see page 176) to about 30 percent of the sock stitches, then graft the tip.

Toe-Up Sock

For a toe-up sock, start with the stitch count determined by the tables or formulas, but work the Half & Half Toe (see page 176) instead of the Simple Toe shaping (see page 176) that's typically specified.

SITUATION:
THE SOCK TOE IS TOO NARROW

If there's not a significant difference in the circumference at the ball of the foot and the tops of the toes—which is fairly common in wide feet on men—more stitches are needed at the tip of the toes.

Top-Down Solution:

Stop the toe decreases earlier

If you're working a sock from the top down, you'll want to stop the decreases earlier so there will be more stitches—typically 40 percent of the foot stitches—for a wider tip of the toe. To compensate for the shorter length that will result, you'll want to calculate the length of the toe to make sure you don't begin the shaping too soon. Use the formulas below to determine the number of rounds in the toe and its overall length.

Toe Shaping Rounds = (Foot Stitches – Toe Tip Stitches) ÷ 4

Total Toe Rounds = Shaping Toe Rounds × 1.5

Toe Length = Total Toe Rounds ÷ Gauge in Rounds per Inch

For example, let's say we're working at a gauge of 10 rounds per inch (2.5 cm), and our sock has 64 stitches in the foot and that we want to decrease the toe to 40 percent of the foot stitches.

64 foot stitches × 0.4 = 25.6 final toe stitches

Because the shaping is worked in multiples of 4 stitches, we need to adjust this to a whole number that's achieved by subtracting a multiple of 4 stitches from the initial 64 stitches. Therefore, we want to adjust this number to 24 stitches, which means we'll decrease 40 stitches (a multiple of 4).

The next step is to determine how many shaping rounds will be worked. Based on the first formula above, there will be 10 shaping rounds.

(64 foot stitches – 24 final toe stitches) ÷ 4
= 10 toe shaping rounds

Using the next two formulas, we can determine that there will be 15 total toe rounds.

10 toe shaping rounds × 1.5 = 15 total toe rounds

The toe length is therefore 1½" (3.8 cm).

15 total toe rounds ÷ 10 rounds per inch = 1.5. (3.8 cm)

Therefore, we'll work the first round of toe shaping when the foot measures 1½ inches (3.8 cm) less than the desired total finished sock foot length.

I worked this type of toe shape for the Carpita colorwork sock (see page 116) for two reasons: one technical, one aesthetic. I wanted more stitches at the tip of the toe so that the vertical stripe pattern would have sufficient width. Equally important, the stranded-colorwork pattern affected the ratio between the stitch and round gauges (see page 172, which would make the standard shaping too long.

Toe-Up Solution: Cast on more stitches

If you're working from the toe up, begin by casting on 40 percent of the desired foot stitches, being sure to adjust the original stitch count to factor evenly into the desired number of foot stitches.

For the same example sock as used for the top-down solution, we'd begin by casting on 24 stitches, then we'd increase every round 5 times to 44 stitches, then alternate an increase round with a "plain" round 5 times to the desired 64 stitches.

SITUATION:
THE TOE IS TOO WIDE

Although this situation isn't common, if the curve of your toes is extreme or if your shorter toes are are significantly shorter than your longest toe(s), the toe cap may be "baggy."

Toe-Up Solution

For a toe-up sock, cast on fewer stitches and work more shaping rounds—the Half & Half or Barn Toe shapings (see pages 176 and 177) are best for this situation, as they increase stitches more quickly at first, which creates more of a curved shape.

Top-Down Solution

The basic top-down sock pattern uses the Half & Half Toe (see page 176), which is fairly curvy. If you need more curve, use the Barn Toe (see page 177) or adjust the Barn Toe by removing some of the "even" rounds.

Toe Shapings

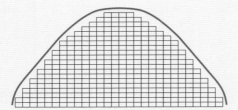

Half & Half Toe

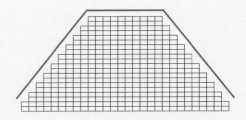

Simple Toe

The Half & Half Toe

This is the standard shape used in the basic top-down sock pattern on page 40. The number of decrease rounds to be worked is divided in half—the first half of the decreases are worked in a 2-round pattern that alternates a decrease round with an "even" round; the second half of the decreases are worked as consecutive decrease rounds.

For example, for a 64-stitch sock that decreases to 8 stitches, there will be 14 decrease rounds. The decreases will be worked as follows: [Work decrease round, work 1 round even] 7 times, then [work decrease round] 7 times.

You can also use this shaping for a toe-up sock if you like the slightly curvier shape it makes. For example, if you wanted 64 stitches in the foot, you'd cast on 8 stitches and work a total of 14 increase rounds. To begin, you'd increase every round 7 times to 36 stitches, then you'd increase every other round 7 times to 64 stitches.

If the number of shaping rounds isn't evenly divisible by 2, you'll need to round the numbers—round up for the longer interval; round down for the shorter interval. For example, if you need to work 15 shaping rounds on a top-down sock, work 8 repeats of the first shaping interval (alternating decrease and even round) and work 7 repeats of the second interval (consecutive decrease rounds). If you're working the sock from the toe up, reverse these intervals—work the first interval (consecutive increase rounds) 7 times, then work the second interval (alternating increase and even rounds) 8 times.

The Simple Toe

This is the standard shape used for the basic toe-up pattern on page 54. It's a very straightforward 2-round pattern of an increase round followed by a plain stockinette round. This toe fits best if the tip of the toe contains about one-third of the total sock stitches.

To use this toe for a top-down sock, alternate decreasing and even rounds until about a third of the stitches remain. Because you're decreasing in groups of four, the final number you hit will be set by the number of stitches in the full circumference.

For example, if you have 60 stitches, the math works out nicely.

$$60 \div 3 = 20$$

$$60 - 20 = 40; \text{ which is divisible by 4}$$

$$40 \div 4 = 10 \text{ shaping rounds}$$

If you've got 70 stitches, however, the math is a bit messier.

$$70 \div 3 = 23.3; \text{ which we'll round to 24}$$

$$70 - 24 = 46; \text{ which is not divisible by 4}$$

You'll need to decrease to 26 or 22 stitches instead.

To end, graft the remaining stitches together; this toe cannot be cinched together.

The length of this toe is 2 times the number of shaping rounds, divided by the number of rounds per inch, as follows:

Shaping Rounds = (Sock Stitches – Final Stitches at Tip) ÷ 4

Number of Rounds in Toe = 2 × Shaping Rounds

Length of Toe = Number of Rounds in Toe ÷ Gauge in Rounds per Inch

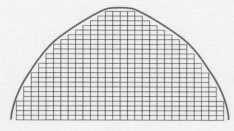

Barn Toe

The Barn Toe

The Barn shaping (so-called because it results in a shape similar to the roof of a barn) creates a nice curve between the full circumference at the base of the toes and 8 to 10 stitches at the tip. This shaping doesn't really work for a grafted closure, and it's best for socks that have at least 10 shaping rounds; therefore at least 48 stitches in the full circumference. (This permits enough rounds to shape a nice curve; if you don't have at least 4 consecutive shaping rounds worked at the tip, the toe shape is fairly pointy.) Although it works in a narrower set of circumstances, it creates a very natural curve.

Worked top down

To use the barn shaping when working from the top down, work as follows.

Work a decrease round, then work 3 rounds even.

[Work a decrease round, then work 2 rounds even] 2 times.

[Work a decrease round, then work 1 round even] 3 times.

Repeat just the decrease round until 8 to 10 stitches remain; cinch the toe closed.

To adjust this shaping for a slightly longer toe, work as follows.

Work a decrease round, then work 4 rounds even.

[Work a decrease round, then work 3 rounds even] 2 times.

[Work a decrease round, then work 2 rounds even] 3 times.

Repeat just the decrease round until 8 to 10 stitches remain; cinch the toe closed.

To adjust the shaping for a slightly shorter toe, work as follows.

Work a decrease round, then work 3 rounds even.

Work a decrease round, then work 2 rounds even.

[Work a decrease round, then work 1 round even] 2 times.

Repeat just the decrease round until 8 to 10 stitches remain; cinch the toe closed.

Worked Toe Up

To use the barn shaping when working from the toe up, you'll first need to calculate the number of shaping rounds.

**Total Number of Shaping Rounds =
(Full Stitch Count – Tip Stitch Count) ÷ 4**

**Number of Initial Shaping Rounds =
Total Number of Shaping Rounds – 6**

To begin the shaping, repeat just the increase round until the calculated number of initial shaping rounds has been completed. Then continue as follows.

[Work 1 round even, then work an increase round] 3 times.

[Work 2 rounds even, then work an increase round] 2 times.

Finally, work 3 rounds even, then work an increase round.

You can also shorten or lengthen this shaping, as for the top-down sock mentioned above.

The **FITZCARRALDO** Knee Sock

FINISHED SIZE
Ankle/foot circumference: 7 (7½, 8, 8½, 9)" (18 [19, 20.5, 21.5, 23] cm).

Calf circumference: 10 (10¼, 10½, 10¾, 11)" (25.5 [26, 26.5, 27.5, 28] cm) at widest point, adjustable to fit.

Leg length: 15¼ (15¼, 17, 17, 17)" (38.5 [38.5, 43, 43, 43] cm) unstretched, adjustable to fit.

Foot length: Adjustable to fit, finished length should be about ½" (1.3 cm) shorter than actual foot length.

Sock shown measures 7½" (19 cm) ankle/foot circumference.

YARN
CYCA #1, Super Fine.

Shown here: The Plucky Knitter Primo Fingering (75% superwash merino, 20% cashmere, 5% nylon; 385 yd [352 m]/100 g): Barely Birch, 2 skeins.

NEEDLES
Size U.S. 1.5 (2.5 mm): set of 4 double-pointed (dpn), two circular (cir) or one long cir, as you prefer (see page 20).

NOTIONS
Cable needle (cn); tapestry needle.

GAUGE
32 sts and 50 rnds = 4" (10 cm) in St st worked in rnds.

I adore a seam on the back of a stocking. This pattern takes that idea and runs wild with it. I've used Bavarian twisted-stitch patterns for that "seam" element, flowing right up into the ribbing. From the front, these socks are plain and simple, but they're entirely different when viewed from the back. The cuff ribbing is twisted for better cling.

Notes

+ This pattern works for any sock yarn that specifies a gauge of 28 to 32 stitches in 4" (10 cm).

+ It's not a bad idea in this case to choose a slightly thicker yarn and knit it tightly; after all, knee socks are a lot of work—you want them to last. The numbers are based on the Basic Pattern on page 54 worked at a gauge of 8 stitches per inch (2.5 cm), with finished sizes of 7 (7½, 8, 8½, 9)" (18 [19, 20.5, 21.5, 23] cm).

+ Choose a size based on foot/ankle circumference, allowing for the usual 10 percent negative ease.

+ Needles with a sharp tip will make the twisted stitches in this pattern easier to work.

THE FITZCARRALDO KNEE SOCK

The Fitzcarraldo Knee Sock is a relatively plain toe-up pattern that allows for easy adjustment. With the exception of the cuff and decorative panel along the back of the leg, the sock is worked entirely in "plain" stockinette stitch. The leg shaping is camouflaged within the decorative twisted-stitch pattern—most of the increases between the cuff and full-calf circumference are hidden between the cable elements. The decreases between the full calf and cuff are worked in the stockinette stitches that border the twisted-stitch panel.

The foot and heel follow the numbers in the table on pages 56–58, based on the stockinette gauge. The number of stitches increased and decreased for the leg shaping is based on the gauge in the twisted-stitch pattern. Because this design is mostly stockinette, it's relatively easy to adjust—you can work more increases or decreases in the stockinette portion to make additional changes to the leg circumferences.

Key sections of the chart are repeated, which allows for length adjustments in 1-inch (2.5 cm) increments in several places. To change the leg length, simply work extra (or fewer) repeats of those portions of the chart as follows.

Rows 31 to 42, which occur below the fullest part of the calf, are designed to be worked twice. To add 1 inch (2.5 cm) of length to this section, work an additional repeat; to reduce the length by 1 inch (2.5 cm), work these rows just once.

Rows 69 to 80, which coincide with the fullest circumference of the calf, are also designed to be worked twice. Again, add or subtract repeats to lengthen or shorten this interval by 1 inch (2.5 cm).

Rows 83 to 94, which are worked from the fullest part of the calf to the ribbing at the same time as the upper leg decreases are worked, are designed to be worked 2 or 3 times (depending on the sock size). Adjust the length in this section by working more or fewer of these repeats.

Toe

Using Judy's magic method (see page 49), CO 20 (20, 24, 24, 24) sts—10 (10, 12, 12, 12) sts each on two needles.

RND 1: Work as foll, depending on the type of needle(s) used.

FOR DPN: K5 (5, 6, 6, 6) with one needle, k5 (5, 6, 6, 6) with a second needle, k10 (10, 12, 12, 12) with a third needle.

FOR TWO CIR OR MAGIC-LOOP: K10 (10, 12, 12, 12) with one needle, k10 (10, 12, 12, 12) with a second needle.

Place a safety pin or marker in the toe to indicate beg of rnd and a second to indicate the center of the rnd.

INC RND: K1, M1R (see Glossary), knit to 1 st before center of rnd, M1L (see Glossary), k2, M1R, knit to 1 st before end of rnd, M1L, k1—4 sts inc'd.

Knit 1 rnd even.

Rep the last 2 rnds 8 (9, 9, 10, 11) more times—56 (60, 64, 68, 72) sts total.

Foot

Work even (knit every rnd) until foot measures 3¼ (3½, 3¾, 4, 4¼)" (8.5 [9, 9.5, 10, 11] cm) less than desired finished sock foot length.

Gusset

Rearrange sts if necessary so that the sole sts are on one needle. Work the gusset incs at each end of the needle holding the sole sts as foll.

SET-UP RND: Knit instep sts, M1R (see Glossary), place marker (pm) for heel, knit to end of rnd, pm for end of heel, M1L (see Glossary)—2 sts inc'd.

RND 2: Knit.

RND 3: Knit instep sts, M1R, knit to end of rnd, M1L—2 sts inc'd.

RND 4: Knit.

Rep the last 2 rnds 9 (10, 11, 12, 12) more times—78 (84, 90, 96, 100) sts total.

Heel
TURN HEEL

Work short-rows (see Glossary) as foll.

ROW 1: (RS) Knit to 1 st before second heel m, wrap next st and turn work (w&t).

ROW 2: (WS): Purl to 1 st before m, w&t.

Working only on the heel sts, cont as foll.

ROW 3: (RS) Knit to st before last wrapped st, w&t.

ROW 4: (WS) Purl to st before last wrapped st, w&t.

Rep Rows 3 and 4 until 8 (10, 12, 12, 12) sts rem unwrapped in the middle, ending with a WS row.

Remove heel markers.

HEEL FLAP

Work the heel flap and dec gusset sts as foll.

STITCH GUIDE

RLI (Right Lifted Increase): Insert the right needle into the st below the next st on the left needle, lift this st onto the left needle tip, then knit it—1 st inc'd.

RLPI (Right Lifted Purl Increase): Insert the right needle into the st below the next st on the left needle, lift this st onto the left needle tip, then purl it—1 st inc'd.

LLI (Left Lifted Increase): Use the left needle to pick up the st 2 rows below the last st on the right needle, then knit this st—1 st inc'd.

LLPI (Left Lifted Purl Increase): Use the left needle to lift the st 2 rows below the last st on the right needle, then purl this st—1 st inc'd.

LT: Sl 1 st onto cn and hold in front of work, k1tbl, then k1tbl from cn.

RT: Sl 1 st onto cn and hold in back of work, k1tbl, then k1tbl from cn.

LPT: Sl 1 st onto cn and hold in front of work, p1, then k1tbl from cn.

RPT: Sl 1 st onto cn and hold in back of work, k1tbl, then p1 from cn.

ROW 1: (RS) Knit to first wrapped st, *knit the wrapped st tog with its wrap; rep from * until 1 wrapped st rem, ssk (final st tog with its wrap and the first gusset st), turn work.

ROW 2: (WS) Sl 1, purl to first wrapped st, *purl the wrapped st tog with its wrap; rep from * until 1 wrapped st rem, p2tog (final st tog with its wrap and the first gusset st), turn work.

Fitzcarraldo chart

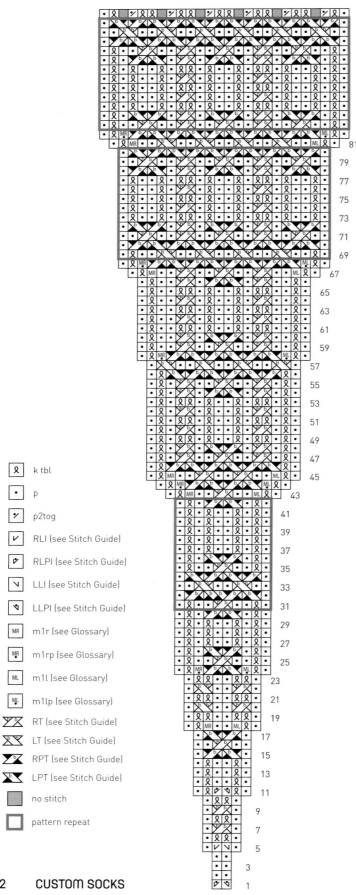

ROW 3: Sl 1, k26 (28, 30, 32, 34), ssk, turn work.

ROW 4: Sl 1, p26 (28, 30, 32, 34), p2tog, turn work.

Rep Rows 3 and 4 until 1 gusset st rem on each side, ending with a WS row—58 (62, 66, 70, 74) stitches rem.

Leg

Rejoin for working in rnds, working in patt across all sts and working the final gusset decs in the first 2 rnds as foll.

RND 1: Sl 1, k26 (28, 30, 32, 34), ssk, work instep sts in patt as set—57 (61, 65, 69, 73) sts. This is the new start of round.

RND 2: K2tog, knit to end of instep—56 (60, 64, 68, 72) sts rem.

RND 3: K14 (15, 16, 17, 18), pm, work Row 1 of Fitzcarraldo chart between last st worked and next st, pm, knit to end of rnd—58 (62, 66, 70, 74) sts; 56 (60, 64, 68, 72) sts in St st and 2 sts in chart patt.

Note: Shaping is introduced while the charted pattern is in progress; read all the way through the foll section before proceeding.

Working chart patt between markers and St st elsewhere, work through Row 42 of chart, rep Rows 31–42 once, work Rows 43–80, rep Rows 69–80 once, work Rows 81–94, then rep Rows 83–94 2 (2, 3, 3, 3) more times, or until leg measures desired length to ribbing, ending with Row 94.

Legend

ℛ	k tbl
·	p
⚋	p2tog
⧸	RLI (see Stitch Guide)
⧸	RLPI (see Stitch Guide)
⧹	LLI (see Stitch Guide)
⧹	LLPI (see Stitch Guide)
MR	m1r (see Glossary)
M̰R	m1rp (see Glossary)
ML	m1l (see Glossary)
M̰L	m1lp (see Glossary)
⊠	RT (see Stitch Guide)
⊠	LT (see Stitch Guide)
⊠	RPT (see Stitch Guide)
⊠	LPT (see Stitch Guide)
▨	no stitch
☐	pattern repeat

NEXT RND: Work Rnd 95 between markers—20 sts rem between markers.

At the same time for all but the largest size, when leg measures 5 (5, 5, 5½)" (12.5 [12.5, 12.5, 14] cm) or desired length to mid-calf, inc as foll.

INC RND: Knit to m, M1R, slip marker (sl m), work chart as set, M1L, knit to end of rnd—2 sts inc'd.

Work 9 rnds even.

Rep the last 10 rnds 3 (2, 1, 0) more time(s)—8 (6, 4, 2) sts inc'd.

Also at the same time when leg measures 11 (11½, 11½, 12, 12)" (28 [29, 29, 30.5, 30.5] cm) or desired length to top of second half of calf shaping, dec as foll.

DEC RND: Knit to 2 sts before m, k2tog, sl m, work chart as set, ssk, knit to end of rnd—2 sts dec'd.

Work 1 (1, 1, 1, 2) rnd(s) even. Rep the last 2 (2, 2, 2, 3) rnds 12 (11, 8, 6, 8) more times—38 (42, 50, 56, 54) sts rem in St st portion.

Third (fourth) sizes only

Rep dec rnd, then work 2 rnds even 2 (4) times—46 (48) sts rem in St st portion.

Cont in patt as set until chart is complete and leg is desired length—58 (62, 66, 68, 74) sts rem; 38 (42, 46, 48, 54) sts in St st portion, 20 sts in panel.

Cuff

SET-UP: Knit to 2 sts before m, k2tog, remove m—57 (61, 65, 67, 73) sts rem. This is new beg of rnd.

RND 1: P1, k1 through back loop (tbl), [p1, RT (see Stitch Guide)] 5 times, p1, *k1tbl, p1; rep from * to end of rnd.

RND 2: P1, k1tbl, [p2, k2] 5 times, p2, *k1tbl, p1; rep from * to end of rnd.

Rep Rnds 1 and 2 for 2½ (2½, 3, 3, 3)" (6.5 [6.5, 7.5, 7.5, 7.5] cm) or desired length, ending with Rnd 2.

Using a stretchy method (see page 52), BO all sts.

Finishing

Weave in loose ends. Block as desired (see page 18).

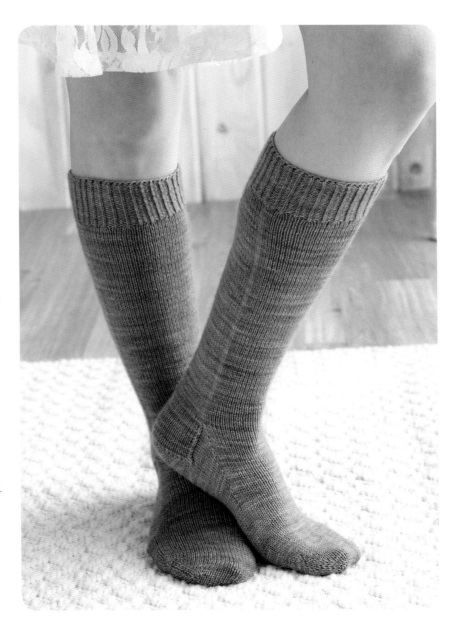

Glossary

Abbreviations

beg(s)	begin(s); beginning
BO	bind off
CC	contrast color
cir	circular
cm	centimeter(s)
cn	cable needle
CO	cast on
cont	continue(s); continuing
dec(s)('d)	decrease(s); decreasing; decreased
dpn	double-pointed needles
foll	follow(s); following
g	gram(s)
inc(s)('d)	increase(s); increasing; increase(d)
k	knit
k1f&b	knit into the front and back of the same stitch (increase)
k2tog	knit two stitches together (decrease)
kwise	knitwise; as if to knit
m	marker
mm	millimeter(s)
M1	make one (increase)
M1L	make one with left slant (increase)
M1P	make one purlwise (increase)
M1R	make one with right slant (increase)
oz	ounce
p	purl
p1f&b	purl into the front and back of the same stitch (increase)
p2tog	purl two stitches together (decrease)
patt(s)	pattern(s)
pm	place marker
psso	pass slipped stitch over
pwise	purlwise; as if to purl
rem	remain(s); remaining
rep	repeat(s); repeating
Rev St st	reverse stockinette stitch
rnd(s)	round(s)
RS	right side
sl	slip
st(s)	stitch(es)
St st	stockinette stitch
tbl	through back loop
tog	together
w&t	wrap and turn
WS	wrong side
wyb	with yarn in back
wyf	with yarn in front
yd	yard(s)
yo	yarnover
*	repeat starting point
* *	repeat all instructions between asterisks
( )	alternate measurements and/or instructions
[ ]	work instructions as a group a specified number of times

Bind-Offs

See page 52.

Cast-Ons

BACKWARD-LOOP CAST-ON

*Loop working yarn and place it on needle backward so that it doesn't unwind.

See page 34 for other types.

Decreases

KNIT 2 TOGETHER (K2TOG)

Knit two stitches together as if they were a single stitch.

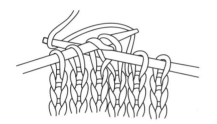

PURL 2 TOGETHER (P2TOG)

Purl two stitches together as if they were a single stitch.

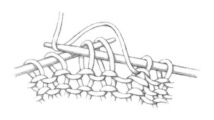

SSK

Slip two stitches individually knitwise **(Figure 1)**, insert left needle tip into the front of these two slipped stitches, and use the right needle to knit them together through their back loops **(Figure 2)**.

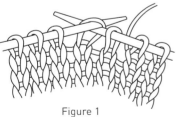

Figure 1

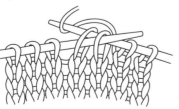

Figure 2

SSSK

Slip three stitches individually knitwise **(Figure 1)**, insert left needle tip into the front of these three slipped stitches, and use the right needle to knit them together through their back loops **(Figure 2)**.

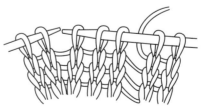

Figure 1

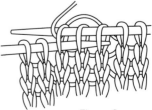

Figure 2

Grafting
KITCHENER STITCH

Arrange stitches on two needles so that there is the same number of stitches on each needle. Hold the needles parallel to each other with wrong sides of the knitting facing together. Allowing about ½" (1.3 cm) per stitch to be grafted, thread matching yarn on a tapestry needle. Work from right to left as follows:

STEP 1: Bring tapestry needle through the first stitch on the front needle as if to purl and leave the stitch on the needle (**Figure 1**).

STEP 2: Bring tapestry needle through the first stitch on the back needle as if to knit and leave that stitch on the needle (**Figure 2**).

STEP 3: Bring tapestry needle through the first front stitch as if to knit and slip this stitch off the needle, then bring the tapestry needle through the next front stitch as if to purl and leave this stitch on the needle (**Figure 3**).

STEP 4: Bring tapestry needle through the first back stitch as if to purl and slip this stitch off the needle, then bring the tapestry needle through the next back stitch as if to knit and leave this stitch on the needle (**Figure 4**).

Repeat Steps 3 and 4 until one stitch remains on each needle, adjusting the tension to match the rest of the knitting as you go. To finish, bring the tapestry needle through the front stitch as if to knit and slip this stitch off the needle, then bring the tapestry needle through the back stitch as if to purl and slip this stitch off the needle.

Insert the tapestry needle into the center of the last stitch worked, pull the yarn to the wrong side, and weave the tail into the purl bumps on the wrong side of the toe.

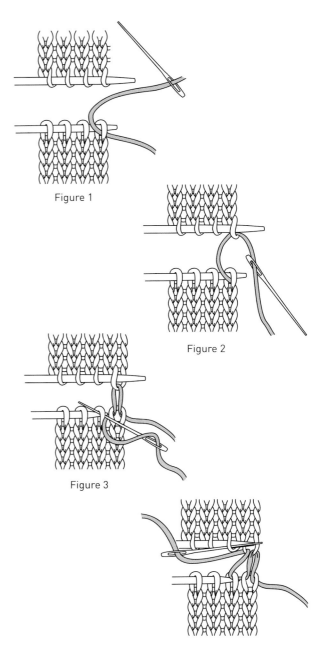

Figure 1

Figure 2

Figure 3

Figure 4

Increases

BAR INCREASES
Knitwise (k1f&b)

Knit into a stitch but leave the stitch on the left needle (**Figure 1**), then knit through the back loop of the same stitch (**Figure 2**) and slip the original stitch off the needle (**Figure 3**).

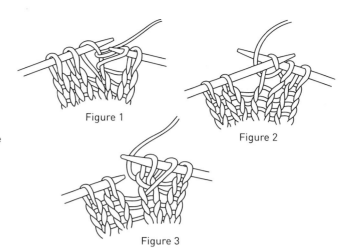

Figure 1

Figure 2

Figure 3

RAISED MAKE-ONE (M1) INCREASES

Note: Use the left slant (M1L) if no direction is specified.

Left Slant (M1L)

With left needle tip, lift the strand between the last knitted stitch and the first stitch on the left needle from front to back (**Figure 1**), then knit the lifted loop through the back (**Figure 2**).

Right Slant (M1R)

With left needle tip, lift the strand between the needles from back to front (**Figure 1**), then knit the lifted loop through the front (**Figure 2**).

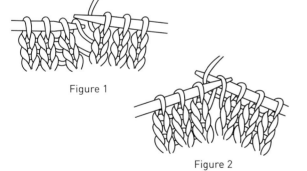

Figure 1

Figure 2

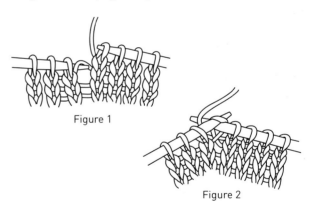

Figure 1

Figure 2

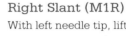

LIFTED INCREASES

Left Lifted Increase (LLI)

Insert left needle tip into the back of the stitch (in the "purl bump") below the stitch just knitted **(Figure 1)**, then knit this lifted stitch **(Figure 2)**.

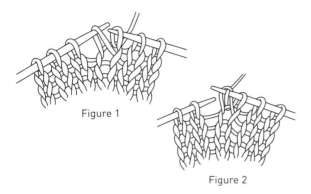

Figure 1

Figure 2

Right Lifted Increase (RLI)

Insert right needle tip into the back of the stitch (in the "purl bump") in the row directly below the first stitch on the left needle **(Figure 1)**, knit this lifted stitch, then knit the first stitch on the left needle **(Figure 2)**.

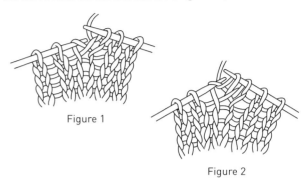

Figure 1

Figure 2

Pick-Up Stitches

PICK UP AND KNIT

With right side facing and working from right to left, *insert the needle tip under the edge stitch **(Figure 1)**, wrap the yarn around the needle, and pull through a loop **(Figure 2)**. Repeat from * for the desired number of stitches.

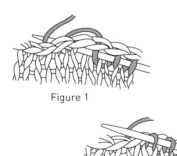

Figure 1

Figure 2

PICK UP AND PURL

With wrong side of work facing and working from right to left, *insert needle tip under edge stitch from the far side to the near side **(Figure 1)**, wrap yarn around needle, and pull through a loop **(Figure 2)**. Repeat from * for the desired number of stitches.

Figure 1

Figure 2

Short-Rows

SHORT-ROWS KNIT SIDE

Work to turning point, slip next stitch purlwise (**Figure 1**), bring the yarn to the front, then slip the same stitch back to the left needle (**Figure 2**), turn the work around and bring the yarn in position for the next stitch—one stitch has been wrapped, and the yarn is correctly positioned to work the next stitch.

When you come to a wrapped stitch on a subsequent row, hide the wrap by working it together with the wrapped stitch as follows: insert right needle tip under the wrap (from the front if wrapped stitch is a knit stitch; from the back if wrapped stitch is a purl stitch; **Figure 3**), then into the stitch on the needle, and work the stitch and its wrap together as a single stitch.

SHORT-ROWS PURL SIDE

Work to the turning point, slip the next stitch purlwise to the right needle, bring the yarn to the back of the work (**Figure 1**), return the slipped stitch to the left needle, bring the yarn to the front between the needles (**Figure 2**), and turn the work so that the knit side is facing—one stitch has been wrapped, and the yarn is correctly positioned to knit the next stitch.

To hide the wrap on a subsequent purl row, work to the wrapped stitch, use the tip of the right needle to pick up the wrap from the back of the right-side row, place it on the left needle (**Figure 3**), then purl it together with the wrapped stitch.

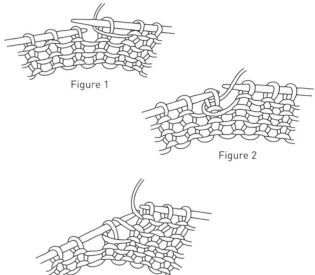

Figure 1

Figure 2

Figure 3

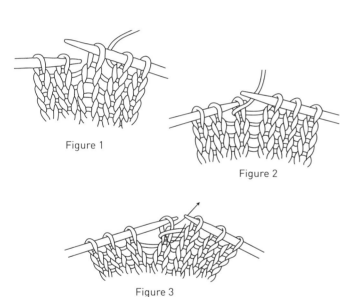

Figure 1

Figure 2

Figure 3

Resources

Books and Media

Budd, Ann. *The Knitter's Handy Guide to Yarn Requirements.* Loveland, Colorado: Interweave, 2004.
Lists yarn requirements for socks at different sizes and gauges.

Bush, Nancy. *Folk Socks: The History and Techniques of Handknitted Footwear.* Revised Edition. Loveland, Colorado: Interweave, 2012.
An excellent overview of sock-knitting history and regional styles and lots of info on different styles of heels and toes. The patterns are gorgeous, but sizing options are limited.

Schoeller + Stahl Yarn Company. *Stahl Socka Book Number 9.*
Published in the early 1990s, this pamphlet was my first introduction to the idea that sock sizing could be generalized. Sadly now out of print, but worth buying used if you can find it at a reasonable price.

International Shoe Size Information:
http://en.wikipedia.org/wiki/Shoe_size

Judy's Magic Cast-On original article:
http://knitty.com/ISSUEspring06/FEATmagiccaston.html

Jeny's Super Stretchy Bind-Off original article:
http://knitty.com/ISSUEfall09/FEATjssbo.php

Yarn

Anzula Luxury Fibers
740 H St.
Fresno, CA 93721
anzula.com

Brown Sheep Company, Inc.
100662 County Rd. 16
Mitchell, NE 69357
brownsheep.com

Garnstudio/Drops
Jerikoveien 10 A
1067 Oslo
Norway
garnstudio.com

Handmaiden Fine Yarns
handmaiden.ca

Indigodragonfly
1946 Kennisis Lake Rd.
Haliburton, ON
Canada K0M 1S0
indigodragonfly.ca

Madelinetosh
7515 Benbrook Pkwy.
Benbrook, TX 76126
madelinetosh.com

Miss Babs Hand-Dyed Yarns and Fibers
PO Box 78
Mountain City, TN 37683
missbabs.com

Patons
320 Livingstone Ave. S.,
Box 40
Listowel, ON
Canada N4W 3H3
yarnspirations.com/patons

The Plucky Knitter
thepluckyknitter.com

Skacel Collection, Inc./ Austermann
PO Box 88110
Seattle, WA 98138
skacelknitting.com

Skeinny Dipping
etsy.com/shop/
SkeinnyDipping

Sweet Georgia Yarns
110–408 E. Kent Ave. S.
Vancouver, BC
Canada V5X 2X7
sweetgeorgiayarns.com

Westminster Fibers/ Regia/Rowan
165 Ledge St.
Nashua, NH 03060
westminsterfibers.com

Zen Yarn Garden
1121 Evett St., Unit 2
Sarnia, ON
Canada N7S 5N3
zenyarngarden.co

Index

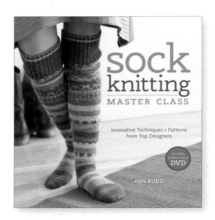
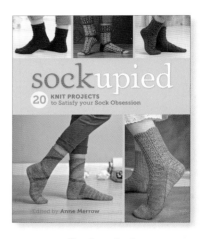 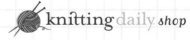